DEATH OF THE SENATE

DEATH OF
THE SENATE

My Front Row Seat to the Demise of the
World's Greatest Deliberative Body

BEN NELSON

Foreword by Trent Lott *and* Joseph Lieberman

Potomac Books
An imprint of the University of Nebraska Press

Library of Congress Control Number: 2021933234

Set in Arno Pro by Laura Buis.

To my daughter Sarah Jane (1970–2016), a precious gift taken too soon, who inspired and encouraged me to write this book;

To my wife, Diane, and kids Kevin, Christie, and Patrick, who always supported me in our political journeys;

To my parents, Ben and Birdella, who taught me to believe that all things are possible and if you want them enough to go after them—they were right;

To the Nebraskans who supported my goal of One Nebraska and made it possible to make Nebraska stronger together.

CONTENTS

ILLUSTRATIONS

FOREWORD

When the Lions Roared

TRENT LOTT & JOSEPH LIEBERMAN

BY TODAY'S STANDARD OPERATING procedure, you'd expect sending a Southern conservative Republican and a Northeaster liberal Democrat to the United States Senate would result in battles on the Senate floor involving recriminations, suspicions and political gamesmanship. But that's not what happened after voters elected the two of us in 1988 and we entered the Senate.

The son of a shipyard worker and son of a liquor store owner took the oath of office, as all senators do, to defend the Constitution from all enemies foreign and domestic. We did not bring boxing gloves, we weren't looking for a fight. We didn't come to Washington and the Senate to make a statement. We came to make a difference. We wanted to tackle problems bedeviling our constituents and country, from taxation to education to job-creation, to lift up the lives of everyday working Americans, and to right some wrongs in our ever-evolving democracy. We aimed to do so—and actually did—by working to build consensus, collaboration and coalitions. We sought support for legislation from colleagues on both sides of the aisle, for with numbers comes power to enact meaningful, durable and bipartisan change. Most of what we achieved that we feel good about—then and now—was bipartisan.

But the Senate doesn't operate that way today. It is a dysfunctional and divided place utterly lacking in the joy and sense of shared purpose we knew. That's why this book by our colleague Ben Nelson matters so deeply. He tells a story worth reading, blending detail, facts, and humor in a sharp and accurate reflection on a special time that was—and could be again if the right circumstances and will emerge in the Senate and country. He's not out to settle scores or to fan the flames of division rampant in Congress and our country, although that would be the easier path, would potentially play well in the far-left and far-right media, and it would fit in the current genre of political tomes that attack anyone perceived as "the others" from the first to the last page.

No, Nelson's got a subtler message. It's rooted in a story his communications director, David Di Martino, shared. After Nelson had been in the Senate for a year or two and had played high profile roles on tax cuts and war and peace issues, he told Di Martino that he'd noticed a slump in his press coverage. He teasingly attributed this to Di Martino's failings as a media master, and asked how this could be fixed. No problem, Senator, said Di Martino, a bit tongue in cheek, "All you have to do is go out there every day and blast President George W. Bush. Your coverage will go through the roof." Nelson responded, "I can't do that!" Both knew that wasn't Nelson's way. He, like us, came to Washington to work *with* Bush whenever possible, to work *with* senators on both sides of the aisle in the same vein and to work *for* constituents who expected results not empty rhetoric.

In this book, Nelson takes us back to a time when the Senate functioned reasonably well, mainly in the 2000s, and—through a series of stories—shows how and why the Senate was able to achieve success on major issues from war to economic stimulus, judicial fights to health care and more. You'll go behind the scenes with key players, formidable people like John McCain and Ted Kennedy and Barbara Boxer and Susan Collins, and see how relationships mixed with real trust and respect were underpinnings that brought senators together to pass bipartisan legislation benefitting the American people. Nelson, finally, lays out recommendations that could restore the Senate to a smoother-running, more congenial and effective body where the word comity again rules.

We need that. Our democracy needs that. Our future needs that.

Today, when political polarization has driven a wedge between millions of Americans, when a pandemic has taken the lives of more than five hundred thousand Americans, and when the scourge of racism has ignited the strongest demands for unity in generations, we need to find ways again to work together—not against one another. When one of the two of us rose up through the Senate to become leader and guide the Republican caucus and the other of us was on the 2000 ticket as Al Gore's vice-presidential running mate and went on to help shape creation of a new federal Department of Homeland Security after 9/11, we measured our successes in our ability to reach across the aisle to develop consensus and deliver what we thought was right and needed for the American people. We were called pragmatists. It wasn't then used as a pejorative.

During our years in the Senate spanning several decades, the upper chamber took on issues such as immigration, welfare reform, education reforms, national defense, trade, arms control agreements and much more, often with bipartisan agreement on legislation. The trains didn't run on schedule every day. But they often left the station loaded with legislative goods aiding our constituents, our communities and our country.

Today, the extreme wings of the parties, which dominate all of Washington, view pragmatists with extreme suspicion. The political center, so robust when we served, has withered away to almost nothing. Senators today have few personal relationships with colleagues in the other party. That's a problem because it's hard to fight with someone whose kids you know, or who you talk with over bowls of Senate bean soup. Our view is that if you're not listening regularly to someone you don't agree with, you aren't learning. And if you aren't learning, you cannot bridge the political divide to pass meaningful legislation. Senators, we believe, should start trying to make friends with those they don't agree with; they might find they can get more done in committees and on the floor.

Another major contributor to today's Senate troubles is how they approach the media, and how the media, especially social media, is constituted. Cable and talk radio are doing very well today by picking out a segment of the market and playing to it ideologically. Social media can share and amplify a senator's offhand comments worldwide in an instant, and trigger a massive bombardment of negative invective from people around the country. This pounding sends the peacemakers running for safety. It would be immeasurably helpful if senators would use and consume social media much less.

At the end of the day, this book isn't one to point out all the flaws and failings of today's Senate. It is about the work we all have to do and why we must. Senators must choose to work more with and develop relationships more with "the other side." You have a job to do, too. You should vote for men and women who pledge to work across the political aisle to get things done for community and country. Ben Nelson did both, with humor and heart, with respect and reserve and always with love of country. In the following pages, he shows how and why we all have a stake in saving the United States Senate, so that once again it becomes the world's greatest deliberative body and a bulwark of our democracy.

ACKNOWLEDGMENTS

JAKE THOMPSON, WHO REPORTED on me for the *Omaha World Herald*, later joined my Senate staff and now helped me write this book.

Thanks also to my Governor's staff, my Senate staff, and colleagues who tolerated my many pranks and made me better through our friendship and association.

INTRODUCTION

Senate Lions

I DEBATED FOR SOME time whether to write this book. As I retired from the Senate in January 2013, I felt a certain sadness. I knew I would miss my colleagues and the familiar interaction with so many of them. Friendships had been established. Relationships developed. I knew it would be different as a former senator. I also believed that the future of bipartisan gangs was limited at best.

The voters were sending those to the Senate who disdained bipartisanship. Several were there solely to build on their plans to seek the presidency. It seemed the political math was changing from addition and multiplication to division and subtraction.

At his first inauguration, in January 2001, George W. Bush said, "I am a uniter—not a divider." I believe he was. But he had some dividers come along with him: the neocons, advocates of intervention in international affairs; and certain staff, promoters of their own agenda. This, however, was overcome by W's outgoing personality and willingness to reach compromise when it counted.

The partisan divide deepened during the two terms under President Obama. In 2016, during the presidential, federal, and state elections, it accelerated. The outcomes of those elections put bipartisanship on life support. The rise of Trumpism divided the country even further into tribal camps distrustful and disdainful of the other side. I decided that maybe I could write about the Senate that I experienced when it worked. And why. I wish I could write it in the third person but, unfortunately, I'm a doer more than an observer. So, I will try to be as objective as I can to tell the story through my eyes. The late senator Daniel Patrick Moynihan of New York is remembered as having said "Everyone is entitled to their own opinion but not their own set of facts." What might he think today when we now have "alternative facts?" Seems so much easier than to have to deal with a common set of facts. Specious at best, however.

But as long as we are now living in this time where some believe in all things "alternative," perhaps I will be introducing "alternative recollection." It will be my recollection of events, conversations, interaction, motivations, causes and effects and results. Still, I will be trying very hard not to have my recollections "too alternative." Here goes!

If the United States Senate still functioned as the institution that its Founders envisioned, Brett Kavanaugh would not be on the Supreme Court today. This is not wishful thinking. I know this for a fact. Now let me tell you how I know this. And it involves a bit of a backstory . . .

We met in secret. Away from the press, away from most of our staffers, and away from curious Senate colleagues hoping to overhear our deliberations. They were right to be curious, because we had the numbers. The numbers gave us power. And, then as now, power was a commodity that never lost its value on Capitol Hill.

We were dubbed the Gang of 14—seven Democrats and seven Republicans. We looked ordinary enough—men and women in dark, sober suits with serious looks on our faces. But behind those doors, we were a posse of legislative renegades, and we were in full gallop once again. These periodic gatherings were begun to try to solve a particularly acrimonious issue: the confirmation of federal judges through the obstacle-ridden Senate.

Our agenda was to deliberate the fate of a slew of President Bush's judicial nominees, finding those who weren't on the extremes and could win bipartisan support in the chamber. On this day in 2005 one name jumped out in particular: a young lawyer who had worked in the Bush White House and was a presidential favorite but had no judicial experience—Brett Kavanaugh.

At the time, there were a number of senators who felt that he was too partisan to serve effectively as a federal judge—and these were just the Republicans. Their concern, which I shared, was that Kavanaugh had spent most of his career working in partisan politics and had become associated with the most extreme factions in the conservative legal world. He wasn't the type of nominee the Gang could accept. So, the Gang of 14, including Lindsey Graham, the South Carolina Republican, passed on Kavanaugh, though he later made it to the federal bench anyway. His eventual confirmation was a sign of changing times in the Senate. But if things had worked the way they were supposed to, the way things operated for at least a short shining moment, he would never have gone that far—and the nation could have been spared the great heartache that ensued twelve years later.

In the United States Senate there has always been a healthy appetite for argument. That's just bound to happen when one hundred big personalities try to squeeze into the same small chamber in the north wing of the U.S. Capitol. Debate and discussion sometimes turned into disputation. Still, throughout some 230 years of existence, the Senate maintained a tradition of respectful deliberation that addressed the nation's toughest problems, an essential counterweight to the raucous "People's House" next door.

That time has passed, and I know because I watched it go. I was elected to the Senate in 2000 and served until 2013. My job was simple: to represent the people of Nebraska, for whom I'd served as governor over the eight years prior. I had no way of knowing when I arrived in the Senate that I had shown up for one of the last great eras in the history of the institution—very possibly the last.

The Senate I walked into in 2001 was unlike anywhere else on the planet. It's always been home to big personalities, but I served with some of the biggest. Teddy Kennedy. Robert Byrd. John McCain. John Warner. Dan Inouye. Barbara Mikulski. I learned, too, that when Robert Byrd, well into his eighties, locked you in his gaze from across the Senate floor, he sent out a kind of force field that kept your feet planted in place as he shuffled over to you and grabbed you by the lapels and said his piece. From John McCain I learned how to look at danger from a man who'd stared it in the face and came out the other side (as well as a few tips on anger management). You might call them some of the last "Lions of the Senate."

But no matter how big the personality, there was always room for cooperation. As a red-state Democrat whose political positions leaned toward the middle—and even to the right—I very often found myself in tricky situations that required tough bipartisan efforts to solve. I did my best to be an honest broker between my friends in my own party and my friends among the Republicans. I learned early on, however, that the key to any negotiation at any level is genuine trust. Former president Trump likes to talk about the "art of the deal," but it really isn't an art. In reality, trust is the *heart* of the deal. Mutual trust. And that heart, tragically, is what the Senate has lost.

I knew things were changing when I first met Bernie Sanders of Vermont after he joined the Senate in 2007. Bernie, whose reputation as an aloof loner is well-earned, had first taken a desk next to my own on the Democratic side of the Senate chamber. We got along cordially enough. But it wasn't long before I arrived in the chamber one day to find that my neighbor had moved and had taken a desk further in the back. Was I that terrible of a companion? As usual, I figured it was best to defuse awkward situations with humor, so I just walked up to Bernie and asked what was so wrong with sitting down by me. Was it my voting record? He smiled sheepishly, and pointed up toward the C-SPAN cameras mounted in the gallery. "Oh, no," he said, "the camera angle is better up here." The celebrity culture of the Senate was now firmly entrenched—with so many of my colleagues wanting to be noticed rather than accomplishing something out of the limelight. Running for higher office, Bernie?

A bigger and more damaging change began during my time in

the Senate, and it has nearly erased the opportunity for bipartisanship, collegiality, and compromise. It's the rise of ideological groups on the far right and far left who punish people who deviate from their view. They expect 100 percent compliance, 100 percent of the time, on 100 percent of the issues. Sure, there have long been far left and far right groups, but they did not dominate political debate the way they do today.

Now if a senator dares to digress from the far right or left view—and how is it possible to please either, ever?—they will recruit a primary opponent and raise a ton of money to be poured in against your next race. This has weakened the parties and undermined the center. Gone is the concept of a big tent, for either party. Back when I served, if a senator from either party held different views from the majority of their party in a particular issue, they were not ostracized nor punished. It was accepted that the senator was representing his or her state and had an obligation to use the best judgment to serve constituents back home.

I see the changes most vividly in the same people I served with years ago and who continue to come across my television screen. The Lindsey Graham I see on TV today is not the Lindsey Graham I remember from yesterday. The man I served with had his ambitions, sure. He's had an eye on the U.S. attorney general slot for some time. But he was not prone to gin up outrage just for the benefit of the cameras. Graham's transformation shows what has happened across the whole Senate—the once-serious workhorses have given in to a culture of grandstanding.

Susan Collins, too, surprised many when she voted in favor of Kavanaugh's confirmation to the Supreme Court. The Susan Collins I served with was a true Republican moderate, a centrist unafraid to go against her party when she felt deep-down that it was the right thing to do. I saw her do it, and more than once! I have no doubt that she is still a smart, dependable legislator. In fact, I know she is. But when the Republican caucus lurched to the right, it left centrist Collins stranded in the center with very few Democrat centrists partners, because others had been pulled to the left of the party or been defeated. The formerly nearly three dozen Centrist Caucus members of 2002 had been hollowed out. The very few remaining had moved away from the center to their party's ideological right or left. In 2018 Susan Collins formed the Commonsense Caucus with West Virginia Democrat Joe Manchin, but they don't have a large bench of supporters. The center in the Senate became, and still is, a no-man's-land—an unsafe zone that attracts attacks from both the far right and the far left.

The march toward extremism continues. I don't watch it with anger toward my former colleagues. I watch it only with sadness. I wish the Grahams and other centrists that I knew and served with were still the ones holding those seats in the Senate. I wish more senators followed the examples set by bipartisan groups like the Gang of 14. The soil of today's Senate is not nearly fertile enough for such collaborative efforts to take root. A great institution has been steadily eroding before our very eyes. Robert Byrd, one of my first friends in the Senate, impressed on me the importance of protecting the institution to keep it from turning into a smaller version of its rough-and-tumble neighbor, the House. I'm afraid Byrd's worst fear is coming true.

The part that makes me angry is this: I know we can do better. I was there when we did.

I want to share lessons from a time when men and women of honest good faith worked together to get things done despite their honest political differences. This was a time when principle came before politics. It was a time when "compromise" was not yet a dirty word and before "primary" became a verb used to scare elected officials out of doing the right thing. It was a time when integrity meant something, and a time which, if we are not careful, we may never see again. It was a time when the men and women who roamed the marble halls of the Capitol were truly worthy of the title Senator.

Recently I traveled with my wife, Diane, to a family event in Argentina. One day, while waiting for a taxi to the airport to return to Nebraska, Harry Reid called me out of the blue. He just wanted to chat. This was classic Reid. When I was in the Senate he would do this all the time. He even called me twice when I was on my tractor back home. I didn't tell him that's where I was because he'd try to get off the call thinking he was interrupting me, and I knew what he had to say was far more important than cutting the last blade of grass. On this day when he reached me in Argentina, he seemed to want to talk about the good old days. He told me, "I'm still a little miffed about the Gang deal," which I well understood. "But you always were in the center of things," he said. We talked about working together for a couple very intense weeks on the bipartisan 2009 stimulus bill. It was controversial, sure. But it helped put the economy back on its feet and people back on the job. "That's when we used to get things done," I said to him. "Yes," Reid agreed. After a pause I added, "That was the time the lions roared."

And they might just roar again. I know there are good people in the Senate, and not just the ones I served with. There are young up-and-comers in both parties who have the credibility and the temperament to work effectively with their colleagues across the aisle. Some of them even still do so, but quietly, behind the scenes, because they don't want to anger the extreme factions of their party and risk a primary challenge. This is the attitude we have to change, and that's why I felt compelled to write this book. History is important. I served at a time when the Senate worked, and there are lessons to learn that can help restore it. Why does that matter? If the Senate cannot work effectively for the American people, then the government doesn't work. And if the Senate cannot serve as a responsible, credible check on the powers of the president—as it was meant to—then our democracy can't work. If our democracy can't work, our country will decline and our people will suffer. There's a lot on the line in getting the Senate to function again.

As a former United States senator I still retain the privilege to go back to the body, and I have done so. I have met with former colleagues and new members of the Senate since I retired. Many of them, if not most, agree with the blunt assessment I intend to offer here. But they are afraid. Many Republicans still live in a climate of fear—of Donald Trump and of their own voters. They don't dare make decisions that Trump and his supporters might not like. That's a terrifying abandonment of their duties, and they know it. And it's not just the Republicans. Democrats, too, feel stuck between getting things accomplished and catering to a base that is pulling the party to the extreme on the other end. If there is no one willing to move to the center, then democracy plain and simple cannot work.

The dysfunction in the Senate prompted me to join seventy former senators in sending a letter on February 25, 2020, to current senators, urging that they form a bipartisan group of some sort to begin the progress of coming together. As much as I am encouraged by our outside "intervention," I am saddened that this didn't originate within the Senate itself. Can't someone step forward and reach across the aisle to a colleague and say "Let's do another 'Gang' or some form a new center-oriented bipartisan coalition?" It hasn't happened because it is broken. Not possible. Hopelessly fractured. As I discuss the reasons why, I hope to illustrate what used to work and why it worked so that it can be a template for moving forward in the future.

So, I intend to use this book not to just tell old war stories, but to offer lessons for the future. Not to shame my colleagues in the current Senate to do the jobs they were elected to do but to warn Americans about the danger if they don't. It's not just up to our elected officials to change the climate in Washington. It's up to all of us.

DEATH OF THE SENATE

ONE

A Nebraska Centrist

I GREW UP AN ONLY CHILD. This oriented me, from an early age, to look outward. It taught me to seek equal favor from my parents, Benjamin Earl and Birdella Nelson. My mom worked in a doctor's office and helped in the school cafeteria. My father was an electrician for Nebraska Public Power and the assistant chief of the town's volunteer fire department for thirty years. In my world both of my parents were right, both worthy of respect. I didn't favor one over the other, or seek more from one or the other, or have to vie with a sibling for attention. As an only child I was raised as an adult. I got my parents' full attention and they mine.

When I was older sometimes one of them would tell me something they wanted the other to know, using me as a neutral go-between. Being an only child is often thought of as a negative thing, but, for me, it was a blessing because both of my parents were very loving and supportive. At the same time, they were demanding, encouraging me to do my best in everything in which I became involved. You could say this upbringing shaped my bipartisan, or nonpartisan, outlook in life and politics, and my drive to excel. Like in golf, I only had to compete against myself.

Before kindergarten, my mother homeschooled me. When she turned me over to my kindergarten teacher, Mrs. Maxine Morrison at West Ward, I already knew how to count and could read at a basic level. Mrs. Morrison was later to become First Lady of

Nebraska when her husband, Frank, a local attorney, was elected governor in 1960.

My mother continued to encourage me to read and took me to the McCook Carnegie Library to check out books. I still have my first library card (number 266), signed by the librarian Miss Millicent Slaby, who was right out of central casting for a librarian (white hair and a stern look). She used a quill pen dipped in an inkwell. It was fascinating.

My father taught me the outdoors, hunting, fishing, and sports. We played catch nearly every night after school and we both thought it best for me to study hard and work for a scholarship rather than count on a pro baseball career. Our weekends consisted of fishing, with baseball games tossed in.

My mother, who decided that I was a modern-day Tom Sawyer, sometimes asked me, "What are you up to, Tom?" I loved the outdoors and thrived in the Boy Scouts. My lifelong love of practical jokes was born in McCook, and I pulled off several memorable ones at my mother's expense.

Our home was in town but still close enough to cornfields and undeveloped land that critters found their way into our backyard. My dad taught me how to catch snakes. Rattlesnakes. Which I kept in large pickle jars on the piano until I could release them away from our house. I was concerned that they presented a danger to my dog, Spot, and wanted to keep them out of the yard. Killing them was not an option. Relocating them was. My mother was OK with this but didn't want the snake to visit more than a day or two.

On one occasion, I came home from Junior High football practice and my dad met me at the door. "The snake got out and Mom's at the neighbor's." I explained that I had come home at noon and released it. He smiled and said, "Good, let's go get a cheeseburger and a malt. We'll tell Mom when we get back." When we arrived back from Loose and Smith's Pool Hall, which served the best burgers in the county, my mom was waiting, outside the house. While my dad and I had a hearty laugh explaining the empty jar, my mother sighed in relief. She suggested I leave a note next time.

A short time later I caught another rattler—a very big one. This time I talked my parents into taking me to the zoo at Kugler's Truck Stop in nearby Culbertson to see if they would pay me something for the snake. They offered a trade—a baby racoon for the snake. My parents reluctantly agreed. So, "Susie" became my latest friend and shared my room with Spot and me. Susie rode in my paper bag on my bike on my paper route, peeking out. She won over the household and lived with us for two years until I knew it was time for her to be a free racoon. My dad and I released her in the woods near the river. We were sad to see her go, and we knew it was the right thing to do. Soon she would again be a wild racoon.

At age fifteen I became an Eagle Scout thanks to my mother's reverse psychology. I was just three merit badges (out of twenty-four) away from becoming an Eagle Scout when I stalled. My mother said, "You've been overcome by fumes—car fumes and perfumes—so I will finish these last three merit badges. But I get to wear the Eagle pin." I knew what she was doing. It worked. I completed the badges and learned the most valuable lesson for everything else in my life since then. Completion! Finish what you set out to do and you'll never have to explain. Fail to finish and you will be explaining the rest of your life. By the way, before my mother passed, I gave her my Eagle pin as a symbol of my gratitude for her wisdom and perseverance. It's true that I did the work, but it seemed most fitting to share it with her to honor what we both did together to earn it.

In 1958, as a senior in high school, I was elected Boy Governor of the Nebraska Statewide Hi-Y Model Legislature, an annual youth legislative simulation open to high school students. Students from all over the state came to the State Capitol in Lincoln and served as state senators in the legislative chamber. They sponsored bills, ran committee hearings, debated bills all to learn about Nebraska's unique Unicameral.

I was elected Hi-Y governor from among the four student candidates, one from each congressional district. Since the governor, Victor Anderson, had just lost his reelection weeks earlier and was out of the state, I had the office to myself. As Hi-Y governor, I sat in the governor's chair in the governor's office for two days, signing and/or vetoing bills. I remember saying to myself that one day I will be back and sit at this desk again. On this side. In this chair. As governor of Nebraska. The dye was cast.

Two decades later when Diane and I married, I warned her I would, at some point, run for governor. Like others, she skeptically said to herself "Sure."

I attended the University of Nebraska at Lincoln, earned a bachelor's degree in philosophy, earned a master's degree and taught logic in the philosophy department, and then earned a law degree. I worked for an insurance company, was named the director of the Nebraska Department of Insurance in the 1970s, helped out on the campaigns of Democratic presidential candidates in 1976 and 1980. In the 1980s I was named CEO of the Central National Insurance Group and in 1982, executive vice president of the National Association of Insurance Commissioners, the association representing the states' top insurance regulators, Republican and Democrat, elected and appointed.

In 1981 and 1985, I was rumored to be considering a run for governor, but Diane and I felt the timing wasn't right for our blended family. But in 1989, with three of the kids in college and the fourth graduating from high school, I decided the time had come. I would jump into the 1990 gubernatorial race against the incumbent, Republican governor Kay Orr. First, however, I had to win the Democratic primary.

So, I hired a DC polling firm to conduct a Democratic party statewide base line poll in November 1989. The pollster called me with the results. It showed that out of eight hundred Democrats who were given background information about me, only two of them (not 2 percent) thought I should be governor. The pollster said, "It's a good thing your wife and mother were home," apparently trying to cheer me up. It didn't work. I explained both were still registered Republicans, hadn't changed their registrations yet and weren't in the polling pool. Anyway you summed it up, I had next to zero support. Undaunted, I hired staff and filed to enter the Democratic primary in early 1990.

I faced five opponents: Lincoln mayor Bill Harris; former Omaha mayor Mike Boyle; U.S. Sen. Bob Kerrey's former chief of staff Bill Hoppner; former state senator Don Eret; former regent Bob Prokop; and Rob Nemec, who filed, but was unable to pay the filing fee. (He claimed he could make it rain—that's a valuable claim in Nebraska where droughts are common.) A tough lineup anyway you frame it. My last election was twenty years earlier, in 1969, when I was elected president of the Nebraska Law School student body. I really had my work cut out for me.

Nobody expected me to win and I never expected to lose. My opponents underestimated how important this was to me and how much I wanted to win. Even under a negative siege from my opponents near the end polling showed me ahead. I won by just forty-two votes out of several hundred thousand cast. The narrow margin triggered an automatic recount. Several weeks later after the recount I was ahead by thirty-seven. The partisan board in an unprecedented move, voted to have a second recount which ended the week of July 4. The margin? Forty-one votes. Not waiting for another recount, I filed a Writ of Mandamus action with the Nebraska Supreme Court which met over a weekend and ordered the State Elections Board to declare me the Democratic nominee. I went on to launch a general election campaign and defeated Republican incumbent Governor Kay Orr. No recounts!

In January 1991, Diane and I moved into the governor's residence in Lincoln, just across the street from the State Capitol. In my inaugural address I outlined a vision of "One Nebraska." During my tenure as governor, we bridged the political and geographic divisions in the state as we tightened the state's fiscal belt by several notches, expanded trade, improved education and helped usher in strong economic growth. I won reelection in 1994 with 74 percent of the vote, attracting more Republican votes than my popular Republican opponent. I had made good on my campaign pledge to rein in spending. We had cut the growth of state spending, cut the state income and sales taxes, and provided property tax relief.

I was active in the National Governors Association, co-founded the National Governors' Ethanol Coalition with Republican Terry Branstad of Iowa, and Tommy Thompson of Wisconsin. I chaired the Council of State Governments, the Western Governors Association and Midwestern Governors Association. I took on the federal government in a fight against unfunded federal mandates, the onerous practice where the Congress passes laws or regulations ordering states to take certain actions but provide no funding to meet the requirements. I considered them heavy-handed but empty-handed orders from Washington. So much so, that I had T-shirts printed with the message: "The states are not branch offices of the federal government." This idea would inform my work as a senator later.

In 1996, U.S. Sen. Jim Exon, a fellow Democrat, former governor, and friend, announced he was retiring. I jumped into the open-seat Senate race to replace him. That fall, I suffered a surprising loss against Republican businessman Chuck Hagel. It was tough. But I moved on and finished my second term.

My fondness for pranks landed me on a 1997 episode on the old TV show *Candid Camera*. Here's what we did. I had a desk placed in a corner of the governor's office and staff invited random visitors in the Rotunda to come over, meet me and hear about an idea I had. When each one sat down across from me, I said, "You know, the name Nebraska has served this state so very well. But it's time to move on to a different name. Look at Standard Oil. Now you've got ESSO, you've got AMOCO, you've got all these shorter and more modern names. It just seems to have worked very well for them. So, I've thought about changing the name of the state from Nebraska to a more modern one. I'd like to run this by you. What do you think of a name like 'Quintron?' Or maybe 'Zenmar?'" And mouths would drop open. Usually people just laughed a bit. One woman, though, immediately crossed her arms and gave me a stern look as if to say, "Have you lost your mind?" When I told the others and her that she was on "Candid Camera," and pointed to the hidden camera nearby they all laughed with relief.

I finished out my second term as governor and left with the state's fiscal house in solid order.

Then, in 2000, another friend and fellow former governor Bob Kerrey surprised many by announcing he would retire from the U.S. Senate at the end of his second term that year. I knew I wouldn't get another shot for quite a while. I entered the race, unopposed on the Democratic side. Against Republican attorney general Don Stenberg, who'd lost the 1996 GOP primary to Hagel, I ran hard. That November of 2000, I won one of the closest Senate races in the state's history, edging out Stenberg 51 percent to 49 percent, picking up 15,096 more votes of nearly four hundred thousand cast, even as George W. Bush won the state with 62 percent of the vote. I was grateful for Nebraskans' support. I was on my way to Washington.

Nebraska has been dominated for years by the Republican Party. Over the recent decades, party registration has shifted even more, Democrats have lost ground, Republicans have gained and Independents have surged. When I entered the Senate in 2000 there were 537,605 registered Republicans; 392,344 Democrats; and 153,088 Independents. By 2018, there were 576,916 registered Republicans; 362,203 registered Democrats; and a hefty 256,375 Independents. My 2000 race proved that a Democrat with a moderate streak could maintain a Democrat base and still pull enough votes from Independents and Republicans to win statewide. I never forgot that broad coalition of voters that trusted me to represent them in the Senate. I said at the time I refused to be a lap dog for anyone. I would be an independent-minded leader for all Nebraskans, those who voted for me, and those who didn't. That I would continue to be a fiscal and social conservative. That I would be open-minded to solutions because that's how we got things done during my days as governor. In Washington, I would be willing to cross party lines, to be constructive, to support the president when I thought he was right, oppose him when I didn't, but not obstruct. I would always look for ways to advance progress for Nebraska and our country.

7

In the Senate I was a centrist. It felt natural to me from my days as governor and as a way to represent, fairly, the range of Nebraskans who elected me. Being a centrist isn't being a sellout. Nor is it being a moderate, a label too often attached to me in my Senate career. A centrist isn't necessarily a moderate. But most moderates are centrists. I wasn't a moderate; I was pro-life, pro-Second Amendment, and a fiscal tightwad. These weren't political positions to me, they were core values guiding my personal life.

IN THE 1970S MY late first wife, Marcia, and I adopted two children at birth. I am pro-life, from before birth to all the days on Earth. I'm an avid hunter and have a lot of trophies to show for it. I keep a sharp eye on my spending, my investments and my family's financial bottom line. Always have. My staff liked to tease me that I'm tighter than three coats of paint. So, in Washington, I wouldn't give up those core values, but I would look for ways to bridge differences, to find creative ways to reach goals, and perhaps most important, to listen to what others offered in the way of compromise to get something done. I would be willing to cross party lines; I would try to be constructive.

The Founding Fathers established the Senate to be a kind of fence against the "fickleness and passion" often seen in the public and members of the House of Representatives. George Washington, according to historical lore, told Thomas Jefferson that the framers of our country had created the Senate to "cool" House legislation just like a saucer was used to cool hot tea.

The Senate I entered in 2001 for the 107th Congress was split 50–50 along party lines, with Vice President Cheney expected to be on hand often to cast tie-breaking votes. This compelled senators to work together. Democratic leader Tom Daschle of South Dakota and Republican leader Trent Lott of Mississippi were privately friendly, publicly respectful of each other (and remain so in 2021), which set a tone at the top that the parties would try to work together on issues, until, or unless, they couldn't.

There were many of my colleagues who could be considered moderates, many who operated as centrists, and from that crew there were many willing to work together on a bipartisan basis. Those open to bipartisan collaboration included, on the GOP side, Ted Stevens, John McCain, Ben Nighthorse Campbell, Richard Lugar, Olympia Snowe, Susan Collins, Mike DeWine, George Voinovich, Pete Domenici, Gordon Smith, and Lincoln Chafee. On the Democratic side, those willing to sometimes cross party lines included Blanche Lincoln, Joe Lieberman, Tom Carper, Zell Miller, Max Cleland, Jeff Bingaman, Evan Bayh, John Breaux, Max Baucus, John Edwards, Byron Dorgan, Kent Conrad, and Tim Johnson.

While the two Senate leaders, Daschle and Lott, could fight for their party's positions like heavyweight pro wrestlers, they never made it personal. My how things have changed as I write this in 2020, especially under the leadership of Senate majority leader Mitch McConnell, a man I never trusted one iota. I had fully trusted Trent Lott as Senate Republican leader; he was a straight shooter and a believer in the tradition of the Senate as the place where hot-tempered partisan House-passed legislation was considered by cooler heads. The same was true for Lott's successor as GOP leader, Sen. Bill Frist. You had to work hard to pick a fight with Frist. He was almost too nice to be a party leader. But McConnell was a major departure. He operated with one goal: To secure and maintain a grip on political power and partisan advantage, come hell or highwater.

And the centrist/moderates? Everyone I served with has retired, been defeated, or in the case of Lindsay Graham, swapped progress for hyper-partisanship. Sens. Susan Collins and Tom Carper remain from when I arrived in the Senate in 2001 but only a few colleagues are willing to cross the isle and serve with them today. Some senators today talk a good game about working with the other party. They profess bi-partisanship, but when it comes to voting, when it really matters on big issues, they rarely deliver. Others don't even bother to talk to their colleagues across the aisle and never miss an opportunity to land a partisan punch over even the most mundane matters.

When I entered the Senate, I immediately set the stage for how I would operate by working with the White House to scale back President Bush's first big initiative, a proposed $1.6 trillion tax cut that I helped negotiate to a more responsible $1.3 trillion tax cut. In the ensuing months, I worked with colleagues on both sides of the aisle on budget issues, health care, veterans, national defense, and, after 9/11, on homeland security and war.

Capping my first year in the Senate, the Associated Press reported that, according to a Congressional Quarterly study, I had lived up to my campaign promise of not voting just the party line. I had opposed my party 42 percent of the time and supported President Bush 74 percent of the time. Only Zell Miller of Georgia departed from the Democratic party line more than me. "I don't think the Democratic Party is right 90 percent of the time," I told the *Lincoln Journal Star*. I didn't think the Republican Party was right 90 percent of the time either. "It seems to me when I'm voting with the president, I'm being bipartisan," I added. "I'm a Democrat, but I'm a Nebraskan first. I vote for good policy over politics. I will not put the party first." Then I finished with, "I think Nebraskans want a senator to be a leader, not to play follow the leader."

That trend continued throughout my career. A *National Journal* congressional vote study in 2007 ranked me to the right, yes, the right, of eight Republican colleagues—Gordon Smith, Olympia Snowe, Arlen Specter, Susan Collins, Lincoln Chafee, Richard Lugar, Norm Coleman, and Mike DeWine. Mary Landrieu of Louisiana was the only other Democrat to rank to the right of any Republican on key votes, and she was to the right of just one of them, Lincoln Chafee. For the 2010 *Congressional Quarterly* study, the publication found that in 2009 I was the Senate Democrat most likely to vote against my party, which I did 37.1 percent of the time. No other Democrat, by this time, was more likely to cross party lines more than me.

Finally, if you're lucky enough to get elected to the Senate, you ought to show up. Sure, there's overwhelming pressure to raise money for your campaigns, and some use the Senate floor as a launchpad for higher office, but I believe it's important to show up for votes, to cast your vote for the people who send you to Washington. Over my twelve years in the Senate, while I missed some votes for various reasons, I showed up and cast my vote about 98 percent of the time on more than thirty-seven hundred recorded roll call votes, according to a report from the Democratic Policy Committee. Showing up, doing your job, matters.

As governor, I had learned to work with politicians of all stripes. While some viewed compromise as a four-letter word, I did not. Compromise is about finding middle ground. It's working in shades of gray. It's almost always not about principles, it's about implementation of a law or policy. You don't have to bring the country to its knees to bring it to its senses. You just have to be willing to listen to other ways to achieve a shared goal. My understanding of compromise wasn't always shared. I remember one time when one of my colleagues asked if I could support a proposal she had and asked to come see me. "Of course," I answered. She came to my office. After the usual greetings, she got down to explaining what she was proposing. I didn't see how I could support it, explaining why I thought it wouldn't work for Nebraska. We continued our discussion and she tried to persuade me she was right. She suggested there was a possible compromise, and offered it. The implication being I was known for finding middle ground, so what was wrong with me? "Well," I finally said to her in a teasing tone, "you and I have different ideas of compromise. Your idea of compromise is for me to abandon my position and adopt yours." She sat quiet, then said with a small smile, "I think maybe you're right." We both laughed. We went back to work on it.

I had some guiding practices that helped me in the Senate, and I believe would be useful for today's and tomorrow's members of the Senate to consider.

First, relationships matter. They help bring people together. When I arrived in Washington in 2001, I accepted as many invitations as I could, from colleagues, from the White House, from those seeking legislative change in Washington. I went to nearly everybody's social gatherings or get-to-know-you chats. I came to think that spending Monday nights at the White House with the president was common for everyone, because I had been invited to several. In relationship building, you have to establish common ground with both presidents and colleagues. I remember former House Speaker John Boehner once lamenting it was challenging to work with President Obama because it was hard negotiating with someone chewing Nicorette and drinking iced tea while you're chain smoking and drinking bourbon.

Second, it's beneficial to play both an inside game and outside game. Inside, I worked with the Senate Centrist Coalition founded by John Breaux and Joe Lieberman, which counted thirty-three members in 2002. Breaux and Lieberman formed a centrist political action committee that contributed to my campaigns. Some colleagues would show up once in a while to our weekly centrist meetings, check the box and disappear. I attended most of its meetings. I also talked with the members all week long, week-in-week-out on and off the Senate floor. For the outside game, my staff and I reached out to leaders and groups in Nebraska, their national counterparts and allies in both the business and labor communities. I could at times be the bridge to bring opposing sides together because of this practice.

Third, for me, I never left my governor days behind. Once a governor, always a governor. As a governor, you have to get real things done. You don't have the luxury of being the party of no. You can't obstruct for political gain. From the very beginning, I came to Washington suited up, not wanting to sit on the sidelines.

Fourth, I always remembered my core principles and tried to never trade them away. Of course, one has to have principles in the first place, something not universally observable in today's Senate. One of those core principles should always apply to anyone serving in the Senate. Remember your constituents, the people who elected you and expect you to deliver results for them, for their benefit, for the improvement of their lives. For me, this meant that I couldn't just cut all federal taxes and force the capitols in Lincoln or Des Moines to raise state taxes to pay for federal responsibilities. That's not fair. It doesn't make lives better. It makes them harder.

Finally, I hoped to be likable, approachable, and never mean-spirited. As my dad used to say, you couldn't make people like you but you could make it hard for them not to. A practical joke or teasing comment thrown in here or there helped to break the ice. I remember soon after I got elected, I found myself sitting near Sen. Jim Bunning of Kentucky, who I had not yet met. But I knew his reputation. Bunning had been a Hall of Fame major league baseball pitcher known for his hot temper and brushback pitches aimed at batters' heads. When I sat near him now as a senator, it was clear Bunning was steamed about something. He made a pointed crack, he looked angry. Just about then, another colleague introduced us. I took a breath. I reached out my hand and said, "I haven't had the pleasure of meeting the senator from Kentucky. But I see he's still got his fastball. I just hope he doesn't still have his bean ball." Bunning glared, then broke into a smile. We were friends ever after.

In this book I aim to explain how some big bipartisan deals came together, my views on why that has become rare, and offer ideas to get back there. My dealings with Jim Bunning illustrate how friendships and alliances can be used to translate into bipartisan partnerships on issues that, sadly, today is altogether rare.

In 2003 the federal Centers for Medicare and Medicaid Services published a proposed rule on what was called the "75 percent Rule" that would have jeopardized patients' access to inpatient rehabilitation services at a number of hospitals around the country, including Madonna Rehabilitation Hospital in Nebraska, a premier facility offering specialized care for those who had suffered brain injuries, strokes, sand spinal cord injuries. The CMS actually tried to close more than a handful of these hospitals, which prompted a bipartisan and bicameral group from states affected to join together, to fight back. Bunning, who had a relative who was a doctor at one of the rehabilitation centers, joined me. So did a group of conservatives and liberals that included Sen. Rick Santorum (R-PA), and House members Nita Lowey (D-NY) and Frank LoBiondo (R-NJ), who all had these facilities in their states. We held press conferences together and signed joint letters to the CMS, practices that are much rarer today.

The CMS wasn't convinced the services provided were worth the cost in reimbursement, but we were. When the CMS refused to budge, we introduced legislation in both houses that would enable the rehabilitation hospitals to remain open. The bills moved through Congress and in 2007 we succeeded in passing the legislation that would enable the rehabilitation hospitals to continue receiving reimbursement for services they provided, and to keep their doors open.

Jim Bunning once even helped me pull an elaborate practical joke on my wife during a bipartisan Senate congressional trip, which are known as CODELS on Capitol Hill, to Russia in the summer of 2002. Our group included Bunning, Trent Lott (R-MS), Robert Bennett (R-UT), Craig Thomas (R-WY), me, and our wives. When we arrived in Moscow my wife, Diane, was on guard. She had been coached by a friend familiar with Russia and with the Russian government. He told her all the hotels were "bugged." I assumed this was true and I knew Diane's concerns, so when we entered the hotel room I made a few loud and extremely derogatory comments about Russia. She nearly fainted, saying, "Don't say that! It's not funny." She was even inspecting the TV because she had been told that that's where the bug was located. She unplugged the TV. Shortly thereafter a hotel employee knocked on the door and said he wanted to check the TV, and plugged it back in. After he left she said to me, "See what I told you."

At dinner I quietly suggested to Bunning that we get a waiter to write on a piece of stationary something in European cursive. He hailed a waiter and tipped him to do it. The waiter wrote, "Meesus Nelson, please tell your husband we are not bad people, signed

Yuri." Jim was chuckling so hard he could barely read it to me. He asked the waiter that it be slipped under the door about 2:00 a.m.

Diane was so spooked she was changing her clothes in the bathroom, in the dark. After being in bed for a while, I heard the note being slipped under the door. Diane heard it, too. She jumped from the bed, grabbed the note, and with her ever-present small flashlight got back in the bed with the covers over her head, to read. She poked me and said, "Read this! I told you that wasn't funny." How I managed to keep a straight face, I'll never know. Under the covers, with her flashlight, I read the note, too. I didn't say much.

At breakfast that morning with the whole group, Diane commented about the note and at that point learned about the prank. A good sport, she took it well and enjoyed the joke. But Jim Bunning, who chuckled when we were planning it, now fairly howled with laughter, as did the others. No harm. No beanball. He had a great sense of humor too.

Friendship, honesty, partnership, and humor: they made all the difference in my Senate years.

TWO

The World's Greatest Deliberative Body

WHEN I SHOWED UP in Washington as a new U.S. senator from Nebraska, I had no idea what to expect. Nobody ever does. I'll let you in on a secret: there's no cheat-sheet they pass out on the first day titled "How to Be a Senator." Everybody has to figure it out as they go along. And for former governors like me, the transition can be especially tough. You go from being the chief executive of a state, working with a legislature to enact policies and pass laws that directly affect every resident, to a junior member of a national legislative body where seniority is everything—and we had some very senior members in the U.S. Senate.

But this chapter isn't going to be that much about me. Instead, I'm going to share the history and character of the United States Senate going back to 1789. Don't worry, I don't like dry, boring histories any more than you do. This will highlight some of the biggest personalities and toughest debates from the Senate's first two hundred years or so, including some with whom I served. I will share the stories as I learned them, so that readers get to know the Senate through the eyes of a brand-new senator just figuring things out for himself.

One thing that struck me immediately was a respect among many in the Senate for bipartisanship and for crafting legislation from consensus. Lots of people today talk about the need for bipartisanship, but when I first joined the Senate there were many, more than two dozen, who regularly worked across the political aisle to push good legislation through the upper chamber. I learned there was a robust Centrist Caucus, made up of Democrats and Republicans who often met to try to advance bills that bore a bipartisan stamp of approval—back when that meant something. That bipartisan spirit would fade, flicker, and die in the next dozen years for many reasons, as you'll read in later chapters.

In my first days, there were all kinds of new people to meet, like my fellow freshman Democrat, Hillary Clinton of New York. I first got to know her in the early 1990s, when I was governor and she was First Lady, in charge of President Clinton's proposed health care overhaul, which bore her name, Hillarycare. Once, in a small private White House meeting, I pressed her top aide, Ira Magaziner, for the overall cost of the health care proposal. Magaziner launched into a long-winded discussion about the plan, its improvements and its impact, then stopped abruptly when I cut in, "I heard what you said. But I didn't hear an answer." Hillary shot me a steely glare.

Years later I got to work with her when she was elected to the Senate. It's often said that senators are either workhorses, those who learn the nuances of federal policy and toil behind the scenes to get things done, or show horses, those who seek the spotlight, even borrow it from the real workhorses when it suits their political ambitions. Hillary Clinton clearly was a workhorse. She was always prepared, always serious and often accompanied by a circle of aides toting armloads of background materials.

That's not to say she didn't show an occasional spark of humor and mischief. I remember the day of our swearing-in on January 3, 2001, when we freshmen senators were lined up alphabetically by state. Everyone had brought their own Bible to take the oath of office. The oath is weighty. You get nervous before speaking these lines: "I do solemnly swear (or affirm) that I will support and defend the Constitution of the United States against all enemies, foreign and domestic; that I will bear true faith and allegiance to the same; that I take this obligation freely, without any mental reservation or purpose of evasion; and that I will well and faithfully discharge the duties of the office on which I am about to enter: So help me God."

As I prepared to take that oath, I noticed that Nebraska and New York were close enough in line that I could chat a bit with Hillary Clinton. I couldn't resist. I asked her, with a straight face but jokingly, this question: "What Scripture are you going to read?" Her face paled. She had taken me seriously. "Scripture!" she said in a panicked voice. "Nobody told me I had to read Scripture!" I paused a moment. Then reassured her that I was joking. She took it well, but with a mischievous glint in her eye, she looked over as if to say "Go get Corzine." And so, Jon Corzine, the Wall Street financier and future New Jersey governor who was standing nearby but missed our whole exchange, found himself my next victim of the practical joke. He fell for it, too, and we three had a good laugh afterward.

I wish my fellow Nebraskans could see the Senate the way I was fortunate to see it and come away with the same impressions— like with Senator Clinton, my guess is most of them would have preferred to let her into their homes for a visit than "lock her up," if only they had met her. Not only was it a place where collegiality still reigned, but it was a time when there were still "Lions of the Senate." By serving with them, I became a staunch institutionalist. I have Robert Byrd, one of those last lions, to thank for that.

Byrd was a contradiction in many ways—like other senators of a certain age he had begun his career as a segregationist. He later disavowed those past views and apologized for the error of his ways. But by the time I met and got to know him, it was crystal clear to me that Byrd was fiercely devoted to protecting the Senate and its crucial role in our fragile democracy so that it would best serve the interests of all Americans. With his combed white hair, hawkish face, and often stern demeanor, Byrd looked like Central Casting's idea of a modern-day Roman senator, upholding the great tradition of oratory and debate against an incoming tide of sloth, petty politics and small-mindedness.

As we became friends, I learned how important it was to keep the Senate as it had long been, a deliberative, fairly collegial, at least publicly, body, so that it didn't become a miniature version of the fractious, raucous, and tribal House. Unfortunately, it has been sliding toward that tribal House state over the last decade, and more. In my view, the Senate is a grand institution, essential to the republic, fundamental to our democracy and worth our efforts to save.

I was born in 1941 in McCook, a farm community on the western plains of Nebraska established in 1882 whose population has remained around seventy-six hundred over the last eight decades. In McCook, we had for years one of the earlier Senate lions living in our midst, George W. Norris. Norris passed away in 1944 and his home, which became a historical museum, was not far from my parents' home. He had been a dominant figure in Nebraska politics, a friend of Franklin Roosevelt, a nationally renowned progressive statesman, and congressional maverick in both the U.S. House and Senate. Norris epitomized what a leader should be. He was trustworthy, pragmatic, honest, possessed of strong beliefs, willing to consider alternative ideas, committed to the public good, and tough.

For forty years, from 1903 to 1943, Norris served in the U.S. House of Representatives and Senate, thirty of those years in the upper body. During his career, he championed the transformation of the Nebraska Legislature into a one-house Unicameral to curb the ideological flames of partisanship and because he hated the bicameral conference committees in Congress, which he thought duplicative and unnecessary. Years later when I served as governor, I benefitted from Norris's vision in working directly with the Unicameral's forty-nine senators. People run for those seats with no party designation. Once in office, everyone generally knew who was a Republican or a Democrat. But it wasn't uncommon for members of both parties to chair important committees. Later still, when I served in the U.S. Senate, I got to see firsthand what Norris disliked about the congressional conference committees.

When the House and Senate pass bills that are similar, or even nearly identical, they are sent to a joint conference committee to come up with one unified bill. What I witnessed was conference committees functioning like a fumble and a pileup on the football field where the ball changes hands five times before the referee blows the whistle. They're messy. Good provisions get stricken from the final package with no fingerprints. Bad provisions that many want to be pulled out in conference somehow survive with no explanation. There's a lot of back room deal-making with no public oversight or accounting. Conference committees often add confusion to a final product. The sum of two parts often is not an improvement. One plus one somehow often equals less than one. You'll read in a following chapter how a conference committee was used to strip out a provision I fought for in the 2001 tax cuts battle that might have helped avoid a return to huge federal deficits that have plagued the taxpayers, the federal budget, and our country ever since.

Norris also created the Tennessee Valley Authority, a vast federal enterprise that provided flood control, economic development, and electricity to most of Tennessee and parts of Alabama, Mississippi, and Kentucky. Nebraska benefitted, too. Today, Nebraska is the only state where every home and business receive electric service from publicly owned utilities, run by boards of directors elected by the people they serve to provide electricity in the best interests of customers, not shareholders.

But it was Norris's independent streak and willingness to buck his party and his constituents to do what he thought right that made him exceptional. It landed him in then-senator John F. Kennedy's *Profiles in Courage*. The book addresses eight senators in American history known for their integrity and political bravery.

Kennedy tells several stories revealing Norris's true character. In 1917, in the lead-up to World War I, Norris, who was a vehemently antiwar Republican, resorted to filibustering, a tactic he disliked, to try to block a bill authorizing President Wilson to arm American merchant ships. Norris thought it was the camel's nose under the tent that would draw America fully into a war with Germany. He led a lengthy highly publicized filibuster. That earned him excoriating criticism from his constituents, from leading Nebraska newspapers, from his colleagues, and even the president of the United States. But Norris's filibuster succeeded. The bill could not advance. Norris was not victorious in the end, however. Wilson subsequently declared that a careful examination of the statues confirmed that executive power already allowed him to arm the ships without Congressional blessing, and so he did. Norris was viewed as a traitor playing into the hands of the Germans and many predicted his political career was finished.

Norris decided he would explain his goals, reasoning, and purpose in the matter directly to his constituents back home. He traveled to Nebraska, rented a large hall in Lincoln, and one evening walked into a packed room that, as he strode onto the stage fell deathly silent. Norris looked out on his audience and began with the words, "I have come to tell you the truth."

Incredibly, applause burst out. He went on to acknowledge that many in attendance likely thought he should have stood by his president. But he wondered aloud, "has the time come when we can't even express our opinions in the Senate, where we were sent to debate such questions, without being branded by the moneyed interests as traitors?" When he concluded his ninety-minute speech, the crowd cheered boisterously. A hero! The governor soon dropped his plans to ask the state legislature to launch a special election to recall Norris.

In years following, Norris's fame grew, as did his differences with his own Republican Party. They were never enough to persuade him to switch parties and register as a Democrat. Instead, he became an outlier and progressive leader, but still willing to take up an improbable cause. In the 1928 presidential election, he campaigned for Al Smith, a Democrat and Catholic from New York who favored the repeal of Prohibition—which Norris, a Protestant and "dry," supported. Norris fought for Smith convinced he was right on law enforcement and economic issues. Norris again was vilified far and wide. Smith lost. No matter, George Norris could not abandon his convictions for any reason.

His courage and conviction were so renowned that other office-seekers often made the trip to McCook seeking his endorsement.

Walt Sehnert of Sehnert's Bakery recalled in a piece he wrote for the *McCook Gazette* that in the 1932 presidential race, New York governor Franklin D. Roosevelt made the journey to our small town to secure Norris's backing. At a large rally at the fairgrounds, Norris, then a Republican, dwelt at length on the dangers of extreme partisanship. Norris quoted George Washington who once said, "Party spirit, while necessary should be kept in subjection, especially in a democratic government, else the flame intended to warm should consume the very foundation of our government structure." For his part, Roosevelt lavished praise on Norris: "He stands forth as the very perfect gentle knight of American progressive ideals."

In 1933 Roosevelt became the first president inaugurated under the Twentieth Amendment, sponsored by Norris. He had fought for this "lame duck" amendment to shorten the long time a defeated president or member of Congress continued to serve before they were replaced. He wanted to limit the amount of legislation a defeated officeholder could jam through as they went out the door. The amendment moved the beginning of the term of the president and vice president from March 4 to January 20 and members of Congress from March 4 to January 3.

In 1936 Norris won reelection as an Independent but lost his last election in 1942 and passed away at his home in McCook on September 2, 1944. He is perhaps best remembered for this declaration: "I would rather go down to my political grave with a clear conscience than ride in the chariot of victory as a Congressional stool pigeon, the slave, the servant, or the vassal of any man, whether he be the owner and manager of a legislative menagerie or he be the ruler of a great nation."

For me, Norris loomed large. My aunt Grace lived near the Norris home and was good friends with his wife. My father worked for McCook Public Power, a cooperative that provided electricity to our area, which later became Nebraska Public Power District. He was well-acquainted with Norris's support for public power and creation of the Tennessee Valley Authority. Every Decoration Day, now Memorial Day, my family would drive to the McCook cemetery to pay our respects to family, those who served our country and others. We always drove by George Norris's grave. My father would point and say, "There is the greatest United States senator we have ever had."

While McCook also was home to other Nebraska politicians—Govs. Frank Morrison and Ralph Brooks—Norris was the center of my world. I gained my political views largely from him. From his role in shaping the Unicameral, which wasn't heavily partisan, I learned to work with legislators of both parties. I did that as governor and senator. My slogan when I ran for governor was more than just a catchy bumper sticker. It was my goal for all of the people of our state: One Nebraska.

Many other senators over our 240-plus years fought for their beliefs and yet found ways to work with colleagues of other ideologies and parties, without giving up their core values. They worked to improve the lives of their constituents and the nation. In 1959, then-senator John F. Kennedy presided over an induction of the "Famous Five," to a hall of fame where their portraits would be placed in Senate Reception Room's five open spaces. The ornate reception room lies just off the Senate floor and is where senators meet with visitors, constituents, journalists, and colleagues. A special Senate committee had weighed recommendations from an advisory group of 165 scholars from around the country who offered sixty-five names. Their top choice? George W. Norris.

You might think that would seal the deal. But Norris's inclusion was blocked by three senators, including Nebraska Republicans Roman Hruska and Carl Curtis. To this day, I don't understand their vindictiveness. They were partisan ideologues. Curtis and Hruska should have been better than that. The Senate today, and tomorrow, should be better than that. Members should rise above reflexive loyalty to party, and put the country and our Constitution first. They especially should in the post-Trump era.

So, bypassing Norris, Kennedy led the induction of Sens. Henry Clay (KY), John C. Calhoun (SC), Daniel Webster (MA), Robert

Taft (OH), and Robert La Follette Sr. (WI). In 2004 the Senate added Arthur Vandenberg (MI) and Robert Wagner (NY). These are outstanding senators, which should include George Norris, chose politically risky paths to stay true to their principles.

To this day, Norris has not been properly honored in the U.S. Capitol. I call on the members of the Senate to do so now, to make a symbolic and historic gesture that acknowledges the independent authority of the Senate. Whether it's with a statue, a bronze bust, a painting, George W. Norris deserves recognition as one of the finest examples of what it means to be a United States senator. Everyone who visits the Senate should see, as my father said, "the greatest United States senator we've ever had."

Among senators in recent decades whose courage and effectiveness I'd like to call out are Lyndon Johnson, Barry Goldwater, Bob Dole, Robert Byrd, Ted Kennedy, Barbara Mikulski, and John McCain. I served with the latter four.

One of Lyndon Johnson's greatest virtues was his earnestness. When he was for something, he was 1,000 percent all-in. Sometimes he went astray, for sure. But he's widely viewed as the Master of the Senate, perhaps the most powerful Senate leader in our history. Johnson's workaholic drive, his relentlessness, and his practice of berating, imploring, even bribing colleagues to get his way, is legendary. Despite suffering a serious heart attack in 1955, Senator Johnson went on to push through civil rights legislation and beef up funding for the U.S. space program—issues that also would shape his presidency.

Barry Goldwater might not be an obvious choice. The irascible Arizonan, five-term senator and 1964 Republican presidential nominee, was a staunch conservative. He also carved out a role as an expert in defense and foreign policy. It's his role as a patriot under trying circumstances I would like to draw attention to. On August 7, 1974, with the Watergate scandal engulfing the nation and talk of impeachment in the air, Goldwater, a party elder, joined House GOP leader John Rhodes and Senate GOP leader Hugh Scott, for a meeting with President Nixon. Goldwater told

Nixon he had just sixteen to eighteen Senate supporters left. That was too few to avoid ouster in a Senate trial that would follow impeachment by the House. Nixon asked the men where they stood. Goldwater, sitting directly in front of Nixon, responded, "Well, you don't have my vote."

"I've got a very difficult decision to make," concluded Nixon, according to Woodward and Bernstein's account in their Watergate book. It was clear he'd lost congressional support, including from the most influential members, like Goldwater, who felt compelled to put the good of the nation ahead of party. Today, I wish we had more senators like Barry Goldwater in the Senate. The last four years have been eerily similar with a president endangering national security for political gain.

Goldwater's love of country has at least one connection to Nebraska. One late June day in 1985, the first B1-B bomber swooped over Offutt Air Force Base south of Omaha at six hundred miles an hour and roared in for a landing. The bomber was entering the Air Force's active forces thirty years after the last U.S. bomber, the B-52, was introduced. When the B1-B stopped, Goldwater, chairman of the Senate Armed Services Committee, got out along with the flight crew. He called the B1-B's debut "a great day for America."

Standing on the tarmac, Goldwater poked a thumb over his shoulder at the hulking bomber behind him. "That's a helluva plane."

Goldwater always loved planes. He had served as a pilot in World War II, flying supplies into and out of U.S. military installations and giving rides home to America to weary soldiers.

Down on the ground during that war was another future senator, Robert J. Dole of Russell, Kansas. I didn't serve with Dole but did serve with his close friend and World War II veteran, Sen. Daniel Inouye. Dole and Inouye were like brothers. Inouye and I once traveled to Tuscany in Italy and visited the gravesites of many of those with whom he had served.

Seeing him mourn and pay tribute to those who had fallen beside him in battle taught me something I could never learn from a book or a classroom. Without saying a word, Senator Inouye gave me a heightened respect for the shared purpose and camaraderie among those who serve in America's Armed Forces. We would be allies.

Like Inouye, Dole was grievously wounded on the battlefield in Italy. He spent several years in recovery and never regained full use of his right arm and hand. Later, as county attorney, Dole often worked late into the night, signing welfare checks for poor families. He never forgot the gnawing feeling of dread after his injury that he'd never be able to land a good job. He also remembered the hardships those less fortunate endured.

These two elements came together in the mid-1970s when Sen. George McGovern, a liberal Democrat from South Dakota, approached the conservative former GOP chairman and vice-presidential candidate to invite him to team up on food aid programs, domestic and international. Their partnership extended the food stamp program to all U.S. states, and expanded international food aid programs. Together, they both helped lift the markets for American farmers, help hungry people put food on the table and extend the best of American diplomacy to developing nations. Dole knew the importance of putting country ahead of party. Both he and Inouye served in the Senate to help struggling Americans, not just their own self-interests.

Bob Dole and I share a love of humor as an icebreaker to ease tensions in politics. In the often-stuffy Congress, he remains renowned for his quips and one-liners, delivered deadpan and frequently self-deprecating. He once said, "If you're hanging around with nothing to do and the zoo is closed, come over to the Senate. You'll get the same kind of feeling and you won't have to pay."

Then there were senators who could put the fear of God in you. By the time I entered the Senate the senator everyone looked up to was Robert Byrd. He'd been the Senate Democratic leader during some of Dole's GOP Senate leader days, would become the longest serving senator in U.S. history and always was a fiery defender of American democracy. I can still hear his voice ringing out as he exited the elevators and headed to the Senate floor for a vote: "Make way . . . for Liberty!"

In the 2000s Byrd served as the unofficial keeper of the Senate's traditions and decorum. Author of a five-volume history of the Senate, Byrd addressed each new class of senators with a short history and an entreaty to protect the traditions and role of the world's greatest deliberative body, and the treasured Constitution of the United States of America. He gave me, and probably many others, a pocket-sized copy of the Constitution. His courtly, old-school ways and my penchant for practical jokes had occasion to cross paths.

Byrd forbade female senators from wearing open-toed shoes on the Senate floor. During one rare Saturday morning vote, with senators smelling jet fumes and longing to head home, I spied Sens. Blanche Lincoln, Debbie Stabenow, and Amy Klobuchar. They were hiding out at the farthest corner of the floor near a door, looking nervous. I'd been talking with Byrd about some legislative matter and sauntered over. Time for fun. "Boy," I told the women with a straight face, "somebody's sure got him upset about decorum." They looked uneasy. "Oh," I added looking down, "you've got open-toed shoes. No wonder he's upset." I paused a beat while they fidgeted. "Gotcha!" I beamed. They looked relieved but rueful. Each would remember that day and repay me with their own practical jokes.

I wasn't immune to Senator Byrd's ability to strike terror. Once, when I was still new to the Senate, I learned I was due to sit in the presiding officer's chair that day and run the Senate. I had on a colorful tie, not appropriate for presiding. I knew Byrd wouldn't like it. I also knew Byrd would critique my handling of the presiding officers' job. His assessment would be less favorable, for sure, if I wore that wild tie. So, of course, I drove downtown to a clothing store and bought a new tie. Then, I took my seat at the head of the Senate. I think Byrd noticed that I showed up dressed to show respect for his beloved the Senate. Small but important gestures like this paved the way for our later partnership on an issue crucial to the fundamental nature of the Senate, the Gang of 14 agreement on judicial nominations.

Another who could put the fear of God in you is Barbara Mikulski. She is slight of height but strong of heart. As the first woman to chair the powerful Senate Appropriations Committee, Mikulski made sure that the budget process worked. I served on the Appropriations Committee with her and remember her toughness but also her empathy for the people of Maryland she served. When she retired in 2017, one colleague said of her, "We often talk of the lions of the Senate. Barbara Mikulski ranks among them. I will miss her fierce advocacy, her counsel, her commitment, her tenacity, and her grit."

I got to know one of the other Senate lions just after I got to the Senate. Sen. Edward M. Kennedy and I sat beside each other at the weekly Democratic caucus lunches, held behind closed doors in a room just off the Senate floor. Republicans have similar caucus lunches. At ours, lunches were often sponsored by a senator and themed with fare from their home states. We enjoyed each other's company and discussed action on the Senate floor—all out of the eye of the public and, for the most part, our staff.

Ted Kennedy's humor could match or exceed mine. One day, he sat down and before him was a can of the nutritional drink Ensure. People sometimes use it to lose weight. Kennedy seemed to feel he needed to lose some pounds. "Is that stuff very good?" I said to him with a half-frown-half-smile. "Well," he responded, "you look like you could use some of that, too . . . Next week, I'll bring two!" I hadn't expected that; he was, sadly, right. He did bring two Ensures.

The following week I brought two. Then we started trading weeks and debating what flavors were best. This delighted colleagues at our table and sparked talk about who else was losing weight, should be or was cheating on their diet. Fun as it was, I longed for Nebraska beef. This simple act of connecting on a personal level, a human level, helped me work on serious policy issues with Ted Kennedy. Although we didn't always see eye to eye—after all, I'm a right-of-center conservative and he was a far-left liberal—we engaged in civil, friendly, and open discussions about matters ranging from national security to health insurance to education.

The same could be said for my relationship with Sen. John McCain, who could easily match his former Arizona colleague Barry Goldwater for intensity, a hot temper, and righteousness. One day early in my Senate tenure, when I was still getting to know the place and its players, I spoke out on the floor raising questions about a proposed Patients' Bill of Rights that Kennedy, McCain, and others were promoting. I know a bit about health insurance, because of my earlier career in insurance. The proposed federal bill I spoke about on the floor would have preempted states' efforts to shield patients. I couldn't see any good reason for preemption. Kennedy's chief of staff contacted my chief of staff, Tim Becker, and asked if I would suspend a bit, and come to a meeting. "I think they want to talk to you because you're winning," Becker told me. I said I'd be happy to talk with the bill's backers.

The meeting was held the next day. I came in open-minded about finding a way to bridge our differences. When I walked into McCain's inner office, Kennedy was seated on a sofa to one side. I found a seat. We all looked at McCain's desk. He was hidden behind an open newspaper he held in a death grip. Suddenly, he slammed the paper down. His face red, he shouted, "Did you see what that f— Larry Craig said about me!" It wasn't a question. So, I decided to plow ahead and shared what I was interested in to modify the bill as a possible amendment. McCain looked furious. He then launched into a tirade about what he viewed as an attack by me on his effort to protect patients in the bill, as it was then written. It went on a while. I had been warned about his temper.

When he paused to catch his breath, I jumped in. "Senator, are you about done?" I said. "Because I don't want to interrupt a perfectly good rant. But if your intent is to try to intimidate me, you can't. I dealt with the Nebraska legislature for eight years. And, Senator, compared to their rants, you sound like an amateur."

Silence. I noticed Kennedy was holding a sheaf of papers before his mouth. His eyes twinkled. Then, as if nothing had happened, McCain dove into a discussion about how we might hammer out a compromise. We didn't work it all out that day, but we made progress. As we left the meeting, in the hallway Kennedy doubled over laughing. I chided him, "Well, you weren't much help in there!" Barely able to talk, he said, "You didn't look like you needed any!" Through the rest of my time serving with McCain we never had another testy or cross exchange.

A few months later, I saw the heart of what made John McCain great, his bravery. One day not long after the terrorist attacks on September 11, I was in a meeting just off the Senate floor. Suddenly, deafening warning alarms went off. I didn't know it at the time, but a pilot of a small plane had inadvertently flown off-course and breached the Capitol's protected air space. As though we were under attack, Capitol police ran through the halls yelling loudly for everyone to evacuate. It made the hairs on my neck stand up. Instinctively, I jumped up, and bolted into the hallway, ready to run. Behind me I heard McCain calmly say, "Slow down, Ben. If I was going to be dead, I'd be dead by now." I knew his knees weren't as good as mine. But that wasn't the issue. I held up and we walked safely outside. I'll always remember that walk beside a true American hero. That we became friends, and partners, was even more an honor. He was a Republican budget hawk, a proponent of less government and a strong military, a man of principle, with the background and spine to prove it. He was another of the last lions.

Our bond was never broken, not even when McCain made a play during my Senate career to move the headquarters of U.S. Strategic Command from my state of Nebraska to his state of Arizona. Both of us were on the Armed Services Committee, and someone had persuaded McCain that he might be able to steal away the heart of America's strategic offensive and defensive hub against nuclear war from where it had been for more than four decades, the Omaha area. No way, if I had anything to do with it. I told him privately there was no good reason for the move and

I'd fight him tooth and nail if he kept pushing for it. Then, he just shrugged. He dropped the ploy. We respected each other.

Later in this book you'll read about how McCain and I walked in lockstep partnership for three high-stakes weeks. We and a band of Senate brothers and sisters known as the Gang of 14 worked out a way to avoid invoking a "nuclear option" to change Senate rules in a way that threatened to fundamentally alter the Senate. After many of our compatriots left the Senate, that sadly came to pass, as you'll later read.

McCain also exhibited another remarkable profile in courage when, in a late-night vote in July 2017, he gave a thumbs down vote to his party's most promising effort to scrap President Obama's signature health reform bill, the Affordable Care Act. I played a pivotal role in the health reform bill becoming law in 2012, and while I thought it had flaws, I got very emotional seeing McCain keep it alive as his own life was nearing an end.

As close as I was with Republican lions like McCain, Trent Lott, John Warner, and Ted Stevens, I remained just as tight with fellow Democrat lions like Barbara Boxer, Dianne Feinstein, Barbara Mikulski, Daniel Inouye, Robert Byrd, and Harry Reid.

In the 2004 elections, Senate Democratic leader Tom Daschle of South Dakota lost reelection and Democrats in the Senate saw their numbers drop to forty-five seats (including one Independent), with Republicans holding fifty-five seats. Not long after, Harry Reid asked me to give the nominating speech for his bid to become Democratic leader when our caucus met to organize for the next Congress. Robert Byrd seconded the nomination. Reid and I considered each other friends, but this was a special honor. Reid recently said that he wanted Democratic senators to know that there would be a new sheriff in town when he took over leadership.

"I wanted to make sure that everyone understood that we were going to accept all Democrats, that we weren't going to have a caucus directed by more progressive members of the Senate," Reid said. "That's why I reached out to Ben, because I wanted the moderate senators, and there were more than people realized, like Joe

Lieberman and John Breaux, to know that they were part of my leadership." Reid added that, "Ben was a person we were glad to have; Nebraska was a terribly difficult state for a Democrat." Reid went a long way to show support.

After he was elected Democratic leader, he heard I had expressed strong interest in being on the Senate Appropriations Committee, one of the Senate's most powerful panels, whose members, many of them seasoned veterans of the Senate, worked collegially to steer federal spending all over the country. It was a plum post. Reid called me into his office. "Ben," Reid recently recalled saying, "my staff tells me that you've been telling people I said you could get on Appropriations . . . and you said you'd been telling people that it would be a big help. We were there just the two of us, nobody else in my office. I thought, 'You know, I'm a leader. Why be greedy here?'"

On the spot, Reid gave up his seat on Appropriations for me. I was shocked but also grateful. I would try to repay him in many ways, but the central way was to always, always keep him informed of my efforts to work in small rump groups with Democrats and Republicans. I did this most notably as part of the Gang of 14 in 2005 and on the 2009 stimulus bill.

Reid was famous for calling out of the blue, talking for a while, then, without saying goodbye, abruptly hanging up. One day he called me when I was home, as was my custom on the weekends, driving a tractor around on my land near the Platte River. I shut the tractor off. He asked what I thought of my Nebraska Republican House colleague Jeff Fortenberry, who I had a decent relationship with and told him so. We chatted a while. Then, to my surprise he said "Bye," and hung up. Not two minutes later, Chuck Schumer, Reid's number two leader, called. "Benno," the voluble New York senator said, using his favorite nickname for me. "I know you've just talked to Harry. I just want to know one thing . . . Did he say 'goodbye'?" Smiling, I responded, "Yes, he did." Schumer sounded like a jealous schoolkid when he shot back, "Damn! He's never said goodbye to me!"

Like Harry Reid, Ted Kennedy never ceased to amaze . . . and delight. One day after the 2004 elections, Reid called a meeting of the senators whose terms would be up in 2006 and who would face potentially tough battles. We were known as the Endangered Species. I joined the breakfast meeting with a handful of colleagues, held offsite at a hotel near the Capitol where we wouldn't be seen. Reid started into his pep talk. After about ten minutes, the door swung open. Ted Kennedy never slipped into a room. His personality was electric. This day, he rumbled in carrying a large bundle of books and papers. The door banged behind him, he plopped his stuff on a chair and started taking off his coat, all noisily.

Reid stopped talking and just watched. He then plaintively said, "Teddy! Why are you here? Are you worried about your race!?" Kennedy was up for reelection, but there couldn't be a safer seat for Democrats. Kennedy kept taking his coat off, and waved the *Washington Post* before his colleagues. "No," he said, "but when I read the newspaper and I see the headlines that my friend Ben Nelson is the Republicans' Number One target in the next election, then I think I need to be here."

He looked around the room and declared, "I will do everything I can to get Ben Nelson reelected. I don't care if I even have to endorse his opponent!" The whole place cracked up. We were the yin and yang. But friends always. And no, he didn't endorse my opponent in 2006. He didn't have to. I won 65 percent to 35 percent.

The 2008 Democratic primary saw three of my Senate colleagues pitted against each other: Hillary Clinton from New York, John Edwards from North Carolina, and Barack Obama of Illinois. Clinton was, early on, the favorite to win the nomination. It was expected that most of her fellow Democratic senators would line up quickly to support the former First Lady. At least, that's what the media expected. Inside the Senate the mood was a little different. While Senator Clinton was certainly respected, she wasn't exactly the senator you rushed to sit next to for caucus lunches. Senator Obama, on the other hand, had only been there a few years but had made friends quickly, and seemed to genuinely respect the institution and its members. (Edwards, for the record, was also a much harder-working senator than people gave him credit for.)

Obama, whose Senate office was near mine in the Hart Building, was a very collegial guy, and got along great with his fellow senators. One of the first times I met him, I jokingly called him "Barry," as I'd heard that used to be his nickname. Well, he stood still and looked at me in a way that showed that would not fly. "Barry" had grown up into "Barack," no question about it. He said, deadpan: "If you get to call me Barry, then I get to call you Bennie." Well, I'd outgrown Bennie too, so from then on, we understood each other.

I came out early in support of Senator Obama's presidential candidacy. Senator Clinton didn't like that much, but neither of us were under any illusion that I, the junior senator from Nebraska, was some sort of kingmaker. I did understand who was: our colleague from Massachusetts, Ted Kennedy. His endorsement in the primary would be critical, and I worked hard to bring him over to Obama's camp. One time, I told Ted that Obama represented the future of the party and if he wanted to have a big impact, he could make waves with his own endorsement.

At President Bush's 2008 State of the Union address, I arranged for Obama to sit between Kennedy and myself, Ted on Barack's left and I on his right. I was certain that the media would get the symbolism of our seating. The most liberal and the most conservative in the caucus seated accordingly. I don't know if my words or seating arrangements were persuasive, but it worked. Ted came on board, famously endorsing Obama, the first black nominee of a major party.

Over the course of my dozen years in the U.S. Senate, what I learned about how to be a senator can be boiled down to a few words: be honest, trustworthy, and authentic. Also, while I've always taken my work seriously, I didn't take myself too seriously. If you do those things, contrary to common view that you'll be ostracized by party leaders and the public when you break from your party or take a position seemingly outside public opinion, folks will stand by you. That's what Nebraskans did in George Norris's day when he told them the truth from his heart. Even today, I have to believe, people today will accept you, for the most part, as you are.

Among the characteristics for a senator, being authentic ranks high in my book. I can't tell someone how to become authentic. Either you are, or are not. If not, you probably won't succeed in the Senate. Or you shouldn't. The Senate hasn't always been perfect but it's delivered results in legislation and policy that help Americans in their careers, families, and communities.

I was privileged to be part of a time in the Senate when allegiance to the common good was more apparent than not, and much more than today. I know we can get back there. We can return the U.S. Senate to a great legislative body that addresses the challenges facing Americans, from affordable health care to good jobs, from ravages of disease to a good education, from protecting people everywhere from tyranny and dictatorship to shielding our kids from a changing climate. We just need the will to put country before party. Americans first, Americans always. All Americans.

THREE

Napkin Diplomacy

A ZEAL FOR TAX cuts was born during the 2000 presidential contest. With the federal budget holding a rare in the black status thanks to President Bill Clinton and what would turn out to be a tech bubble, the country had a roughly $230 billion surplus. The presidential candidates competed over what to do with the money. Texas governor George W. Bush promised to take the surplus and cut taxes to give people their money back. That's why they call it a surplus, Bush repeatedly said on the campaign trail, because the federal government has taken too much of your money.

He promised a $1.43 trillion tax cut. His rival, Vice President Al Gore, was for tax cuts, too. But Gore argued that about $400 billion was the magic number to stay fiscally responsible. Federal spending for the military and for education, Gore said, might need to rise to both meet the challenges America faced around the world and to educate the nation's children well enough for them to compete globally. Gore was uncannily foresighted, considering the events and aftermath of 9/11.

Americans went to the polls on November 7, but no clear winner emerged because the electoral votes from Florida remained undecided. A recount was ordered. A month-long series of contentious court battles led all the way up to the U.S. Supreme Court, which ruled 5–4 in *Bush v. Gore*, ending the recount and sending Bush to the White House. A decision that served as a harbinger for the political activism to come in the ensuing years at the Court.

Bush made tax cuts his first priority. The narrowness of his victory, and his practice of working with Democrats in Texas, made this deal ripe for bipartisanship. And bipartisanship was still in vogue on Capitol Hill, if for no other reason than the fact that neither party had a commanding control of Congress.

I was new on the job in the Senate as well, and intended to support tax cuts, the question was how large. Cutting taxes, keeping money in the pockets of Nebraskans, had been important in my political races on the state level, particularly the most contentious one. In my 1996 Senate bid, my opponent Chuck Hagel borrowed a page from Republican presidential nominee Bob Dole—with the hope of surprising me news stories later revealed—and called for a major cut in federal taxes. It would be offset, Hagel said, by cutting budgets for federal regulatory agencies, transferring funding and control of welfare and Medicaid to the states, cutting Medicare spending and shutting down the federal Departments of Energy, Commerce, Education, and Housing and Urban Development.

As governor, I had been required by law to balance the state budget each year. Now in the Senate contest I proposed a balanced federal budget plan, along with keeping the Department of Education intact. I lost the Senate race that year, a deep disappointment. In 2000, when I ran again for a seat opened up by Sen. Bob Kerrey's retirement, I battled GOP attorney general Don Stenberg over tax cuts. I won this time, and fully intended to fight for major tax cuts to return money to Nebraskans they deserved. If the money stayed in Washington federal spending would just keep rising, something I wanted no part of. I had *lowered* the growth rate in state spending as governor, and thought that spending in Washington was out of control. Nebraskans wanted tax relief and less government spending, except they wanted to maintain their farm subsidies; I would try to deliver for them.

In his inaugural address, George W. Bush promised major tax cuts. Republican leaders on the Hill had urged the Bush team to start small because of their narrow majority in Congress, 50–50 in the Senate and 229–205 in the House. Secure some modest legislative victories and then move onto big issues, they advised. As governor, Bush was known for his swagger. It continued as president. Bush rejected the GOP leaders' advice, telling Hill allies he would start big, then move onto other big things.

In his first Rose Garden address, held on February 8, 2001, Bush called on Congress to approve a plan he was sending to Capitol Hill to cut income taxes, the capital gains tax, to blunt the estate ("death") tax and so-called marriage penalty and to help students. His tax cut plan totaled a hefty $1.6 trillion over ten years, one of the largest in U.S. history.

"I've been talking about this problem for over a year and will keep talking until we fix it. We need tax relief today. In fact, we need tax relief yesterday. And I will work with Congress to provide it," Bush said. "Our economy faces this challenge: investors and consumers have too little money and the U.S. treasury is holding too much. The federal government is pulling too much money out of our economy and this is a drag on our growth."

Democratic leaders in Congress responded that while tax cuts were needed, they could not go higher than about $400 billion. That soon climbed to $600 billion, and eventually reached a $900 billion ceiling. Bush's team saw they already were winning, and the president held firm. He was determined not to compromise early, aides later said, and pushed his team to fight for the full $1.6 trillion.

For my part, I publicly said I was for substantial tax cuts, I just needed to see the whole picture of the impact of tax cuts on federal spending in the budget. With the Senate evenly divided along party lines, and several Republicans wavering, the president and his team understood they would probably need support from Democrats to get the measure through the Senate. It wasn't long before the White House came calling to a few Democrats on the Hill.

A few days after Bush's Rose Garden speech, I got one of those calls, from the president directly. When we served as governors in the 1990s, George Bush and I knew each other pretty well and often chatted at the annual National Governors Association meetings in Washington. I liked him. He was a straight shooter.

On his call to me, he used the first ten minutes to make his case and went into detail of the elements of his plan. He made it very clear he would like to have my support for the whole enchilada. I reminded him that, as governors, we were forbidden, by state constitutions, to spend more money than we took in, creating budget deficits.

Things are different in Washington, I told the president, who joked back, "Yeah, there are a lot more zeros." I told him that I felt we needed to be cautious in case the federal budget slipped out of surplus back into the red zone. I suggested to the president that he consider devoting part of future surpluses to tax cuts, with other parts devoted to spending on Social Security, ideas Bush heard but did not endorse.

After we hung up, that same day, I joined about fifteen other House and Senate lawmakers for more tax cut pep talks with the president at the White House. Afterward I told a reporter for the *Omaha World-Herald*, "I support a tax cut as part of a larger more inclusive financial plan. You can't just make a pie a piece at a time. And a tax cut can't be an isolated event. It can't be a stand-alone bill." Before I'd throw in my support, I said, I wanted to see how the tax cut would fit with new planned billions in spending to shore up Social Security, for a new prescription drug benefit, to help farmers and to pay down the national debt. I felt we needed to be cautious in case projected federal budget surpluses didn't materialize over the following decade. I wasn't prescient. I was just being cautious!

Still, I made it clear I supported broad income-tax cuts, ending the estate tax and reducing the marriage penalty that affected many couples. I just wasn't ready to commit to $1.6 trillion. Although I'd only been in Washington a little over a month, I'd joined the Centrist Coalition of thirty-seven senators who counted among its leaders John Breaux (D-LA), John McCain (R-AZ), and others, and I wanted to hear what they had to say about the tax cut plan.

In late February, two Republicans announced opposition to the package, saying it was too large, and several others were reportedly uncommitted.

The White House moved ahead to try to peel off one or more Democrats to support the president's plan, knowing that Vice President Dick Cheney could be on hand to cast tie-breaker votes if needed. Sen. Zell Miller (D-GA) announced his support of the $1.6 trillion plan. The Bushies sent their Hill lobbyists to work on me and a few other centrists. Nick Calio and Ziad S. Ojakli, known as just "Z," became such fixtures in and around my office that we joked we should probably put them on my staff. There even was a photograph that appeared in the media once identifying "Z" as a Nelson staffer.

Sen. Phil Gramm (R-TX), a longtime budget expert, was deployed by the White House to become my new best friend. I knew what they all were up to but was interested in trying to shape the tax package so it would help Nebraskans return money to taxpayers and be durable in the coming years.

Because of my worry about future revenues and possible return to federal deficits, in February I began talking up some mechanism to take stock of the tax cuts and revenues in the years ahead, and make adjustment if the country was running into fiscal shoals. Sen. Olympia Snow (R-ME) wanted what she called a trigger, which would fully block future tax rate reductions if surpluses came up short. Our ideas were similar and a number of colleagues expressed interest in some mechanism to revisit the tax cuts if federal revenue projections proved too rosy. A trigger would automatically block the tax cut if revenues were below budget projections and/ or spending exceeded the budget levels, resulting in not being able to pay down the national debt.

My idea, however, was to add a "circuit breaker" to the tax cut package that wouldn't automatically suspend or block payments, but would require Congress to revisit the tax cut in light of the impact on the budget from a shortfall or deficit, including a review of spending as well as revenue. The Congressional

Budget Office had projected a $3.1 trillion federal budget surplus over ten years. There was simply no guarantee that this would actually happen.

My view was to tie the tax cut, debt reduction, and any new spending initiative to a percentage of the actual surplus. If the economy performed exceptionally, the tax cut could be larger than whatever we agreed to. If the economy didn't perform well, the tax cut would be less, breaking the "circuit" before the budget was overloaded. That would eliminate the possibility of returning to the terrible deficits of the 1980s and early 1990s that acted as a drain on the economy.

The White House tried to pressure me to support Bush's full tax cut. Calio and Z were the carrot, and the political office, run by Bush political director Karl Rove, was the stick. The political team helped organize ads in Nebraska pressuring me to support the president's plan, and they persuaded a number of my friends to call me up and ask me to get on board. It was irritating. I tore into Nick Calio and Z on numerous occasions.

I once told them, "Your White House friends are killing me. You want me to help you, we're talking and negotiating, but your White House friends are trying to undermine me. You can't have it both ways. Can't make war and peace at the same time."

On February 28, they brought out the big gun, the president himself. The day after Bush delivered his first address to the nation from the House of Representatives chamber in the U.S. Capitol (the State of the Union in years thereafter), I joined him on Air Force One to fly to Omaha, where he ostensibly sought to sell his budget and tax relief plan in the Heartland.

It was clear as a bell his main purpose was to get Nebraskans ginned up to demand that I back his tax cut plan. Just a few months earlier, in the November elections, Bush had trounced Gore in Nebraska by thirty points as I eked out a narrow 51–49 percent win over Republican Don Stenberg. The political arm at the White House seemed to think they had leverage, and were going to use it on me.

So, when Bush took the stage before a large mainly Republican crowd at the downtown Civic Center, he said of Hagel and me: "The good thing about these two senators is this: I know I'm going to be able to count on them in a pinch." Bush told his audience that, with a large federal surplus and a sputtering economy, the responsible thing to do was to return the surplus to people who could use it to help the economy bounce back.

"The surplus is not the government's money. The surplus is the people's money," Bush said to applause. "And I'm here to ask you to join me in making that case to any federal official you can find. I think we're in pretty good shape with the Nebraska delegation. I certainly hope so. I certainly hope so." As the largely Republican crowd waved tiny American flags, I turned to Hagel and said, "You haven't come out for his tax plan yet, have you?" Hagel, laughing said, "Well, no. But is there any doubt I will?" I felt all eyes were on me. Bush was pinching pretty hard.

We knew that the president was going to try to put me under his thumb. We also knew the entire national press corps was penned up in a small area as part of the traveling entourage of the president. So, my communications director, David Di Martino, developed a plan. As soon as the speech was over, I would make a beeline for the press riser.

Indeed, as the speech wrapped up Di Martino was there telling the national reporters not to move, that I would come over and have an impromptu press conference at the riser. All they needed to do was wait. The plan worked. I raced over and was surrounded. Even the Nebraska reporters stayed to listen. In fact, it solidified the narrative that I was a target and was standing strong for my priorities. My comments were included in every major media story coming out of that event.

We later learned Nebraska's GOP Gov. Mike Johanns and Hagel had scheduled a press conference for immediately after the speech—so they could gang up on me. But literally nobody showed up as they were all at the Ben Nelson show in the back of the giant hall.

Even in between the intense horse-trading on tax cuts, I wanted to try to lighten things up. I'd always found this as a way to ease tensions and sometimes get what I wanted. Plus, I liked to have fun.

The president was well-known for giving aides, lawmakers, and family members nicknames. He called his father "41" since that was his number in the lineup of U.S. presidents. He gave me "Nellie," ugh. I didn't much like it because most people would immediately think of "nervous Nellie," and I may have been keyed up but was hardly nervous. I sent the president a note expressing my desire "to renegotiate it." I added, "How about something more macho, like Tiger, Killer or Rocky? I don't want to lose my image. Keep up the good work!" I didn't hear back from him, but would in a couple of years.

The Republican-led House moved ahead and on March 8, approved a budget measure on a mostly party-line vote with Bush's full $1.6 trillion tax cut. The House's 220 Republicans were joined by ten Democrats. The president took off on another tax cut roadshow with trips to Illinois, North Dakota, South Dakota, and Louisiana—the home states of key moderate Democrats he hoped to persuade, including Kent Conrad, Byron Dorgan, Tom Daschle, Mary Landrieu, and John Breaux.

The "trigger" idea picked up support from five Republicans and seven Democrats who proposed it as an amendment to the budget plan. Both leaders, Republican Trent Lott and Democrat Tom Daschle, objected to the idea, Lott because a mid-course correction due to a shrinking economy should apply to both spending and taxes, and Daschle arguing for a more reasonable, and much lower, tax cut in the first place. "Back then we talked to people on the other side of the aisle. We didn't call each other names," Lott said in a recent interview. "Tom Daschle and I were great friends. I worked with Ben and a lot of Democrats. It was a different time, people were more willing to work across the aisle to get things done."

My circuit breaker idea gained some traction. Unlike the trigger which would have automatically halted the tax cut, the circuit breaker would force a review by Congress of the tax cut and federal spending if the federal budget surplus seemed in jeopardy. Instead of blocking the tax cuts, it would have reopened the whole tax package for reconsideration, including the possibility of higher taxes. Calio and Z told me they didn't see a big problem with it. They didn't but others did. "It's got something for everybody," I said at the time.

Syndicated columnist Marianne Means wrote that a circuit breaker concept might avoid what she called the hypocrisy that bothered previous attempts to keep tax cuts or overspending from creating deficits. She noted that the biggest failure was the 1985 Gramm-Rudman-Hollings Act, which mandated deep spending cuts if deficits rose. It failed because Congress just tweaked various accounting methods under the law to make the budget figures meaningless.

"A 'circuit breaker' would not be a panacea," Means wrote, "but it would offer a more practical tool for political decision-making than wishful thinking." Unfortunately, the Republican assigned to be my "minder" on the tax cuts was Phil Gramm, a co-author of that law and sponsor of budget mischief to keep it from working.

The House-passed tax cut bill landed solidly on the razor's edge of the 50–50 Senate. For days, the Senate engaged in an extended debate and votes adding or subtracting billions of dollars in tax measures for its budget framework. On April 4, with Cheney casting the tie-breaking vote, the Senate defeated a Democratic proposal to reduce the $1.6 trillion tax cut by $158 billion to pay for prescription drug coverage under Medicare. It was clear though that the votes were not there for Bush's full tax cut and a flurry of votes ensued to add and subtract spending measures to the proposed bill.

The White House again tried both the carrot and the stick. Budget Director Mitch Daniels called the *Omaha World-Herald* early in the day to praise my independence, but then called the paper back later with a sharper message, saying of my vote: "It cut severely into the tax relief the president wants for Nebraskans and other Americans. And it adds substantially to federal spending, well beyond what we think is reasonable."

"It did surprise us and disappoint us," Daniels also said, adding that my previous openness to Bush's plan seemed to be "overcome by the pressure he couldn't withstand from his party elders." I was livid being asked for help and being undercut at the same time.

Around that time, I'd joined forces with Breaux and we planned to unveil a new alternative proposal, a $1.25 trillion tax cut. (We later went higher to return $100 billion in rebates to taxpayers.) We called a press conference without giving away the details. Breaux put out the word that at least one other Republican would join the press conference, maybe more. At the appointed time, Breaux, Jean Carnahan (D-MO), and I walked into the Senate radio TV gallery for the press conference—and so did Lincoln Chafee (R-RI). We were desperately hoping that Jim Jeffords (R-VT)—who suggested he might—would also join us. So, Breaux got the press conference underway.

Unbeknownst to us, the Vermont Republican at that very moment was elsewhere in the Capitol meeting with Senate GOP leaders and the White House on a special education proposal they hoped would persuade him to back Bush's full tax cut. Those talks broke off. Breaux started the press conference with Chafee, Carnahan, and me at the podium, stalling. We were sweating bullets. "Where's Jeffords?" we wondered. We knew that his failure to show up when the news media expected him to be there, because we led them to believe that would happen, would not be good. Embarrassing and a whole lot more.

Then suddenly, almost out of nowhere, Jeffords sauntered into the room, a small smile on his face, and took his place alongside us. "I feel very comfortable here," he said. Boy, were we happy to see him and hear that! Our pulse rates dropped back toward normal. The team at the podium now made it clear that our side had the votes to advance a slimmed down tax package.

Unlike most of my Democratic colleagues who didn't want a tax cut north of $750 billion, I publicly spoke during this time period in favor of a tax cut of at least but no more than $1.25 trillion. Just after a vote on April 5, Calio and Z found me and ushered me into a private meeting with Vice President Cheney.

I had known Cheney, a native Nebraskan, for years and once when I was governor and he was secretary of defense under President George H. W. Bush, I presented him with the "Nebraska-lander Award." I also invited him and his wife, Lynn, to stay with Diane and me in the Nebraska governor's mansion, which he said he'd like to do but declined because with his security detail it would be too disruptive for me.

On this tax cut day, I entered a sizable room somewhere away from the Senate chamber where I had not been before. I remember looking around and saw the vice president and leader Trent Lott sitting at a table. Lott recently said he viewed me then as a pro-business lawmaker who wanted a fairer tax code and believed that "if you cut taxes the right way you get more, not less." Phil Gramm, who'd been lobbying me since nearly my first day in the Senate, was seated in a chair away from the table.

I sat at the table, listened to their sales pitch for the $1.6 trillion tax cut and countered with our number of $1.25 trillion. I thought it was reasonable when it was included with a circuit breaker, I told them. It was a very serious but cordial discussion. Finally, when it became clear I would not budge from $1.25 trillion, Cheney took a napkin imprinted with Majority Leader and wrote a number, then some more.

The napkin had "1.6" at the top, "1.25" at the bottom, and in between "1.425." That meant they might be ready to take $1.425 trillion. He handed it to me. I had just negotiated with the vice president of the United States, who did not have the votes to pass his proposal and instead of losing altogether, decided to offer a counterproposal that split the difference. Some might call it a compromise!

For the first time since Bush had started campaigning for a full $1.6 trillion tax cut in early January, the vice president, on Bush's behalf, indicated they might accept less. Now that they were down, they couldn't go back up. Since it was still a larger number than our $1.25 trillion, and I didn't know what others on our side would say about it, I told him, "I'll have to check with my colleagues."

We all thanked one another, shook hands, and I headed out of the room to debrief my staff on the meeting. As I left, I tucked the napkin from Cheney into my pocket. I took it as a keepsake and memento from a fascinating meeting. Little did I know that the napkin would later become evidence and proof during a visit to my office with author Bob Woodward.

My colleagues and I decided to press ahead for a lower number. On April 6, the Senate voted 65–35 to approve a budget with our proposal for a $1.27 trillion tax cut, which helped move the issue to the conference committee process. My circuit breaker provision was part of the Senate package. At the time, the vice president sounded optimistic about the results, saying, "It's a give-and-take process. That's what I've been doing this week."

Sen. Rick Santorum (R-PA) said, "We now know the parameters of the debate—it's between $1.2 trillion and $1.6 [trillion]. Our goal is to get it as close to $1.6 as we can." I said at the time, "This is a major victory for the president. We've broken through a logjam of extreme partisan deadlock." Congress left town for a two-week congressional break. On May 16, the House again approved a $1.6 trillion tax relief bill. The Senate was where the action really was.

While the tax cut drama played out in public, a private drama was about to explode. Jim Jeffords had for quite a while been unhappy in the Republican Party. The Republican takeover of the White House in 2000 made it difficult to take positions against President Bush, and Jeffords was increasingly uncomfortable in the Republican caucus.

On a Monday in late May, Olympia Snowe, the Maine Republican, warned the White House he might defect. The White House scrambled, Bush met with Jeffords and urged him to remain in the party. But Democratic Whip Harry Reid had been actively courting Jeffords for weeks promising that he could chair the Senate

Environment and Public Works Committee, a post he wanted very much, for switching parties.

On Thursday, May 24, Jeffords bolted from the Republican Party and declared himself an Independent. He said he was increasingly at odds with the Republican Party on issues of abortion, the judiciary, tax and spending, and the environment.

This political earthquake would switch party leadership in the Senate from Republicans to Democrats, moving Trent Lott to minority leader and Daschle to majority leader. It gave Daschle power to set the Senate's schedule and agenda, and to be a strong counterweight to the House under leadership from Speaker Dennis Hastert (R-IL), a newfound force with which the White House would have to contend. Bush's political team would consider trying to get Zell Miller and, to a lesser degree, me to switch parties.

On May 25, the House approved the conference report with a $1.325 trillion tax cut and on May 26, the Senate voted 58–33 to approve the conference committee report pushing the final package to cut taxes $1.325 trillion over ten years across the finish line. Unfortunately, I was told that Phil Gramm argued against the circuit breaker and the conference committee took it out. More evidence for why I agreed with Nebraska's great former senator George Norris that conference committees were the bane of good legislation. In this case, Gramm's move to strike the circuit breaker created the worst nightmare for the perfect budget storm to come: 9/11 and the wars of Afghanistan and Iraq blew up military spending and spending to protect the homeland from terrorism. So much for the stewardship by the co-sponsor of Gramm-Rudman. I gritted my teeth and voted for the tax cut deal.

I was one of nine Democrats who voted for the bill, along with John Breaux of Louisiana, Max Baucus of Montana, Jean Carnahan of Missouri, Max Cleland of Georgia, Dianne Feinstein of California, Tim Johnson of South Dakota, Mary Landrieu of Louisiana, and Robert Torricelli of New Jersey. But others in my caucus were not happy at all.

Before the final vote, the Capitol Hill newspaper *Roll Call* reported that Sen. Robert Byrd, the top-ranking Democrat on the

Appropriations Committee, had warned those of us who broke ranks to support Bush's tax cut shouldn't expect to receive funding for projects in our states. On the Senate floor he followed up with a public warning: "Let me say to my colleagues, if you vote for this budget conference report, don't come to the watering hole."

The legislation cut income taxes, repealed the estate tax, gradually doubled the child tax credit, and provided billions in rebate checks headed within weeks to taxpayers—$300 for single taxpayers, $500 for single parents, and $600 for married couples. Bush praised the bill as one that "cuts income taxes for everyone who pays them." At a White House ceremony on June 7, 2001, he signed the Economic Growth and Tax Relief Reconciliation Act of 2001 into law.

The next day, Bush, who had been an owner of the Texas Rangers baseball team and whose father George H. W. Bush played in the College World Series baseball series in 1947 and 1948, flew back to Omaha. There, he threw out the first pitch at the 2001 College World Series. I watched the game with the president from a VIP box.

This is how you negotiate in a bipartisan way to get something done for the benefit of the American people. This deal came together without anyone calling each other names; the president, vice president, their team on the Hill, Calio and Z, their congressional allies, always were cordial, open-minded. We started low and would have taken low. They started high and would've taken high. We found a middle ground a majority could live with. You can't get things like major tax cuts or durable health care reforms or lasting improvements in our national security done with bullying, badgering, and ballistic tweets.

ONE THING ABOUT SERVING in Congress transcends party lines, no matter who is president. You have to be careful whenever you negotiate with any White House behind closed doors. Before the 2001 tax cuts were signed into law but after Congress approved them, the president invited me to the White House for a victory lap. Soon after I returned to my office in the Hart Building, Bob Woodward came in to interview me. The Watergate reporter who had published revealing behind-the-scenes books on the Supreme Court, the CIA, the Gulf War, and the 1996 presidential campaign was working on a book at the time on Bush's first one hundred days.

He got right into it. "I'm interested in the tax cut battle," he told me, "and want to go over one point." Days before, I had been quoted in the news saying that we were negotiating with the White House, and they with us. Sitting across from me, Woodward told me that someone at the White House, he never would say who, had accused me of not telling the truth. The White House says they are not negotiating with me, Woodward said. He asked what did I have to say.

"Oh, okay," I said. I immediately thought of the napkin. I got up from my chair, went to my desk, pulled it out, came back, handed it to Woodward, explained what it was, what the numbers meant and that Cheney had written them on this napkin. "Well," I said, "that's my side of the story. I should've asked him to sign it, but I didn't take it as evidence. It clearly shows they were negotiating with me. They negotiated $1.425, I hadn't accepted that. We came back and our side went a little higher, their side a little lower, and we got it through the Senate."

Woodward sat there, looked slowly from me to somewhere in the distance, looked back at the napkin and, ever so slightly, shook his head as if to say, "I can't believe it." I still have the napkin. It's framed with a nice note from the president, and a pen he used to sign the tax cut package into law.

After the tax cut passed and the pleasant occasion at the College World Series with the president, there were more carrots and a stick. Republicans began pressuring me to change parties. Sen. Chuck Grassley, my friend and longtime ally on promoting ethanol as a cleaner burning homegrown fuel, approached me on the floor of the Senate. The Iowa Republican, who was now the ranking minority member on the Senate Finance Committee thanks to

Senator Jeffords switching from Republican to Independent said that if I would switch from Democrat to Republican it could pave the way for me to become chairman of the Finance Committee. I knew how much the chairmanship meant to him, and how he'd like to lead it again, and I was impressed by his sacrifice.

There was just one problem. It was very hard for me to entertain the idea of changing parties. Typically, a politician in America leaves their party when the party leaves them. For my part, I felt no animus toward the Democratic Party, or my fellow Democrats, particularly my colleagues in the Senate. I genuinely liked a lot of them and respected all of them. Democrats always accepted me, on many issues, as being somewhat to the right of center. But we had a very solid relationship where I remained comfortable, and still remain comfortable, being a Democrat. Back home, I was comfortable with the Nebraska Democrats. I told Grassley thanks for the kind offer, but no thanks to taking it up.

Around that time, the two Chucks of Nebraska put a stick in the spokes of the wheel rolling to try to get me to switch parties. Republican state party chairman Chuck Sigerson and my Senate colleague Chuck Hagel declared that they were stoutly opposed to me joining the GOP, much to the chagrin of Trent Lott and others who suggested I should change parties. I was asked on CNN a bit later what I thought of Hagel's frequent criticisms of me during my first year in the Senate. Referring to the 1996 contest, I said, "Well, I got over losing. But I guess he hasn't gotten over winning."

I went right on after that time working in a bipartisan fashion of bringing people together, looking for compromises and alternatives, with the goal of helping the American people, and keep my promise to find solutions.

TAX CUTS WOULD RETURN to the fore in 2003. By this time, the economy had fallen into a recession after the end of the late 1990s tech boom and the terrorist attacks on September 11, 2001, and the federal budget went back into the red, running up deficits. Oh, how I and others longed for that jettisoned 2001 circuit breaker. On January 7, 2003, President Bush announced an "economic stimulus plan" to strengthen the economy that proposed a new round of tax cuts, including an extension of some of the 2001 tax cuts and expansion other tax cuts.

"If Congress thought it was good enough in '01 to let people keep more money, they ought to think it's good enough in '03 to let people keep more of their own money," Bush said in a speech before employees of the National Capital Flag Co. in Alexandria, Virginia. The White House cast the president's proposed $674 billion, ten-year plan as giving the economy "a timely second wind" by putting more money in the hands of consumers and entrepreneurs. He proposed lowering the current tax rates of 15, 28, 31, 36, and 39.6 percent with rates of 10, 15, 25, and 33 percent; a doubling of the child tax credit to $1,000 per child; eliminating the estate tax; a reduction of the marriage penalty; expanding a charitable deduction; and incentives for small business growth.

Like in 2001, Democratic leaders on Capitol Hill wanted a much smaller plan, this one totaling $136 billion, which they said would be designed to have a more immediate and positive impact on the economy. They specifically criticized the president for backing away from providing money for struggling states. "The states have a total of $80 billion in deficit spending," said Sen. Chuck Schumer (D-NY). "What are they going to have to do? Well, they are either going to have to cut programs, which will drag the economy down, or they are going to have to raise taxes, which will drag the economy down."

I would never say tax reform isn't needed, but I wanted to try to ensure that any stimulus plan advanced would create or retain jobs, keep the doors of small businesses open, increase production, and increase sustainable wages. I wanted to know how much the package would cost, and for how long it would last.

The president soon rolled out a plan intended to shore up the baby boomer-strained Social Security system. In early February, Air Force One headed back to Nebraska. The president again would try a little friendly pressure on me. Speaking before about ten thousand people in Omaha's Quest Center, Bush made his pitch to a large audience and singled me out. "I am proud that Senator Ben Nelson is here. He is a man with whom I can work, a person who is willing to put partisanship aside to focus on what's right for America. Senator, thanks for coming." My political team loved that endorsement from the president like nothing other. That was political gold. They would share it frequently with journalists for years as a reminder of just exactly what the Republican president thought of the Democrat senator from Nebraska. I'll admit, it made me feel pretty good, too.

After the event, I rode in the presidential limousine with Bush, Karl Rove, and Rep. Jeff Fortenberry (R-NE) back to Omaha's Eppley Airfield. I told the president I was open-minded about his plan and wanted to see the calculations for how it would work. It was a friendly conversation.

One great benefit of the trip was I got to engage in a lighthearted renegotiation of my presidential nickname. I knew that he favored "Nellie," and I had mentioned to him that reminded me of what the late sports announcer Keith Jackson said on at least one occasion during a football game, "Whoa, Nellie!" It was in reference to a runaway horse. The president responded that, in his mind, it referred to the famous White Sox second baseman Nellie Fox.

I suggested that he and I were probably among the few who knew that factoid. I suggested something more masculine, like "Hunter." We went back and forth. "Nellie" and "Bennie" were out the window. The president finally declared that from then on, he agreed to call me "Benator." What a victory!

Bush continued pushing for his Social Security revamp in trips around the country, but back in Washington his focus returned to his economic stimulus plan. I supported some form of economic stimulus and tax cuts, but I was worried about the impact on states that were struggling financially. I heard Republican senator Susan Collins raising the same concerns about the impact on her home state of Maine, and we got together and began trying to come up with a solution. Our staffs researched the issue and we agreed upon pushing for $20 billion of the tax cuts to go to struggling states.

Susan Collins—or "SueCo," as she's known on the Hill—and I reached out to other centrists to build support for including our state fiscal relief plan in the tax cut package. We worked with George Voinovich of Ohio, Olympia Snowe of Maine, and others. Sometimes when you know you are doing the right thing, don't expect others to cheer you on. Our proposal for state fiscal relief was sharply criticized by some Republicans in Nebraska as not needed.

On May 13, the president again flew to Nebraska, this time to pressure me to support his tax cut plan. The House had scaled Bush's $726 billion plan down to $550 billion and the Senate cut it to $350 billion. Congress was in the middle of coming up with a figure all could agree upon.

After the president's speech I told reporters there that I was still open to supporting tax cuts larger than $350 billion, if it included the $20 billion in fiscal relief to struggling states like Nebraska, mostly to come through the FMAP, or Federal Medical Assistance Percentage, program. The White House signaled that it was open to our offer. The bipartisan co-chairs of the National Governors Association, Democrat Paul Patton of Kentucky and Republican Dirk Kempthorne of Idaho, wrote to the Senate Finance Committee leaders, Chuck Grassley of Iowa and Max Baucus of Montana, pressing them to support aid to the states to help deal with their growing financial crisis. "The inclusion of state fiscal relief is critical," they wrote, "to help states manage this crisis and meet our needs in addressing underfunded state-federal partnerships."

Two days later the *New York Times* reported that a bipartisan group of senators reached agreement with Republican leaders on the $20 billion state aid plan, giving strong momentum to Bush's stimulus and tax package. The plan would give $10 billion to states to offset higher Medicaid costs, $6 billion in unrestricted grants to states and $4 billion in unrestricted grants to cities and counties.

I was among those endorsing the plan and told the *Times*: "We've got states removing kids from the health care rolls, and seniors worried that they'll lose their nursing homes. This assistance will go a long way to resolving those problems." I made it clear that I would support the dividend exclusion if we could get that state fiscal relief, and having done that, "I guess I'd better be prepared to take yes for an answer."

Back to the battle, Collins, Jay Rockefeller of West Virginia, and I sent a letter to congressional finance and spending leaders, Chuck Grassley on the Senate side and Bill Thomas on the House side, urging them to include the $20 billion in state fiscal relief in the House-Senate conference report. We noted that states faced deficits of $70 to $85 billion for the next year, and $26 billion in the current year. At the same time, nearly 1.7 million Americans were at risk of losing health care coverage.

"Our states face the worst financial crisis in several decades," we wrote. Fiscal relief from increasing FMAP would help avoid adding to the ranks of the forty-one million Americans uninsured, we reasoned. Jay Rockefeller was critical to getting our plan through the Finance Committee, of which he was a member. Grassley agreed to include it and offered to talk to reporters about the state relief package. Grassley gave my staff his cell phone number and we shared it with the *Omaha World-Herald*.

Grassley flew back home to Iowa, got on his tractor and kept his phone under his seed cap, so he'd know it was ringing. He took a reporter's call to say that I was doing the right thing, from his tractor. Collins, meanwhile, was taken to the woodshed by Vice President Cheney and House and Senate GOP leaders. Cheney, she says, offered to do a deal that put in FMAP money for just the state of Maine, but she told him no.

She was fine when she came back from meeting with them. She was shaking a bit, but she had remained strong. We all but high-fived her. I and my staff and she and her staff gathered together for celebratory drinks at Charlie Palmer's steak house. During this time, she and I went over to the National Governors Association to see what they thought. Governors almost uniformly greatly appreciated our efforts on FMAP. They also liked my line that "states are not the branch offices of the federal government, but the laboratories of democracy."

Ten days later, the House and Senate—with Cheney casting the tie-breaking vote in the 50–50 tally—approved the final bill. Zell Miller and I cast the only Democratic votes for the bill. It provided $350 billion in tax cuts and $20 billion in state fiscal relief. The bill increased the child tax credit for the middle class, and provided broad tax relief. Taxes or dividends and capital gains were reduced and tax rates in the highest brackets were lowered faster than in the 2001 tax bill. The legislation was signed into law by Bush on May 28, 2003.

"It was incredibly hard, incredibly hard to get support," Collins recently said. "And we felt so strongly that it was needed." She noted that she and I represented rural states, both had experience prior to the Senate in insurance—as state regulators—and brought that knowledge to the Senate. "It was a great partnership, we hung in there together, and I think it made a difference for the country."

One closing thought is important for centrist-minded politicians to remember. As I mentioned, sometimes when you know you are doing the right thing for your state, don't expect others to cheer you on. My colleague Chuck Hagel labeled it a gift, said states must make tough decisions to control their spending, but then voted for my plan.

Back in Nebraska while the tax bill was moving through Congress, some Republicans, including the Nebraska governor, Mike Johanns, sharply criticized our bipartisan proposal for $20 billion for the states as unnecessary, unwanted, and part of the unsavory Washington deal-making voters deplored. It didn't matter, apparently, that the bipartisan leaders of the National Governors Association had strongly endorsed the state fiscal relief plan, writing that it "is critical to help states manage this crisis and meet our needs in addressing underfunded state-federal partnerships."

Just eight months later, on January 16, 2004, Johanns gave his State of the State address, which disclosed his plan for closing a $211 million state budget shortfall. Nearly half of the money—totaling $101 million—was coming from *those same* state fiscal relief funds that came to Nebraska in the federal tax bill. The money came from the same state fiscal relief I had fought so hard for and he had fought so hard against. Taking and using the money would keep Johanns from violating the Nebraska constitution requiring a balanced budget. The governor's press release on the issue included this line: "Gov. Johanns proposes utilizing federal fiscal relief funds provided to Nebraska, which will avoid the need for harsh reductions in essential government services."

Bipartisan teamwork in Washington was valuable and helpful in Nebraska after all, even if Johanns refused to acknowledge how he benefitted.

THE PRESIDENT AND I remained on very good terms and he seemed to understand that it was better to work with me than to work on me. But the White House political shop didn't get the memo. By late 2004, it was scheming about a swap to boost its power. The thinking seemed to go something like this: Getting me out of the Senate could increase the GOP's advantage beyond its narrow 51–48 seat edge.

So, my cell phone rang one Friday afternoon in November. It was Bush's political director, Karl Rove. This is how these dances go. Rove asked me what, if the president were to offer me the post of Secretary of the U.S. Agriculture Department, would I say. The White House had recently forced out Agriculture Secretary Ann Veneman, and this should be a plum job for someone from an agriculture state like Nebraska. Would I take the job, Rove asked.

I thought about it for a while and called back. Nope, I'm not interested, I told him. Rove seemed nonplussed. He told me he'd give me the weekend to think it over. Fine, I said. But I don't need the time. I'm happy where I am, in the Senate. Then, the White House, I assume, leaked details of the call to the media and my life got interesting. Media stories portrayed me as under intense pressure. I felt little of it.

From their perspective, it might have looked like a sweet deal. If I took the Ag job, Gov. Johanns, a Republican, would get to appoint my successor, beefing up the Senate GOP majority. The farmers of the country would welcome a farm-state former governor at the USDA. The White House could claim it had more bipartisan representation in the president's cabinet in addition to Democrat Norman Mineta, serving as Transportation Secretary. Also, they wouldn't have to negotiate with me again to push their proposals through the Senate because I'd be out of the way and a new Republican from Nebraska, grateful for the opportunity, would certainly be more compliant than me. Voila! It looked perfect, from their perspective. But not from mine.

First and foremost, you always feel honored to be considered for attractive jobs and a cabinet post was among the most attractive in the country. But I didn't really want the job. The next agriculture secretary would have to go to farm country and tell farmers that the Bush administration was cutting their federal support through budget cutbacks. A farming life is always hard, the profit margins are always narrow, and farmers need the government to back them up when sudden trouble arrives, like a drought, floods or trade problems. So, they wanted me to be the bearer of bad news in bad times. No, thanks!

Second, and equally important, I greatly enjoyed working with Senate colleagues on both sides of the aisle on matters of war and peace, on tax policy, on health care, on public safety and national security. They were men and women with smarts, savvy, and a commitment to the people of their state and the nation. They took public service seriously. When I had headed to the Senate with trepidation in 2001, I'd worried that it'd be frustrating for a former governor to struggle to get anything good done.

In fact, I'd found just the opposite. It certainly wasn't easy street, but the Senate functioned well and addressed the issues that concerned Americans most—their jobs, their health, their families, and their sense of security. I was having a good time, far too good to leave for a thankless job of telling farmers, many from my state, and many whom I counted as friends, no.

So, early the next week I let the White House know I really did not want the agriculture job. Much to my surprise, someone else held up his hand publicly and announced he was interested: Mike Johanns, the governor of Nebraska. Within a few short weeks, he was nominated, fully supported by Hagel and myself, confirmed by the Senate and became the fourth Nebraskan to hold that post. He served very effectively as agriculture secretary from 2005 to 2007. Republican David Heineman became governor of Nebraska.

Rove didn't quit, though. He traveled to Nebraska and recruited Pete Ricketts, the son of Ameritrade Founder Joe Ricketts, to run against me in 2006. I won that contest 63.8 percent to 36.1 percent. I would return to the Senate for a second term.

At an event not long after the elections I ran into Rove. He'd heard an earful from my Republican friends that I was frustrated that I apparently was good enough for the Bush team to offer me a cabinet post, not good enough to remain in the Senate, where I might continue to be an ally, for the right cause.

"I hear I owe you an apology," Rove said. "No," I responded. "An explanation . . . How can you expect me to work with you and the president when you mistreat me like that?" He didn't have an acceptable answer. No matter. On many subsequent issues I continued supporting the administration and the president continued to call me Benator.

During the Bush years, some of my Democratic colleagues were wary sometimes around me, sending out a vibe that I seemed a little too close to the Republican president for their tastes. What an opportunity!

One evening before one of Bush's State of the Union addresses to Congress, we senators gathered outside the Senate chamber to prepare to walk across the Capitol together to the House chamber for the big speech. For most State of the Union addresses, under a president of either party, most everyone in Congress is keyed up beforehand, eager to hear the president's spin, proposals and plans. This one was no different.

As we were waiting to head across the Capitol, one of my fellow Democrats announced, with some excitement, that he had just gotten an electronic copy of Bush's speech on his Blackberry. Who wants it? "Nah," I said to the group, "I've already read it." We were walking and they all stopped in their tracks and several shot me dagger eyes. As if to say, "We knew it! You are *that* close to Bush!"

I just smiled. After a couple second pause, I said, "Gotcha!" Everyone groaned, ready to strangle me. They'd been had—again.

FOUR

War and Peace

JUST A FEW MONTHS into my time in the Senate, blinding change came out of a clear blue sky. For the entire nation, September 11, 2001, would never be forgotten. Per my usual routine, I had returned the day before from Omaha to Washington. I got up early that Tuesday the 11th, a brilliantly clear and warm day, to attend a business breakfast near the Capitol. A member of my staff picked me up afterward to head to my office in the Hart Senate Office Building and, as we passed La Colline, a well-known gathering place for senators, lobbyists, and reporters, we heard something on the radio about smoke blowing this way and that way. Probably a house fire, I thought.

We parked in the Senate Hart Office Building basement, rode up the elevator to the seventh floor and strode into my office, finding everyone there gathered around a TV, raptly watching coverage of one of the World Trade Center towers in New York City, the top of which was billowing with smoke and fire. Suddenly, a jet flew across the TV screen. It smashed into the other World Trade Center tower and burst into flames. In an instant we knew the crashes were not accidental. Over the next hour we watched the towers burn, and saw them collapse in a horrifying heap of twisted metal and clouds of toxic dust that marked the death of thousands trapped inside and aboard the planes.

Everything went haywire. Local news coverage in Washington at one point blurted out that smoke had been seen at the Pentagon, then at the State Department, then there was a rumor that a plane had crashed not far from the White House. We got no credible information from any branch of law enforcement. We waded through misinformation on the radio, TV, and online, as the media struggled to determine what was happening and why. I and my staff were worried there might be more attacks. In a rush to leave but realizing we might not be back for a while, everyone grabbed laptops, cameras, Blackberry devices, cell phone chargers, and other equipment to set up a makeshift office in my kitchen at my home a few blocks away. We watched the news coverage on TV, took calls from reporters, and I checked in with Diane and the children and grandchildren back in Nebraska.

This was a crazy few hours. We thought we were in danger. We were shocked as it became clear that terrorists had used four large commercial jets loaded with passengers and fuel to attack our country, killing more than three thousand people in explosions at the World Trade Center, the Pentagon, and a field in Pennsylvania. This act of terrorism forever changed America.

President Bush, who had traveled to Florida, began September 11 visiting the Emma E. Booker Elementary School in Sarasota and heard as he entered the school that an airplane had crashed into the World Trade Center. As he was reading to the children, his chief of staff informed him a second plane hit the second tower and that America was under attack. Bush left the school, Air Force One flew to Barksdale Air Force Base, then to U.S. Strategic Command at Offutt Air Force Base, just south of Omaha, and returned to Washington DC that evening. That Friday, the president spoke at a National Day of Prayer and Remembrance at the National Cathedral, then flew to New York City and while visiting Ground Zero, with weeping families around him, he climbed atop a pile of torn metal, and when they called out they couldn't hear him, he accepted a bullhorn handed to him and memorably responded, "I can hear you! The rest of the world hears you! And the people who knocked these buildings down will hear all of us soon!"

Late that week, after the grounding of all civilian flights was lifted, I flew back home to Nebraska through Milwaukee.

The 9/11 attacks pushed much of Bush's domestic agenda off the table and thrust national security into the forefront of all of Washington's focus. I served on the Senate Armed Services Committee, and our work got a whole lot busier. As we prepared our military response to these attacks, I worked with Republicans like former secretary of the Navy John Warner and John McCain—a man who had experienced war up close—to wage the War on Terror in a responsible way. President Bush launched the hunt for the mastermind of the terrorist attacks, Osama bin Laden, and ordered American troops into Afghanistan to defeat the Taliban and al-Qaeda, believed to be linked to bin Laden.

On September 18, Congress approved and Bush signed a joint resolution authorizing a military response against those behind the 9/11 attacks. That fall Congress also approved, and Bush signed, creation of the new Department of Homeland Security and the USA Patriot Act, moves designed to protect Americans and allow law enforcement to suspend some privacy protections in the pursuit of information about those who would seek to do us harm.

In October the U.S. unleashed Operation Enduring Freedom, the official name for the Global War on Terrorism. The mission initially sent airstrikes and thousands of U.S. troops into Afghanistan to defeat al-Qaeda and the Taliban, to capture bin Laden, and to help establish a democratically run government. Some favored expanding the war in Afghanistan to Iraq, but there was division. Secretary of State Colin Powell opposed expansion, while Vice President Cheney and Defense Secretary Donald Rumsfeld backed ousting Iraqi leader Saddam Hussein as a key element of the War on Terror. The president, reportedly, declined to expand the war to Iraq though expected to come back to the issue when Afghanistan was more under control.

IN EARLY 2002, AS a member of the Senate Armed Services Committee, I traveled to Afghanistan on what is known in Washington as a CODEL, an official congressional delegation trip. We initially flew into Uzbekistan and then drove into Afghanistan. Even with tight military security I was a bit nervous. We were the first U.S. congressional delegation to travel by road and it was bomb-pocked. Security instructed us to be cautious. They said if we came under attack, they would yell "scatter, scatter!" and we should exit the vehicle fast, not to run to the ditch (ditches were full of landmines) but instead head directly to the vehicle behind us and see if we could get in.

All at once this war became very real. I remember rehearsing those instructions with Olympia Snowe (R-ME) as we rode along the roads. We were deadly serious because we knew there would likely be no time to think—only react. We saw burned-out Russian tanks from the lengthy war with Russia which the Afghans had won. This was not a "AAA approved" route through pleasant scenery. This was an active war zone.

In Kabul we went through a crowded market teeming with people, shops consisting of small tents and "gas stations" with no pumps but glass bottles filled with fuel. We were on edge. We arrived at the abandoned U.S. Embassy where a few Americans were putting tables and chairs back into offices. We were greeted at a front door that still had a bullet lodged in it. A reminder of a not so long ago, prior time. Plumbing was not operational. Probably electricity was out, too.

We left and went to the palace, which had been occupied by the Taliban, and were hosted by Hamid Karzai to an Afghan lunch at the same table where the Taliban had likely enjoyed the same food he was now serving us. The bullet, the abandoned embassy, and this meal made the whole U.S. endeavor in Afghanistan very real. This was no movie set. Karzai was friendly and willing to talk diplomacy, making it clear that the U.S. couldn't pull out like it did last time leaving the country vulnerable to another outside crowd like the Russians or Iran.

After our time in Afghanistan, our plane flew to Islamabad, Pakistan. In Islamabad, we stayed at a Marriott, later bombed by the local opposition, and went to meet with the president—Gen. Pervez Musharraf. Fortunately, there would be more security. Musharraf had granted air space rights to the U.S. for the war easing access for our military aircraft to take us out of the country.

When we met the subject of Pakistan's nuclear arsenal came up. I asked Musharraf, "How certain are you that you have all of your arsenal secure?" He looked at me, paused for a second, and said, "Ninety-five percent." That ended the topic. He was friendly, blunt, and engaging.

A few years later, in 2008, on my next meeting with President Musharraf in his office, he looked at me with a twinkle in his eye. "Senator Nelson," he said, "you asked me how certain I was we had our nuclear arsenal secure?" I responded, "Yes, I remember." Musharraf said, "How certain are you that yours is secure?" Hmmmh.

This was not long after the disturbing news that Air Force personnel had unknowingly loaded six live nuclear warheads onto a bomber in North Dakota which flew to Barksdale Air Force Base in Louisiana, where they sat unguarded for a day and a half. He had me. Not to be outdone, however, I said "Ninety-six percent." We both chuckled. A teaching moment for Musharraf. A learning moment for me.

ONE MORNING IN MID-MAY of 2002, I traveled from my home near Capitol Hill to the Pentagon for what was billed on my schedule as a breakfast briefing with Secretary of Defense Donald Rumsfeld. As a member of the Armed Services Committee, I got to know Rumsfeld pretty well. He testified often before our committee about the War on Terror and called me directly so often it drove my communications director, David Di Martino, nuts. I'd casually mention that I'd just talked to the secretary of defense and David would shoot back, "What'd Rumsfeld want?" The interesting thing was the one-on-one calls seemed to be, at least to me, mainly temperature-taking outreaches.

On the May morning as I walked into the Pentagon I expected more of that, and I expected to join a handful of Armed Services colleagues meeting with Rumsfeld. When I got to his rather imposing suite of offices, I didn't see anyone else waiting in the hallway. I must be late, I thought. A military aide ushered me inside and I was surprised to see a table set for just two people, Rumsfeld and me. He greeted me warmly and over breakfast we talked about the war in Afghanistan, about geopolitical relations in the region and general matters. There was never an ask. Although, as you'll read soon, the Bush team was starting to think beyond Afghanistan, Rumsfeld did not sound me out on further intervention in places like Iraq.

That's how a number of the top policy team in the Bush administration operated. They tried to first establish personal connections with members like me in settings devoid of asks, or requests for action. Those might, and often did, come later. The personal connections made the policy conversations far more collaborative than confrontational. It was a style I respected.

By the summer of 2002, with the war in Afghanistan progressing, the Bush administration began publicly raising the idea of invading Iraq. Administration officials argued that Iraq and its dictator Saddam Hussein posed a threat to the region and the world because the country continued to possess and manufacture weapons of mass destruction (WMDs) and supported terrorist groups including al-Qaeda, the architects of the September 11 attacks. Iraq's invasion of Kuwait in 1991 ended in its defeat by a broad U.S.-led coalition in the Persian Gulf War.

Saddam Hussein clung to power, brutally suppressed uprisings by the Kurds and Shi'ites, and flouted United Nations sanctions and bans on weapons of mass destruction. This led to U.N. weapons inspectors uncovering weapons and barred technology in the 1990s, orders from President Bill Clinton to bomb military installations and a refusal by Saddam Hussein to allow inspectors back into Iraq. Now, in 2002, the Bush administration, led by its neocon wing, a group pushing for a more interventionist role in international affairs, alleged that Saddam had kept a stockpile of chemical and biological weapons in hiding, violating UN resolutions, that he might give them to terrorists, and was trying to develop nuclear weapons.

Many of us in both parties in Congress were skeptical about shifting the U.S. focus away from Afghanistan. I was among those concerned that the neocons were just trying to finish what they felt was left open-ended after the Persian Gulf War of 1991–92—Saddam's expulsion from power and an attempt to plant a seed of democracy in an unsettled region we depended on for oil. These neocons appealed to Bush to take Saddam Hussein out, once and for all, because he had in the early 1990s plotted to assassinate Bush's father, President George H. W. Bush. The neocon crowd acted like they had everything figured out about the dangers Iraq posed and how the U.S. military would be received if it invaded, like long lost uncles and aunts. Certainly, the neocons were smart, in a thirty-thousand-foot theoretical way, but they had no common sense, no real grasp of how a war might unfold. Few, if any, had ever seen combat. I hadn't either. Being a sergeant major in the Air Force ROTC at the University of Nebraska didn't count. That's why I wanted to hear what our military leaders had to say, and would query them again and again in Armed Services Committee public and private hearings over the next years.

In August 2002, the administration stepped up its case for action against Saddam Hussein. The Defense Department's Douglas Feith, undersecretary of defense for policy, one of the neocons, gave a radio interview broadcast in Iraq, calling for the Iraqi people to overthrow Saddam. "The future that we see from Iraq is a future that would be based on the Iraqi people freeing themselves from the oppression they are now suffering," he said.

Vice President Cheney became the point man, and delivered the administration's argument for invading Iraq in a speech to a Veterans of Foreign Wars convention. He warned that Saddam would have nuclear weapons "fairly soon," and wouldn't wait long before unleashing his most lethal weapons upon neighbors and the world. While Cheney conceded that the administration might never know exactly the breadth of Saddam's efforts to develop weapons of mass destruction, he said it would be incredibly risky to misread a dictator who has already used such weapons.

"There is no doubt that Saddam Hussein now has weapons of mass destruction," Cheney said. "There is no doubt that he is amassing them to use against our friends, against our allies, and against us." I would long remember those words. Un-truths travel farther and faster than the truth.

The administration was aware of nascent opposition from lawmakers about going to war in Iraq when we were so heavily engaged in Afghanistan. The Bush team said it would "consult" with Congress, but declined to say whether it would seek authorization for war as Bush's father did in 1991 for entering the Persian Gulf war. Almost immediately, my Nebraska colleague Chuck Hagel, a combat veteran of the Vietnam War, began pushing the Bush administration to seek formal authorization for war from Congress. It pushed back. The administration's position was that it did not need Congress's blessing for the commander-in-chief to protect our national security.

Hagel's basic argument—that a president should seek the support of Congress, duly elected by the people of our nation, and even want that support to bolster his position before putting American lives and treasure at risk in a war—found support from Republicans and Democrats, including me. The Iraq issue put all of us in a delicate situation.

If Saddam indeed had weapons of mass destruction and might use them or give them to terrorists, shouldn't we intervene to protect innocent lives? Should we give a blank check to go to war? Or should we demand that the administration take more time, for investigations in-country by UN weapons inspectors and for more international and diplomatic leverage to force Saddam to disarm, or at the very least stop his bellicose threats against others in the region.

We held hearings in the Armed Services and Foreign Relations committees in the early fall, seeking to ascertain how much of a threat Saddam posed to the Middle East region, and the world. We sought to learn whether elevated pressure from the international community could determine the presence of weapons of mass destruction in Iraq. And we sounded out our military leaders on how a war might be waged, if it came to that.

The Bush administration eventually recognized that it needed Congress on board for war with Iraq, if for no other reason that it controlled the purse strings the administration would need to loosen to fund an invasion to overthrow Saddam Hussein. On September 12, one year and one day after the attacks, President Bush addressed the United Nations, and spoke of threats of further terrorism hiding in many countries, including the United States, then got down to business.

"In one place, in one regime, we find all these dangers in their most lethal and aggressive forms—exactly the kind of aggressive threat the United Nations was born to confront," Bush told leaders from around the world. That place was Iraq. He continued, "With every step the Iraqi regime takes toward gaining and deploying the most terrible weapons, our own options to confront that regime will narrow. And if an emboldened regime were to supply these weapons to terrorist allies, then the attacks of September 11 would be a prelude to far greater horrors . . . We cannot stand by and do nothing while dangers gather. We must stand up for our security and for the permanent rights and the hopes of mankind. By heritage and by choice, the United States of America will make that stand."

It was a well-spoken argument for intervention in a sovereign state; it just wasn't backed up by the facts, we would later learn.

In early October the House and the Senate engaged in a multiday debate over Iraq's threats, a war resolution, options for peace, the need for weapons inspectors to scour Iraq, and the role the UN could or should play in the growing conflict.

On October 8, I spoke on the floor, along with colleagues Arlen Specter (R-PA), Max Cleland (D-GA), another Vietnam War veteran, and Ted Stevens (R-AK). I noted that Secretary of State Colin

Powell was alone among Bush's advisers suggesting that putting weapons inspectors back into Iraq and making sure they could do their job was the right course to pursue, and I talked about how to guarantee those inspectors unfettered access to determine, once and for all, the existence or absence of WMDs, and disarm Iraq if needed. I spoke about what a congressional resolution should be, and what it should do. In part, I said:

> In concert with a focus on disarmament, a Congressional resolution should also strongly urge the president to exhaust all diplomatic efforts within and outside the United Nations. Total disarmament of Iraq should be a multinational effort. Nevertheless, we must reserve the right, and give the president the authority, to act unilaterally provided the presence of an immediate and grave threat to the United States.
>
> This Congressional resolution should not give the president an immediate and unconditional pass to wage war but should place an emphasis on his diplomatic effort to resolve the issue of disarmament without the loss of life. If Saddam's defiance leads to war, we must also focus on what we will need to do to accomplish, after the war, in order to ensure the stability of the region. More thought must be given to the effort that will be required to maintain peace and provide for the Iraqi people in the event that Saddam fails to resolve this issue peacefully. We seek no quarrel with the people of Iraq and the international community must be prepared to assist them.

A couple days later Congress gave Bush the green light. The Democrat-led Senate voted 77–23 (I voted aye) and the GOP-led House voted 296–133 to authorize Bush to go to war in Iraq. A handful of Republicans in both houses opposed the war resolution. West Virginia Democrat senator Robert Byrd, one of the Senate lions, warned that the measure was just another Tonkin Gulf measure handing the president unchecked power. "Remember the Constitution!" Byrd fairly roared. From the opposing side of the issue another lion roared back. Arizona Republican senator John McCain said that giving peace a chance only gave Saddam Hussein more time to prepare for war at a time of his choosing and "in pursuit of ambitions that will only grow as his power to achieve them grows."

The resolution authorized Bush to use America's armed forces "as he determines to be necessary and appropriate" to defend our country from "the continuing threat posed by Iraq" and to enforce "all relevant" United Nations Security Council resolutions concerning Iraq. It required Bush to report to Congress within forty-eight hours of any military action.

This was a tough issue, a tough vote, one that I've mulled since many times. We were so misled by so many—the Bush team, our intelligence services, the intelligence services in other nations, leaders in other nations, and mystifyingly by Saddam Hussein, who chose bellicosity rather than honesty, with disastrous consequences. I do not regret voting for the war. I regret that the misinformation was so bad.

I would later feel that if they had hoodwinked Secretary of State Colin Powell, how could anyone in Congress really see the truth? As we would ruefully learn later, there were no weapons of mass destruction in Iraq, no nuclear weapons buildup. What we found in Iraq, however, would prove to be a huge challenge, one of the unanticipated consequences of war.

In the end, however, bipartisanship helped Congress do its job. And you'll soon read bipartisanship paved the way for congress asserting its constitutional role of oversight for the war and chaos that ensued. It was important, at this moment, that members of Congress in both parties had weighed in, provided the checks and balances on the president's power required by the Constitution, and set the stage to play an active role in the prosecution of the war. This became all the truer as the war dragged on for years, taking thousands of U.S. lives and hundreds of thousands of Iraqi lives, costing hundreds of billions of dollars of taxpayers' money and shredding any semblance of stability in the region. To this day much of the region remains in chaos and immense suffering marks the lives of so many of its residents.

Fast forward to present times. What did Congress do in 2019 when President Trump announced he was abruptly withdrawing U.S. forces from protecting the Kurds from attacks from forces loyal to Syrian president Bashar al-Assad? Even when that withdrawal led to the slaughter of Kurds? Nothing. Or what did Congress in early 2020 do when Trump decided, without informing Congress, to order the killing of Iranian Gen. Qassem Soleimani, prompting a retaliatory attack from Iran's regime on a U.S. base injuring our soldiers? Nothing. Again. In modern times, congressional Republicans kowtowed to Trump's many whims, cast aside their constitutional duties as members of the legislative branch and ceded power to the president. That's wrong. People, especially Republicans, need to develop a little more spine and take those duties back, for America's sake. We can't put our soldiers' lives on the line, put them in harm's way or ask them to make the ultimate sacrifice through the edict of a communication limited to 240 characters.

COLIN POWELL ADDRESSED THE United Nations in early 2003, laying out the Bush administration's rationale for war in Iraq, backed by what he said was unassailable intelligence that Iraq was hiding chemical and biological weapons and working to develop a nuclear capability. The U.S. prepared for war. The vice president sounded an upbeat tone at the time and predicted that, "We will, in fact, be greeted as liberators." In mid-March, Bush issued an ultimatum for Saddam to vacate his country within forty-eight hours.

Late the next day, on March 19, I walked off the Senate floor into the cloakroom nearby, where I found Joe Biden and sat down to chat. We happened to be alone. His phone rang, he stepped away. When he came back, Biden, quietly said. "That was Colin Powell. He said to turn on the TV in five minutes. All hell is going to break loose." And it did. Shock and awe. We watched live coverage of the bombing of Baghdad, the kinetic sound of bombs resounding over the thousands of miles. It was obviously a courtesy call to Biden, then the chairman of the Foreign Relations Committee. I was just a lucky beneficiary to the heads-up notification.

The "shock and awe" campaign started the invasion of a U.S.-led international coalition that sent nearly 180,000 troops into Iraq, 130,000 of them U.S. troops. They engaged in battles throughout Iraq to seize control from Saddam and his loyalists, and free the people of Iraq. Initially, things seemed to go all right. Retreating Iraqi forces largely chose not to resist the coalition forces, though battles were held in southern Iraq. Saddam's Republican Guard defended Baghdad against heavy bombardment from the coalition forces, eventually they were routed and Baghdad came under coalition control. Battles in other parts of the country through April achieved more successes and Bush declared the end of major combat on May 1 in a televised speech from an aircraft carrier near Iraq, a large banner behind him declaring, "Mission Accomplished."

In early July, I joined a bipartisan congressional delegation trip, to Iraq with Sens. John Cornyn (R-TX), Susan Collins (R-ME), Jay Rockefeller (D-WV), Jack Reed (D-RI), Mark Dayton (D-MN), Carl Levin (D-MI), and Pat Roberts (R-KS). All of us served on the Armed Services Committee except Rockefeller, who was on Intelligence. On the trip, we took a windshield tour through downtown Baghdad, one of the last times members of Congress would take that risk to drive around the city as the violence in the streets with improvised explosive devices, IEDs, turned it into a no man's land.

We traveled to Kirkuk and toured the bombed-out city center and neighborhoods. We also examined areas where Iraq had oil fields. On the whole, Iraqis we met with were amiable, hopeful and pleased to be freed from Saddam's autocratic rule. But the dictator, in hiding somewhere in Iraq, still retained the power to strike terror. I remember meeting one Iraqi official who was an absolute delight until one of us mentioned Saddam Hussein. His face went white. He fell silent.

Over the ensuing months an insurgency took hold in Iraq, security devolved, the Ba'thist regime fell, sectarian strife rose, the insurgency grew, the conflict dragged on, and the coalition forces struggled to restore law and order and a semblance of peace. Casualties, which at the war's outset had been light, rose during this time to more than one thousand U.S. soldiers killed by the time of the 2004 presidential election. Casualties kept climbing in the following years to more than three thousand by early 2007. Thousands more were severely wounded and faced grueling recoveries. At the same time, several hundred coalition soldiers were killed, along with untold numbers of Iraqis. Estimates ranged from forty thousand to more than six hundred thousand Iraqis killed. The word "quagmire," from the Vietnam War, now was attached to the conflict in Iraq.

We had gone to war with Iraq because we were told they had weapons of mass destruction, including that Saddam had used poisonous chemicals on his own people, and we were unsafe. Members of Bush's security team cautioned us all that Iraq had centrifuges to develop nukes in firing missiles loaded with nukes. They had them and we needed to find them and stop them, they had said.

Well, as it turned out, they didn't. What ensued was a mission where we were told we would be welcomed and greeted by the Iraqi people with open arms. We would win their hearts and minds. There were surges and debates about stabilizing or leaving. Sides were taken. Vice President Cheney said we were winning. As did the neocons. Sen. John Warner, ranking member of the Senate Arms Committee on which I sat, returned from a trip to the Middle East and said "The war is going sideways." My Nebraska colleague Chuck Hagel claimed we were losing. Three distinguished Republicans looking at the same war all seeing a different outcome in the making. They couldn't all be right. It didn't take a Venn diagram to see the conclusions: Winning. Sideways. Losing. Not helpful.

There must be an objective and verifiable means to evaluate how the war is going, I thought. Given that there was no consensus on why we were there, whether we should stay or pull out, or how to measure success or failure, I began to wonder if we could develop an agreed-to set of benchmarks or metrics to quantify such conclusions? Reminiscent of the kids in the car asking, "Are we there yet?" "No, we have a hundred more miles to go." Of course, in the "are we there yet" example we had a departure location and destination and distance. So, in the case of benchmarks for Iraq, perhaps we could agree as to where we were (location) and where we wanted to be (objective). Could we begin to agree and/or disagree about how close we were to achieving our objective? 25 percent, 50 percent, 0 percent? This approach appealed to me because I taught logic (Philosophy 10) in the Philosophy Department at the University of Nebraska from 1964 to 1966 (MA, 1966).

As 2007 dawned there seemed to be no end in sight, no end to U.S. casualties, no end to funneling billions of dollars of taxpayer money into Iraq, no end to the sectarian violence, no sign of what victory might look like. Americans and members of Congress were getting tired of being in Iraq. In Congress, many wanted more oversight. Leading Democrats, and some Republicans, began calling for an exit strategy, for a gradual or complete withdrawal of U.S. forces from the Iraq theater. Republican leaders and the Bush administration countered that setting a date certain for withdrawal would send a clear signal to the enemy when we were going to leave. All they had to do was hunker down and rise up to seize control after we departed. Some even said that we were, in fact, close to achieving our objective of turning Iraq over to the new Iraqi leaders. I couldn't figure out what was the truth. My three trips to Iraq since the beginning of the war made no clearer what the U.S. should do now.

Here was the crux of the dilemma. Cheney, Warner, and Hagel represented three broad views in Washington: winning, sideways, losing. Everyone was looking at the same set of facts in Iraq—and drawing different conclusions. They all couldn't be right. Back then, facts were facts. This was long before President Trump and his acolytes brought the ludicrous notion of "alternative facts" into fashion.

Back then, in Iraq, I felt we needed some way to evaluate, in a dispassionate way, the facts, the tactics, the strategies, and the goals at play in the continued U.S. engagement. I started talking up my idea of establishing metrics, or benchmarks, as a way of measuring progress. I felt that Congress should push the administration to outline the tactics, goals, and strategies in Iraq and tell us how far along we were to achieving success. For example, if our goal was to strengthen internal security forces in Iraq to the point they could operate effectively and independently, where were we: 20 percent? 40 percent?

I took the idea to John Warner. I said: this is what three leaders from your party are saying—winning, losing, sideways. You can't all be right about the same set of facts. Maybe we might work together to set metrics, I suggested, to measure U.S. objectives and a requirement that the administration give Congress an estimation of progress, as a percentage. If you can't establish measurements, the question is why are you there? I brought up the fact that our military leaders warned against setting a date for withdrawal and Congress was all over the place on whether, when, and how to pull U.S. troops out of Iraq. We might draw bipartisan support for metrics. I had the uneasy feeling that establishing metrics made so darn much sense, why hadn't someone thought of it before? Well, maybe we should try them now. Warner stared at me, a lightbulb seemed to turn on in his mind, he put his hands on my shoulders. "Yes, yes, that's the way to go," he said. "Let's do it."

We then reached out to Susan Collins, who also served on Armed Services and embraced the idea. We then officially changed the title from metrics, which some on my staff suggested might make people think we were somehow shifting to the metric system, to benchmarks. Benchmarks for Iraq.

In early 2007 our bipartisan team pushed to have benchmarks included in a major Iraq war spending bill. Democratic leaders in both houses demanded that Congress set a timeline for withdrawing U.S. troops from Iraq and battled with the Bush administration over spending measures that included timelines for withdrawal. Bills were advanced to end combat missions in either late March 2008 or that fall. The White House resisted. In March a proposed nonbinding resolution setting a goal for removing combat troops by March 31, 2008, led by Senate majority leader Reid, was defeated 50–48. That was twelve votes short of the sixty votes required for passage.

Sen. Mark Pryor (D-AR) and I were the only Democrats opposed. I favored a measure establishing "conditions for staying," with benchmarks that the Iraqi government had to meet for U.S. troops to remain. "We cannot win their Iraqi civil war," I said. "The Iraqis have to do that for themselves."

My staff and I, working with Warner and his staff, and Collins's staff, joined with leader Reid's staff to lay out our bipartisan proposal to establish a series of benchmarks for Iraq. We proposed a Sense of Congress resolution. Our focus was to propose a revision of the United States policy on Iraq that would support U.S. forces, transition the mission to a phased redeployment, protect the U.S and coalition personnel, back training for Iraqi forces, conduct targeted counter-terrorism operations, and develop a comprehensive diplomatic, political, and economic strategy to bring stability to Iraq.

A memo from the time described several benchmarks specific to actions expected from the Iraqi leadership. It stated: "Achieving success in Iraq is dependent in large measure on the Government of Iraq meeting specific benchmarks, as reflected in previous commitments made by the Government of Iraq including:

Deploying trained and ready Iraqi security forces in Baghdad;

Strengthening the authority of Iraqi commanders to make tactical and operational decisions without political intervention;

Disarming militias and ensuring that Iraqi security forces are accountable only to the central government and loyal to the constitution of Iraq;

Enacting and implementing legislation to ensure that the energy resources of Iraq benefit Sunni Arabs, Shia Arabs, Kurds and other Iraqi citizens in an equitable manner;

Enacting and implementing legislation that equitably reforms the de-Ba'athification process in Iraq;

Ensuring a fair process for amending the constitution of Iraq;

Enacting and implementing rules to equitably protect the rights of minority political parties in the Iraqi Parliament."

In mid-March, Reid agreed to add the bipartisan Warner-Collins-Nelson benchmarks provisions to the spending bill. Those benchmarks required the Iraqi government to meet certain responsibilities, such as quelling violence in Baghdad, training Iraqi security forces and dividing oil revenues equally among the country's religious and ethnic groups. Our provision called for America's top commander in Iraq, Gen. David Petraeus, to deliver regular reports to Congress on conditions in the country.

On March 28 the Senate approved a $122 billion war spending bill stating that U.S. troops must begin withdrawing from Iraq that year and to halt combat missions by the end of March 2008. I supported it. It had our benchmarks for the Iraqi government to meet in assuming control of the country. The Bush administration remained adamantly opposed to setting an "arbitrary" timeline for troop withdrawal.

Late in April, I led a congressional delegation trip to Kuwait and Iraq. I invited my Nebraska House colleague, Republican Rep. Lee Terry, and California Rep. Devin Nunes, who I remember was very quiet throughout the trip, much unlike the Trump attack dog he became. Also on the trip was Sen. Jeff Sessions (R-AL). Why would I invite Jeff Sessions on CODEL Nelson? Because he was my ranking member on the Senate Armed Services Committee's Subcommittee for Strategic Forces, which I chaired. And he accepted the invite. Bipartisanship still functioned in the Senate.

Our crew hoped to gain more strategic forces information from the ground in Iraq. Meeting with our commanders and the Iraqi president and prime minister was important in planning and budgeting. Jeff Sessions and I worked together and when we disagreed, it was never partisan. While not Saturday night dinner partners.

Jeff and I had a personal and a professional relationship. I even coerced him to join me atop the high board of Saddam's empty swimming pool for a picture or two. Talk about mutual trust! Representative Terry was from Nebraska's Second District, the Omaha area, and served on the House Energy Committee; it was he who suggested inviting Congressman Nunes, a former dairy farmer from California's Twenty-Second District and a member of the House Ways and Means Committee. Bipartisan, bicameral courtesy.

And we cemented the partnership, at least for a while, with a practical joke I played on my communications director, David Di Martino. During our trip, I slipped a rock into David's shoulder bag without his knowledge, then two, three, and more. By our last day, he was complaining that the trip was wearing him out so much that his bag was feeling heavier and heavier. As we boarded our military jet to leave, David collapsed into his seat.

I casually mentioned that I'd lost one of my cufflinks. Maybe it fell into his bag? Ever dutiful, David fished inside and with a puzzled look pulled out a rock. Then another and another. Soon a bunch of rocks were piled on the floor and David gave me a dismayed and knowing look. "Gotcha!" I said. Watching the whole thing from their seats nearby, Sessions, Terry, and Nunes laughed uproariously.

In Iraq we met with U.S. commanders and Nebraska troops and checked up on the security situation. At this time, Sunnis, Shiites, and Kurds were continuing to have trouble working out a power-sharing arrangement needed to build a working government. This time we couldn't travel in the streets of Baghdad. We toured the area by helicopter. On the helicopter tour we heard machine gun fire below.

The trip, I would tell the media, "only deepened my belief we have to have conditions on the Iraqis for staying." But now I didn't want to tie benchmarks to funding for America's soldiers: "I do not think the troops should be unfunded or underfunded in any way whatsoever." I suggested support for limiting U.S. foreign aid that the Iraqi government relied on for reconstruction work. "I think tying things as a carrot, rather than as a hammer, would make a lot of sense. If they don't meet the benchmarks . . . I think the aid and other assistance has to be held in abeyance," I said.

U.S. troops were performing extremely well under extremely trying circumstances. But the Iraqi government, led by Prime Minister Nouri al-Maliki, a Shiite, continued to struggle in uniting the country. During my trip there, I had told Iraqi officials that they must show "commitment, effort, and progress" toward taking control of their country. The American people were wearying of the war. It had cost more than thirty-three hundred U.S. lives and thousands more were wounded. I told the *Omaha World-Herald* that the debate in Washington about troop withdrawal had been useful because Iraqi leaders now understood that a serious fatigue factor was setting in within the minds of the American people. "We've been dangerously close to creating a cycle of dependence here," I said.

In late May, Congress passed the war funding bill with almost $100 billion for military operations in Iraq through September. The bill did not include a timetable sought by Democrats for pulling troops out of Iraq. It did include a provision, written by Warner, Collins, and myself, requiring the Iraqi government to meet a series of benchmarks as a condition of receiving more funding for American reconstruction aid. The House voted 280–142, with 86 Democrats in favor and 140 opposed. The Senate followed, voting 80–14, with three potential 2008 Democratic presidential candidates lining up in opposition, Hillary Clinton of New York, Christopher Dodd of Connecticut, and Barack Obama of Illinois. Another possible contender, Joe Biden, the Delaware Democrat, voted, as I did, to support the bill.

I said at the time that the benchmarks would clearly signal to the Iraqi government that it must stabilize the country. "As our men and women are there, fighting and dying for the preservation of a democracy, it is not too much to expect that the Iraqi government take a greater role in this endeavor?" I asked.

The benchmarks provision also included the requirement that the administration report to Congress in July and September about its strategy in Iraq and independent assessments of the Iraqi government's performance. In July, Gen. David Petraeus delivered the initial benchmarks assessment report on eighteen specific measures. He conceded that some objectives were not met, including improvements in the ability and political neutrality of the Iraqi security forces and the Iraqi government. For the first time, we had a forthright and detailed analysis about a clear set of facts on the ground in Iraq.

"The significance of the report is shown in that everyone is talking about it today, analyzing it, reacting to it," Collins said when the interim report arrived in Congress. "Prior to it, there was no commonly accepted milestone to assess the progress the Iraqi government is or is not making." She and I expressed pessimism about prospects for improvement over the next months.

Asked by the media who deserved the most credit for requiring the report, Collins said with a smile, "In Nebraska, I think Senator Nelson deserves the most credit. In Maine, I would be happy to take it, and in Virginia, we'll give it to John Warner."

General Petraeus delivered a more detailed, and upbeat, final report that fall. He testified on The Hill that "the military objectives of the surge are, in large measure, being met." Other objectives, he said, were on the road to success, and recommended a gradual drawdown of U.S. forces in Iraq. Before he delivered his testimony, rumors circulated that it had been written by the White House, insinuating some spin was incorporated at its behest.

Petraeus insisted that he'd written his own testimony, assessments and assertions all, without clearing it with anyone at the Pentagon, White House or Congress. Democrats blasted the report as fiction, Republicans commended Petraeus for a forthright assessment of the situation in Iraq. Everyone reacted to the same set of facts, though, they didn't make up their own to push their point of view. This was progress.

I would revisit the idea of benchmarks, this time for the ongoing conflict in Afghanistan. In the summer of 2011, I brought them up in an Armed Services hearing on the confirmation of Leon Panetta to be President Obama's defense secretary replacing the retiring Robert Gates. I told Panetta I was introducing legislation to require benchmarks on the transition to Afghanistan's leaders assuming responsibility for their country.

Those benchmarks would go into progress reports the Pentagon provided regularly to Congress. I saw them as a way to avoid gray areas about whether the U.S. was winning or losing in Afghanistan. I asked Panetta what benchmarks would be helpful. He responded with four areas: levels of violence, the stability of individual districts, development of Afghan security forces, and the government's responsibility. The reports provided to Congress already addressed those issues. I wanted the new benchmarks to focus specifically on progress in transferring responsibility to the Afghanis, rather than the overall mission.

What a contrast to the way President Trump operated on military matters, really on about everything—from trade to border security, tax cuts to the deadly coronavirus outbreak. Trump's alternative facts are not the truth; they are "spin" to artificially make the president look good, and correspondingly make his critics look weak or confused. Alternative facts use government disinformation in an attempt to use the levers of government to sow discord, confusion, and political division, and score partisan political points by knowingly spreading lies and denying facts.

This reckless practice does much more damage. It fosters division, one side taking facts, another taking alternative facts. It devalues the institutions that hold our society together and unite us as Americans. It undermines our democracy. And it undermines the presidency, which could spell disaster in the future if our allies and our adversaries cannot believe what the U.S. president is saying—or tweeting.

THE EVOLUTION OF THE military's policy regarding gay people serving in the military is a good example of how bipartisan compromise and consensus can develop good outcomes. Back in early 1994, the Clinton administration formally adopted a Defense Department directive establishing the official U.S. policy on military service by gays, bisexuals, and lesbians, known as "Don't Ask, Don't Tell." It prohibited military personnel from discriminating against closeted homosexual or lesbian servicemembers, while also prohibiting openly gay, bisexual, or lesbian from serving in the military. This policy arose from a law passed in 1993 that further prohibited them from disclosing their sexual orientation or from speaking about any homosexual relationships, including marriages, while serving in the armed forces.

Finally, the policy said that that any service members who discloses that they are homosexual or engage in homosexual conduct should be discharged from the military except when the individual's conduct was "for the purpose of avoiding or terminating military service" or when it "would not be in the best interest of the armed forces." In the following years numerous legal challenges were filed challenging the Don't Ask, Don't Tell policy.

In the 2000s, public opinion shifted from a majority opposed to gays serving in the military to a strong majority, around 70 percent supporting their service. Servicemembers themselves also were growing more comfortable serving alongside gay and lesbian servicemembers, polling showed. With hundreds of thousands of Americans in the military, and in active combat in Afghanistan and Iraq, our forces were stretched thin.

In 2007 retired chairman of the Joint Chiefs of Staff, Gen. John Shalikashvili, broke new ground by announcing that he opposed keeping DADT in place. "I now believe that if gay men and lesbians served openly in the United States military, they would not undermine the efficacy of the armed forces," Shalikashvili wrote, adding that with the U.S. military so heavily engaged in overseas conflicts, it needed everyone who wanted to serve. Still, it took a while for Congress to take up the issue.

Finally, in early 2010, Congress was ready. The Senate Armed Services Committee held a hearing to discuss the Pentagon budget and to consider whether to repeal Don't Ask, Don't Tell. There was division throughout Congress and among our military leaders. Through the spring, I was identified as a potential key vote on possible repeal. I listened to all sides. It came down to this: I didn't want to undermine the military and I didn't like discriminating against anyone. After much staff discussion I concluded with was a military values issue.

The U.S. military held among its highest values honesty and integrity. But this policy pushed people to lie, either the service member who knew someone who was gay and serving, or a gay person in uniform who could not disclose their sexual orientation. "Nebraskans don't want the 'Don't Ask, Don't Tell' policy to continue," I said in a March press release. "It encourages people to be deceptive and to lie. It encourages others to be suspicious and senior officers to look the other way."

Later that very day, by happenstance, I was having lunch at a restaurant near the Marine barracks near Capitol Hill when a Marine officer came up to me to thank me for what I'd said, because he was tired of being forced to lie to his comrades about who he was. I got his card, and years later I was proud to learn he'd had a successful retirement from the Corps while remaining true to himself.

Later in 2010 debate heated up in Congress over legislation to repeal Don't Ask, Don't Tell. The bill had a requirement that the policy would stay in force until the president, defense secretary, and the chairman of the Joint Chiefs of Staff certified that repeal would not disrupt military readiness, which could occur on September 20, 2011.

The Senate Armed Services Committee held a lengthy hearing on the bill on December 2, featuring Adm. Mike Mullen, chair of the Joint Chiefs of Staff, Defense Secretary Robert Gates and other service leaders. The debate was vigorous, the hearing was packed. When it was my turn to speak I said, "To me the issue seems to be not whether to allow gays to serve in the military, but whether to allow them to serve openly. But permitting them to serve, but not openly, undermines the basic values of the military: honesty, integrity, and trust. And when that's undermined anywhere, it's undermined everywhere. It also seems that our military is expected to say, 'I don't want to lie, but you won't let me tell the truth.'"

I asked Admiral Mullen, "How do we square this circle? I think there are those who are legitimately concerned this will adversely affect readiness and national security and yet we have the report that seems to be somewhat overwhelming in some areas saying it is time to change the law. Can you help me understand how we move to something where it's now possible to tell the truth? I say that because I hear everyone saying to one degree or another you've served with people who were gay. But if you knew they were gay and didn't turn them in, were you lying, or is honesty sort of a mobile commodity?"

"I think, Senator Nelson," Mullen replied, "from my perspective you've hit at the core issue. I can't square the circle. Certainly, historically we have not been able to. And I think that your comment about if it exists anywhere it exists everywhere, and that's been the case with respect to gay and lesbian service for my whole career, including under this law. I think it does fundamentally undermine who we are because we are an institution that is so significantly founded and based on integrity. So, I can't square it."

I then turned to Secretary Gates saying that I'd seen comments from him suggesting that he believed the core values of honesty and integrity needed to prevail in the military. "Doesn't the current system undermine those values?" I asked. Gates replied, "Yes, sir, it does."

This changed the paradigm from who serves to maintaining the core values of the military. Thus, for some senators who may have been apprehensive about gays serving, that issue had already been decided when Don't Ask, Don't Tell was approved. It was not whether, but how. They had to serve deceptively. With this change the how became now they could do it openly and honestly, and the military would no longer be violating its own core values by looking the other way and by requiring the soldiers to lie.

About two weeks later, on a rare Saturday session, the Senate voted 65–31 to repeal the outdated Don't Ask, Don't Tell law. Six

Republicans voted for repeal, Susan Collins and Olympia Snowe of Maine, Scott Brown of Massachusetts, Lisa Murkowski of Alaska, Richard Burr of North Carolina, and John Ensign of Arizona.

I was glad to see the Senate finally get rid of the policy. It went against my principles and I was uncomfortable with it. I also was pleased that the two-step process for repeal would remove politics from the issue by moving its effective date until after the 2010 elections.

Henceforth, service members would not have to lie to each other, or look the other way. Honesty, integrity, and trust would be restored at all levels of our military. Our country would be stronger. Acknowledging our shared values and reaffirming our respect for everyone who calls themselves an American was the right thing to do.

1. Sens. Joe Lieberman (I-CT), Nelson, Susan Collins (R-ME), and Arlen Specter (R-PA) talk with reporters in the Capitol on February 7, 2009, about ongoing negotiations to pass a stimulus bill. Courtesy E. Benjamin Nelson, *One Nebraska, One Nation*.

2. Nelson with Carl Levin (D-MI) (*left*), chairman of the Senate Armed Services Committee, and John Warner (R-VA), ranking member of the committee. E. Benjamin Nelson, *One Nebraska, One Nation*.

3. "Down the Aisle and Down the Runway." Created by Jeff Koterba. E. Benjamin Nelson, *One Nebraska, One Nation*.

4. Nelson accompanied by his wife, Diane, after being sworn into office by Vice President Al Gore, January 3, 2001. E. Benjamin Nelson, *One Nebraska, One Nation*.

5. Nelson aboard a C-130 during a trip to Afghanistan. E. Benjamin Nelson, *One Nebraska, One Nation*.

6. Nelson with President Hamid Karzai of Afghanistan. E. Benjamin Nelson, *One Nebraska, One Nation.*

7. Nelson talking with President Barack Obama in the Oval Office, February 4, 2009. E. Benjamin Nelson, *One Nebraska, One Nation.*

8. Nelson with Sen. Joe Lieberman (I-CT) on the set of CBS's *Face the Nation* on Sunday, December 13, 2009. The two were joined by Sen. Jay Rockefeller (D-WV) to discuss health care reform. Nelson said: "I want to be a friend of the process." E. Benjamin Nelson, *One Nebraska, One Nation.*

9. Humor has served Nelson well in his official capacity. This photo, taken on January 28, 2004, shows Nelson before the start of a hearing on Iraq to the Senate Armed Services Committee, bringing smiles to the faces of fellow committee members Hillary Clinton (D-NY), Ranking Member Ted Kennedy (D-MA), and Chairman John Warner (R-VA). E. Benjamin Nelson, *One Nebraska, One Nation.*

10. Nelson walks off the Senate floor on Capitol Hill in Washington, Tuesday, February 10, 2009, after the Senate approved President Barack Obama's economic stimulus measure. AP Photo/J. Scott Applewhite.

11. Nelson on *Meet the Press*, March 13, 2005. Author's collection.

12. Nelson speaking at a news conference regarding his ACA vote.
Author's collection.

13. Nelson outside Senate, reviewing comments before conference.
Author's collection.

14. Seven members of the Gang of 14, on *Hard Ball* news program.
Author's collection.

15. Impromptu Halloween dinner with Pres. George W. Bush.
Author's collection.

16. "Senator E. Benjamin Nelson: Nicknames and Titles."
Created by Jeff Koterba.

17. Nelson at press conference for stimulus package. Author's collection.

18. 112th Congress—Senate. Author's collection.

19. Nelson at Eagle Scout Court of Honor, with parents, Birdella and Ben.
Author's collection.

20. "Independence." Created by Jeff Koterba.

21. Iraq CODEL on the phone "calling home." Author's collection.

22. Nelson family statue in front of the Nelson family home (now a museum), only four doors away from the family home of Sen. George W. Norris, also a museum. On Norris Avenue in Nelson's hometown of McCook, Nebraska. Author's collection.

23. Napkin with VP Cheney's proposed tax compromise on first Bush tax cut. Author's collection.

24. A duet with Warren Buffet at Omaha Gridiron Show. Author's collection.

25. CODEL Nelson—Baghdad Airport, Iraq, April 28, 2007. *Left to right*:
Sen. Jeff Sessions, Rep. Lee Terry, Sen. Ben Nelson, Rep. Devin Nunes.
Author's collection.

26. E. Benjamin Nelson with Democratic leader Harry Reid at swearing in,
January 3, 2001. Author's collection.

27. Sen. Mark Pryor (AR) with Senator Nelson, updating the media on the
Gang of 14's internal discussions. Author's collection.

FIVE

Gang Fights

I NEVER THOUGHT OF myself as the "gang" type. I stayed out
of trouble in school, and always tried to stay on the right side of
the law. Anybody back home who heard about me becoming a
"gang leader" would have had quite a shock! But that's exactly what
I became in 2005, joined by thirteen other senators. Indeed, the
thought of a bunch of septuagenarian and octogenarian senators
packing switchblades, greasing their hair, and replacing seersucker
jackets with leather coats is kind of hilarious to consider. But that's
not what I mean.

President Bush's judicial nominees were having a tough time
getting through the Democrat-controlled Senate, and while we
didn't want to confirm staunch partisans, we knew these vacan-
cies had to be filled so the country could have a functioning federal
court system. Senate majority leader Bill Frist (R-TN) insisted on
what he called a "simple principle," a yes or no vote for each nominee. But Senate Democratic leader Harry Reid of Nevada refused
to go along with that notion. "They want all or nothing, and I can't
do that." He insisted that Republicans would still have to get their
nominees through an initial "cloture" vote, which required the Senate to reach sixty votes in favor of moving judicial nominees to a
final up or down vote requiring only a simple majority, fifty-one
votes, for confirmation.

Democrats had filibustered a number of Bush nominees
through cloture, and Frist was visibly frustrated. It so happened

that Martin Gold, an adviser to Frist, had cowritten a law article titled "The Constitutional Option to Change Senate Rules
and Procedures: A Majoritarian Means to Overcome Filibusters,"
which laid out a roadmap to make a change in Senate rules with a
simple majority vote. The Constitutional Option was renamed as
the Nuclear Option. Frist began to threaten to invoke the nuclear
option to push for a vote to change the rules, getting rid of the cloture requirement and enabling a president's judicial nominees to
be pushed through the Senate on a simple majority vote.

For my part, I didn't like filibusters because they were hard to
explain back home where people often viewed them as tactics of
obstruction. Because I'd pledged to avoid obstruction at nearly
all costs when I ran for the Senate, if I were to support filibusters
some might see that as an inconsistency. In addition, as a former
governor, I understood the benefit of letting the executive branch
seat its chosen nominees. At the same time, I viewed the nuclear
option as an extreme reaction that would forever alter the Senate,
blow up what the Founders established, and lead to more partisanship, less bipartisanship, and possibly a slew of unintended consequences. I wondered if we couldn't come up with a deal averting
that catastrophe. With no resolution in sight, the back and forth
continued.

In an interview with a Capitol Hill reporter I said that we didn't
need to invoke the nuclear option to overcome the filibuster. All
we would need would be to get six Republicans and six Democrats
to agree to vote up or down on judicial appellate nominees. This
would negate the effect of the filibuster. Cloture would no longer
be needed; nor could it be used to block a simple majority vote
for the up or down fifty-vote threshold. We could end obstruction.

I said this knowing that some were using the sixty-vote for cloture as a threshold to effectively block a nomination. But my position during my time in the Senate had been to vote for cloture to
move to the up or down vote on most issues, including such as the
McCain-Feingold campaign finance reform plan, which I opposed
but would not block a vote where a simple majority could decide

its fate. On judges, I had supported every nominee who had come to the floor for a vote in four-plus years in the Senate—in excess of two hundred.

I had voted to invoke cloture—suspend a filibuster—all but one time. That once was against Judge Henry Saad for a federal court post, because I and other senators not on the Judiciary Committee were prohibited from viewing sensitive material related to Saad. Because I was not afforded the opportunity to *advise* the president on the merits of his nominee, I could not give my *consent*. Having gone public with my idea of six and six to search for a compromise between the nuclear option and the status quo—where judges were stalled—I thought that would be the last of it.

But the next day the Senate was in session, Sen. Robert Byrd spotted me and was making his way toward me. I had voted for the Bush tax cuts earlier and I knew he hadn't agreed with my vote. I thought, "What now?" I just knew it wasn't going to be good. I expected to get an earful and winced when he grabbed me by my coat lapels. He always called former governors by that title. "Governor," Byrd said, glaring into my eyes, "you've got to do it. You've got to do what you're talking about and get six senators from each side to avoid the nuclear option."

I responded that I was still kind of new to the Senate and not sure if any others would go along with the idea. He shot back, "You need to do it to save the Senate!" I thought, "This will teach me to stick my nose into an area where I have little to no experience." Byrd was the guardian of the traditions of the Senate, from dress code, to asserting its constitutional duties as a check and balance to the executive and judicial branches of government. He came to the Senate in 1959, the year I graduated from high school. He was tradition and duty to country personified, so I listened very carefully. He told me, "I will help." That encouraged me to consider it. I told him I'd see what I could do and we parted.

I walked across the chamber and across the center aisle dividing Democrats and Republicans to talk to Sen. Trent Lott, with whom I'd worked on tax cuts, homeland security and other issues. He, too, had seen my comments in the news story. He pulled an envelope from inside the pocket of his suit jacket to show me that this topic was one of the things he'd written himself a note to do that day—talk to me about what I'd said on TV. He liked the idea of getting a group of senators together to see if we could strike a deal, he thought it was worth trying, and he'd help. The day after that, he came up to me and said he'd have to step aside, pointing out that he didn't want to be seen as undermining Sen. Bill Frist, who had replaced him as majority leader. This caused me considerable concern. But he promised he'd find a suitable Republican replacement.

He recruited Sen. John McCain. "McCain was my agent, even though I was not in there," Lott recalls with a chuckle. McCain was unafraid to buck his party's leadership, having worked on the McCain-Feingold campaign finance bill most in his party loathed. McCain seemed to enjoy giving politicians of all stripes heartburn. I had worked with John on other occasions and was comfortable working with him. We would co-chair the gang. Knowing that having the minimum of twelve left no margin, I had suggested we should have seven and seven, just in case somebody became ill or otherwise felt they had to drop out. Having worked at Sehnert's Bakery in my hometown growing up, I suggested we get a kind of "baker's dozen" of thirteen members. But for political symmetry we made it fourteen. This made sense to both of us and we proceeded to round up others. The Gang of 14 was born.

I first approached Sen. John Warner, my friend and colleague on the Armed Services Committee. He was interested but who did I have on board? When I told him Robert Byrd was, I could see him become more attentive. He agreed to be part of the group. Now I had three lions of the Senate, Byrd, McCain, and Warner, often referred to in that way due to their seniority and respect of their peers. The rest of us were important to the success of the deal, but having the lions gave us momentum and got us noticed. Soon we had the Maine senators, Susan Collins and Olympia Snowe.

In the process of recruiting Mark Pryor, who wasn't sure he wanted to be part of this "gang" thing, I asked him to accompany me to a meeting with Sen. Daniel Inouye (D-HI). Inouye, a combat veteran of World War II, was immensely respected by everyone in the Senate. When we entered Inouye's office and were seated, I explained why I was there and who had joined in on the gang and who we were thinking about asking to join. In response to a question from Pryor as to what he thought about the whole endeavor, Inouye pointed to me and said, "He's my leader." Another lion joining was a sign that we were going to get our Gang of 14. Pryor signed on as well, and would go on to become one of the most enthusiastic participants in our negotiations.

John McCain and I met on the Senate floor during a vote and compared notes. We were making progress. We agreed to confer again the next day or so. When we did, we had our "baker's dozen" of thirteen—plus one, to ensure an even political balance. In addition to the aforementioned, we had on board GOP senators Mike DeWine and George Voinovich of Ohio, Lincoln Chafee of Rhode Island, and Democrat senators Mary Landrieu of Louisiana and Ken Salazar of Colorado. Altogether, we were a posse of legislative renegades, and we would soon be at full gallop. We had the numbers. They gave us power. And, then as now, power was a commodity that never lost its value on Capitol Hill.

McCain, the Navy pilot shot down in the Vietnam War who suffered grave abuse as a prisoner of war that left him with lifelong disabilities, had entered the Senate in 1987. When I got to the Senate, he was either already a lion or was fast becoming one. His stature was secure and was further bolstered by his presidential run in 2000 against George W. Bush where he spoke frankly to voters and as he traveled from town hall meeting to town hall meeting aboard his bus, dubbed the "Straight Talk Express." In our Gang, McCain was a terrific partner and co-chair. I was not sure of my Navy expressions, but he and I knew we were ready to get going and said to this former Naval officer, to his amusement, "John, it's time to set sail."

Around the second week of May, we got the whole Gang of 14 together, but without staff so we could talk openly, plainly, and not risk our discussions becoming public. All of the federal apparatus in DC is notorious for leaks—the federal agencies, the White House, and especially Capitol Hill. It seems every office on the Hill has a leaker, sometimes intentionally. We referred to ours as the "Leakmeister." In recent years, it drove the Trump White House crazy, and the president to declare leaks treasonous.

The best way to avoid them is obvious: Reduce the number of ears in the room until you're ready to go public. Still, that's easier said than done inside the Beltway environment, particularly when there are so many lobbyists eager to grab a morsel to demonstrate their value to their clients, and the ever-present media likewise eager for a scooplet.

Just as our meetings were getting going, we heard troubling news that Frist and Reid, who had been sending each other proposals and counter-proposals, had given up on their negotiations. We were alone, in a race against the nuclear clock. Somehow, we managed to keep a lid on the major elements we were working on.

Initially we actually met in secret, but it didn't take long for enterprising reporters to get wind of the meeting locations. We didn't make the other senators sign an oath of secrecy or anything like that; it was an unspoken agreement among all of us to keep our deliberations private. This helped everyone feel comfortable with floating unusual ideas to see what others thought; and it made us feel like we were all on one team despite our party affiliations and policy differences. John McCain and I would meet with reporters who staked out our meetings and give them a very general update of how things were going. They were our version of the "frank and open" readouts you often hear of private White House meetings. That reduced rumors and speculation. During our senators-only discussions held over about two weeks, I also frequently updated Harry Reid about our discussions to develop a filibuster/nuclear option compromise and I assume my Republican partners were likewise informing Bill Frist.

We began our periodic gatherings to try to solve an acutely acrimonious issue: the confirmation of federal judges gridlocked in the

Senate. Each meeting tended to have a familiar rhythm. McCain would come in late, ornery, and impatient. He'd say something acerbic or unprintable about a colleague who wasn't in the room or, just as likely, about one of us who was. Lindsey Graham, his ever-attendant Sancho Panza, would laugh amiably.

Graham offered interesting ideas at times, so did Ken Salazar and really so did everyone. Susan Collins would listen intently, revealing little about her internal deliberations. The Ohio senators had good ideas. We listened closely to Robert Byrd who would invariably school us on the sanctity of the Senate's procedures and the Constitution. Even if we didn't always see eye-to-eye, trust between the members was always paramount. We knew everyone was negotiating in good faith.

We had only one staffer present, Amy Tejral, a member of my staff everyone trusted, and she mainly took notes and sketched out drafts of a potential agreement we might sign. I told the group at the start that we ought to strive to put something down in writing if we reached an agreement about how we wanted the Senate to sidestep the nuclear option and move some judicial nominations forward.

Back to Trent Lott. Besides Amy, he was the only outsider allowed in. Because of his interest in the success of our gang, Trent would from time to time join our small fourteen-member meetings through a back door, or some secret passage, to avoid being seen by the media. I dubbed him Sergeant Shultz from the old TV sitcom *Hogan's Heroes*, who repeatedly denied knowing about the American prisoners' shenanigans: "I see nothing! I was not here! I did not even get up this morning!" Trent's unannounced appearance and my teasing always brought laughter from the gang. He never sat down with us around the negotiating table; he always stood off to the side, leaning against a wall. "Golly" Lott recalled recently. "That was absolutely true."

The atmosphere of our meetings was both serious and friendly. This Gang of 14 was as bipartisan as any gathering I participated in during my two terms in the Senate. A number of the key negotiations were held in McCain's office around a coffee table. We liked and respected each other. When we were referred to as centrists, Lindsey Graham cheerfully protested and said with a broad smile that he wanted to be known as rabid right-wing conservative.

So, when in future press briefings, the word "centrist" was raised I was certain to exempt Lindsey and some others. We were simply a bipartisan gang with a common purpose and commitment against the nuclear option and obstruction, and for up or down votes. As is often said, "keep it simple" and it was. Robert Byrd was the senior senator in our midst and insisted on walking to wherever we were meeting. He wouldn't have it any other way. A noble gesture from the keeper of the traditions of the Senate. He would remind us of the importance of our efforts. His guidance became the cornerstone of our group. McCain brought moral courage, as did Danny Inouye; John Warner brought gravitas; and others brought a commitment to trust one another, a lot of helpful ideas, and a common goal to see if we could work something out to avoid the nuclear option. Each of us brought something more than a vote. We were seeking a bipartisan solution in a period dominated by acrimony over judicial nominations and threats to use the nuclear option, which we knew would blow up the Senate and continue its slide toward becoming just another version of the eternally divided House of Representatives.

Some days into our deliberations, Joe Lieberman, the Connecticut Democrat, said he wanted to think further about what we were doing. He was uncomfortable with one part of the negotiations and said, "I just don't know whether we should be doing this. I think it's a mistake." McCain pointed and said, "Dammit! What the hell. There's the door."

"Oh, okay," Lieberman recently recalled, "and I got up and walked out."

This was interesting. Joe and John were close. Lieberman had been Democratic presidential nominee Al Gore's running mate in 2000, when McCain challenged George W. Bush in the GOP primary contest. Then, three years after this Gang of 14 effort, McCain would seriously consider putting Lieberman on the ticket as *his* vice-presidential running mate in his 2008 race against Barack Obama.

Back here in 2005, Senator Byrd missed the brief moment, saw Lieberman depart, and said, "What's going on? Where's Joe? Where'd Joe go?" McCain explained, Byrd looked troubled. That day Lieberman flew home and in the airport in Hartford heard from his constituents. They congratulated him for being part of the Gang. "Keep in that Gang, Senator."

Lieberman also remembers McCain also calling him and saying, "Where the hell are you?" And he responded, "Well, you told me if I couldn't agree with this point, I should leave the group." McCain shot back, "I didn't really mean that. Get your *&$ back here." When he came back to DC after the weekend, he showed up for our groups' meeting. "I think I'm back in," Lieberman said. Byrd was delighted, "Joe's back!" It wasn't quite a focus group experience, but did indicate we were on the right track.

Still, we could not reach a DC consensus agreement. Time was running out. On May 18, Frist convened the Senate and, in his comments, brought up the nomination of Priscilla Owen, nominated for a judicial seat on the Fifth District. It was clear Republicans would file a cloture motion soon, setting up a test that could lead to them ending judicial filibusters with what they called the "constitutional option." On Friday the 20th, Sen. John Cornyn (R-TX) filed that cloture motion setting the Senate on course toward the nuclear option. It would happen the following Tuesday.

We labored over finding the right language to avoid a filibuster. In one of our drafts, we said we "would agree to invoke cloture on future members that are not, in our judgement, extremely controversial." That meant that "the majority of, and perhaps all future nominees, will receive up or down votes in the United States Senate." In another of the drafting sessions, we refined the language, adding a clause that would commit the Gang members to, in the future, not obstruct a judicial nominee except under "extraordinary circumstances."

McCain questioned it: "What's this 'except in extraordinary circumstances' clause? How will I know that?" I responded, "Well, it's up to each individual. We have to trust one another that it's not an escape route, but needs to be for a moment when someone feels 'I just can't do it.'"

"Oh," McCain said, then referred to a famous line from Supreme Court Justice Potter Stewart, "Is it like pornography? You know it when you see it?" I said, "Well, it's analogous. When a judicial nominee drains all the blood from your head, you will know it's 'extraordinary circumstances.'" McCain seemed to accept my explanation. There were some in the group who felt they were giving away their vote. But with "extraordinary circumstances," they wouldn't have to.

We drafted a basic memorandum of agreement, which grew to several dozen drafts as we debated and added and subtracted ideas, and listed judicial nominees we would hold votes on or suggest we would reserve the right to filibuster in the future. AP reporter David Espo would write a few days later that Republicans not in our group reportedly viewed the negotiations dimly. Sen. Mitch McConnell (R-KY) and other GOP leaders called it unilateral disarmament that would allow Democrats to filibuster without worry of retaliation. McConnell has always liked to retain an opportunity for retaliation. We felt we had to find a compromise among ourselves, to avert the nuclear option but still get some long-delayed judges votes, and likely confirmation. Frist was on track to hold a vote on the nuclear option on Tuesday the 24th. The heat was on.

Throughout the day on Monday the 23rd, the Gang of 14 traded drafts of who would be considered for votes and the language we would support in our Memorandum of Understanding. In our deliberations, we considered whether to include one judicial nominee: Brett Kavanaugh. Kavanaugh had been an associate independent counsel under Independent Counsel Ken Starr who had key roles investigating the Whitewater case involving President Clinton and the 1998 Clinton impeachment case. Later, he worked as

Staff Secretary in the Bush White House, one of the lawyers working to get Bush's judicial nominations through the Senate.

Originally nominated in 2003 for a seat on the U.S. Court of Appeals for the DC Circuit, Judiciary Committee Democrats struggled over his paperwork for a year, contending that Kavanaugh answered their questions in a nonresponsive manner that bordered on rude, and only made even that effort to address their questions at all after the 2004 elections passed. His nomination had stalled. In the spring of 2005, one of the nominations the White House was pushing and we had on our plate was Kavanaugh's.

At the time, he was seen by several in the Gang of 14—including some of the Republicans—as being too partisan to make an effective federal judge. Personally, I took the integrity of the federal bench very seriously, and always felt that strictly partisan lawyers from one party or the other had no place as federal judges or as Supreme Court justices. I wanted people who would follow the law. I didn't want Kavanaugh in the mix of judicial nominees we would agree to advance for up or down votes in the Senate. Nor did Democratic leader Harry Reid, who along with other Democrats argued that Kavanaugh was too partisan for the important federal bench post.

We refined the language of the memorandum and the language under the heading "Part I: Commitments on Pending Judicial Nominations," adding and subtracting names and the language. The language of the section on the status of other judges on May 18 read: "We acknowledge that signatories who previously voted for or against cloture on the following nominees may do so again." By May 23, that had become: "Signatories make no commitment to vote for or against cloture on the following nominees."

Also by May 23, the list of names had grown. Under the heading "Votes for Certain Nominees" of those we *would* invoke cloture for were: Janice Rogers Brown (DC Circuit), William Pryor (Eleventh Circuit), Priscilla Owen (Fifth Circuit), Richard Griffin (Sixth Circuit), Susan Neilson (Sixth Circuit), and David McKeague (Sixth Circuit). Under the heading *"Status of Other Nomi-*

nees" that the Gang would make no commitment on cloture were: William Myers (Ninth Circuit), Henry Saad (Sixth Circuit), William J. Haynes (Fourth Circuit), and Brett M. Kavanaugh (DC Circuit).

The full Gang of 14 met several times to hash out language and the list. Some Republicans pointed out that the Senate Judiciary Committee had not acted on either Kavanaugh or Haynes, a Pentagon lawyer and author of a controversial memo about interrogation of prisoners at the U.S. base at Guantanamo Bay. Three other nominees were controversial as well, Griffin, McKeague, and Nielson. I have several copies of the draft memorandum dated May 23, 2005, time-stamped from 12:31 p.m. to 4:27 p.m.

Initially, all five were listed in the two categories under the heading "Commitments on Pending Judicial Nominations." Griffin, Neilson, and McKeague made the cut for invoking cloture; Haynes and Kavanaugh were among those we would make no commitment to vote for or against on cloture. And remember, cloture requires sixty votes to advance to a simple majority vote. Our drafts at 12:31 p.m., 1:04 p.m., and 2:54 p.m. carried all five names.

But my final version, time stamped 4:27 p.m., showed a change. All five, Griffin, McKeague, Nielson, Haynes, and Kavanaugh now had a line drawn through their names in black marker. We had cut them from the roster. They would not be part of the final Gang of 14 agreement. The Republicans in the Gang did not want to fight this one or that one in the list. So, Kavanaugh's name did not advance. In fact, his nomination died altogether. It would have to be resurrected by President Bush in the next Congress.

We fourteen senators met in McCain's office at 6:00 p.m. to hash out the last details. With no time to spare, we made it happen. Around 7:30 p.m. we streamed out of his office to tell Reid and Frist that we had a deal. We had reached a final agreement on a memorandum we'd all sign, one that would allow some nominees to move forward, while preserving the cloture requirement with a clause that gave each of us the right to oppose a cloture motion in "extraordinary circumstances."

There was high drama and paranoia that the agreement would get leaked right up to the last minute. My staffer, Amy Tejral, had the only final copy of the memorandum on a computer disc. She put it into a computer in McCain's office, called up the file, went away for a moment to hear of a tiny last-minute recommended change, and when she came back, the screen was blank. Staff had already deleted the file. "Are you really so paranoid about this thing you couldn't even leave it up on the screen until we were done?" she chided the aides, who were sheepish. "What do you think I'm going to do on your computer here? I'm trying to print off the document for everybody to sign." They stuck the disc back in, printed the agreement and Tejral gathered the fourteen signatures.

In the end, Lieberman and I went to Harry Reid, who welcomed seeing the filibuster remain intact but was not excited by the whole deal, because some judges he strongly opposed would get seats on the federal bench. "I didn't like the deal," Reid said recently, "but I knew that I would be better off putting my arms around the deal than saying I didn't like it and worry about how it stood in the caucus. So, when they said they had a deal I said, okay, I'm in favor of it, even though I really wasn't. But I think it was good for the order and worked out well. Like all good compromises, each side had to give a little."

After hearing from the Republican negotiators, Frist was even less pleased. He thought the deal undercut him and complained that not all judges would get the up or down vote he believed they deserved. Our bipartisan bloc was large enough to derail Democratic filibusters of judicial nominees and a Republican attempt to invoke the "nuclear option" to change Senate rules to prevent filibusters from being used. Publicly, Frist declared defeat, complaining that while he was pleased several nominees would finally come to a vote, all judicial nominees deserved an up or down vote. That made things easier for Reid and his team. He publicly said that the agreement was good news for all Americans: "Checks and balances have been protected."

Here's the final text of the Gang of 14 agreement:

Memorandum of Understanding on Judicial Nominations

We respect the diligent, conscientious efforts, to date, rendered to the Senate by Majority Leader Frist and Democratic Leader Reid. This memorandum confirms an understanding among the signatories, based upon mutual trust and confidence, related to pending and future judicial nominations in the 109th Congress.

This memorandum is in two parts. Part I relates to the currently pending judicial nominees; Part ii relates to subsequent individual nominations to be made by the President and to be acted upon by the Senate's Judiciary Committee.

We have agreed to the following:

Part I: Commitments on Pending Judicial Nominations

A. Votes for Certain Nominees. We will vote to invoke cloture on the following judicial nominees: Janice Rogers Brown (D.C. Circuit), William Pryor (11th Circuit), and Priscilla Owen (5th Circuit).

B. Status of Other Nominees. Signatories make no commitment to vote for or against cloture on the following judicial nominees: William Myers (9th Circuit) and Henry Saad (6th Circuit).

Part II: Commitments for Future Nominations

A. Future Nominations. Signatories will exercise their responsibilities under the Advice and Consent Clause of the United States Constitution in good faith. Nominees should be filibustered only under extraordinary circumstances, and each signatory must use his or her own discretion and judgment in determining whether such circumstances exist.

B. Rules Changes. In light of the spirit and continuing commitments made in this agreement, we commit to oppose the rules changes in the 109th Congress, which we understand to be any amendment to or interpretation of the Rules of the Senate that would force a vote on a judicial nomination by means other than unanimous consent or Rule IIii.

We believe that, under Article II, Section 2, of the United States Constitution, the word "Advice" speaks to consultation between the Senate and the President with regard to the use of the President's power to make nominations. We encourage the Executive branch of government to consult with members of the Senate, both Democratic and Republican, prior to submitting a judicial nomination to the Senate for consideration.

Such a return to the early practices of our government may well serve to reduce the rancor that unfortunately accompanies the advice and consent process in the Senate.

We firmly believe this agreement is consistent with the traditions of the United States Senate that we as Senators seek to uphold.

The Gang of 14 signed that deal, sent it to the Senate leaders and held a celebratory press conference in the Senate Radio TV Gallery, nearly everyone giving credit to another of the group. I said at the time, "It's not a contract that's enforceable. It's an agreement that's self-enforcing." On the Senate floor a bit later, I said: "We accomplished this by working together with common purpose and shared concern for the future of this body. Protecting the Senate's minority rights might seem to go against the concept of democracy and majority rule. In reality and without the spin on this issue that the special interest groups from both extremes put on this matter, the Senate's minority rights are part of the system of checks and balances that keep any branch of government from dominating the others."

Robert Byrd found me around this time. He said simply, "You saved the Senate." I demurred, "No, Senator, *we* saved the Senate." He got it. A couple weeks later he sent me a letter in which thanked me and said, "we worked together to save the institution of the United States Senate. Because of your wisdom, the great tradition of debate and freedom to dissent have been preserved in the Senate." With our compromise, everybody won. Those seeking to protect minority rights won. Those seeking to confirm judges won. The Senate won.

The Gang of 14 deal was a high-water mark of bipartisanship during my time in the Senate. Senators crossed the aisle to work together, the Senate leaders didn't interfere or disparage the Gang's efforts while we tried to put together a consensus agreement, everyone mostly didn't run to the media during deliberations, which could have brought outside pressure to scuttle the deal, and we fourteen colleagues treated each other with respect, civility, and honor. After the Gang of 14's agreement held the whole Senate together, the spirit of bipartisanship began to drain away. It would never be that strong again, not until I retired in 2013 and certainly not since.

AS YOU SEE, OUR agreement called for allowing up or down votes on Priscilla Owen, Janice Rogers Brown for the U.S. Court of Appeals for the District of Columbia; and William Pryor for the Eleventh Circuit Court of Appeals. It made no promises on William Myers III for the Ninth U.S. Circuit Court of Appeals or Henry Saad for the Sixth Circuit. Soon after our Gang agreement went into force, Priscilla Owen's confirmation came before the Senate. I had met with her in my office, where she couldn't or wouldn't answer my questions and did nothing to assure me she would be impartial. I voted for cloture, to advance nomination because I didn't see this as a case of "extraordinary circumstances." Then I voted against her in the up or down simple majority vote. She was confirmed on a vote of 55–43. My views on a nominee's ability to be impartial guided other votes.

I was one of just four Democrats to vote in favor of Samuel Alito in 2006 for a seat on the U.S. Supreme Court. I thought Alito, although a conservative, would stick to the law as written and said in a statement announcing my support that his impeccable judicial credentials and pledge that he "would not bring a political agenda to the court" was persuasive. I had become convinced of this by what he told me in a private meeting earlier in my office.

As Alito made the customary rounds of private meetings with senators in the confirmation process, we sat down together. I asked whether he ever had a decision or opinion as a judge that he would do differently. "Was there an example of anything for which you'd like a do-over?" He thought a moment, then said yes. That White House aide accompanying him, whose job it was to keep him out of trouble, looked like she was going to retch. Alito didn't seem to notice.

He said he remembered a case at the appellate level involving abortion and the exception to protect the health of the mother. He had watched the Supreme Court closely and thought he could tell where the high court was heading, so drafted the opinion accordingly. But, later, when the Supreme Court ruled on the case, it overturned the Alito-drafted decision. That's one example, Alito told me. I asked, "Is that like leaning a little too far over your skis?" Maybe so, he answered. I liked his candor. To me, that indicated he would approach decisions on cases before the Supreme Court based on known facts, legal precedent, and the Constitution, not on an interpretation of the mindset of those writing lower court opinions. The Senate voted 58–42 to confirm him to the Supreme Court.

I was the only Democrat in 2010 to vote against Elena Kagan to serve on the high court. Kagan—even though we agreed on many policy issues—seemed too partisan for me to support. She'd been an associate White House counsel and a policy adviser to President Clinton. I issued a statement at the time: "As a member of the bipartisan 'Gang of 14,' I will follow our agreement that judicial nominees should be filibustered only under extraordinary circumstances. If a cloture vote is held on the nomination of Elena Kagan to the U.S. Supreme Court, I am prepared to vote for cloture and oppose a filibuster because, in my view, this nominee deserves an up or down vote in the Senate." The Senate voted 63–37 to send Kagan to the Supreme Court. I voted for cloture, as I said I would, and against her nomination.

SADLY, OUR GANG OF 14 deal didn't hold. Once most of its signers retired, were defeated or passed away, talk returned about ending the filibuster. In 2013 Harry Reid, now serving as Senate majority leader, used the nuclear option to do away with the sixty-vote rule on executive branch nominations and federal judicial appointments, but not for the Supreme Court. Then in 2017, after Republicans gained the majority in the Senate, Republican leader Mitch McConnell used the nuclear option to end the sixty-vote cloture rule for Supreme Court nominees. That enabled him to end debate on the Trump nominee Neil Gorsuch, greasing his path to a seat on the Supreme Court. And that led to Brett Kavanaugh's nomination debacle.

That was a sad day for our country. Not because of my views about Gorsuch's fitness to serve on the high court, or about McConnell's underhanded tactics in blocking Judge Merrick Garland's nomination in 2016 under the Obama administration, which he later boasted was the "most consequential thing I've ever done." It was sad because the Senate had abandoned its constitutional responsibility to provide checks and balances to the political and partisan whims of the executive branch. Those two actions would have far-reaching and negative consequences.

Back to Brett Kavanaugh and to 2006. After the Gang deal averted the nuclear option, the Bush White House renominated Kavanaugh in February 2006 for the judicial seat on the D.C. Court of Appeals. Republicans praised him, Democrats considered filibustering him, and his confirmation hearings were contentious. By the early spring, a number of Bush judicial nominees were stuck in the pipeline, though we had confirmed John Roberts and Samuel Alito to the Supreme Court.

The hallways of the marble-floored Capitol were buzzing with talk again of invoking the "nuclear option" to blow up potential filibusters. On May 3, 2006, the seven senators, myself included, who made up the Democratic side of the Gang of 14 sent a letter to Senate leaders asking for the Judiciary Committee to hold a new confirmation hearing on new issues which had arisen since his initial hearing was held two years earlier. "Perhaps Mr. Kavanaugh would appreciate the opportunity of another hearing to clarify his role, or lack thereof, in issues viewed by some as controversial, such as the White House-approved policy of wiretapping," we wrote. This was a hot issue at the time.

The Judiciary Committee held that confirmation hearing on May 9, during which Kavanaugh was asked about his role as staff secretary in the Bush White House. He denied having any role in a series of White House controversies, saying he wasn't part of deliberations over domestic spying; never met with controversial lobbyist Jack Abramoff; knew nothing about the shocking public disclosure of Valerie (Plame) Wilson as a Central Intelligence Agency spy; nor ever saw the torture memos, the administration's legal memos used to justify abusive interrogation of suspected terrorists.

Our whole Gang of 14 regrouped in my offices the evening of May 10. The Democratic group wasn't pleased with Kavanaugh's answers in his hearing, but largely didn't see a need to filibuster his nomination. On May 26, 2006, the Senate voted 67–30 to invoke cloture; I joined nine Democrats, including Sens. Joe Biden and Barack Obama, supporting the vote to move Kavanaugh to an up or down vote. I didn't see this as an example of "extraordinary circumstances."

Kavanaugh, then forty-one, was confirmed to the U.S. court of appeals post on a vote of 57–36; I voted aye. But Sen. Ted Kennedy (D-MA) said at the time, "I can say with confidence that Mister Kavanaugh would be the youngest, least experienced and most partisan appointee to the court in decades." Kennedy sadly passed away in 2009 and I retired from the Senate in 2013.

On July 9, 2018, President Trump nominated Kavanaugh to the U.S. Supreme Court to fill the vacancy of retiring Associate Justice Anthony Kennedy. This was, of course, after McConnell had done away with the Senate's ability to filibuster nominees to the Supreme Court.

During the televised confirmation hearings, Judge Kavanaugh gained nationwide recognition. So did Chairman of the Senate Judiciary Committee Lindsey Graham. He delivered an Oscar performance. Arms folded to his side, red-faced, uncontrolled anger, Lindsey shouted that in all his years in the Senate he had never seen anyone treated as badly as Kavanaugh. "This is the most unethical sham since I've been in politics, and if you really wanted to know the truth, you sure as hell wouldn't have done what you've done to this guy!" His performance was reminiscent of the perpetually angry cartoon character Yosemite Sam in his cowboy hat and red mustache with steam coming out of his ears, jumping up and down, hootin' and hollerin'.

I don't know for certain what happened to the serious and measured Lindsey Graham I'd served with, but I suspect two things. By the fall of 2018 he had lost his moral anchor when his ally John McCain died from cancer. And the rise of what I call "the Loud Crowd," the Tea Party shrill extremists, pushed him over the edge, into the realm of scary. He also seemed afraid of President Trump, his temper tantrums and his threats.

Before the Senate panel Kavanaugh angrily defended himself against charges of groping, possible rape, drunkenness, and abusive behavior years before, when he was in high school. He was reduced to theatrical griping and his behavior could only be described as astounding and disappointing for a judge on the U.S. Court of Appeals for the Federal Circuit. Kavanaugh threatened the committee Democrats by saying, "What goes around comes around." Not surprisingly, Kavanaugh's attempted intimidation of the Democrats did not invoke a public rebuke from Chief Justice John Roberts akin to the public scolding in early 2020 of Senate minority leader Chuck Schumer for his warning to the Court not to reverse *Roe v. Wade*. Hopefully, Roberts counseled Kavanaugh privately after his confirmation.

So, how did Kavanaugh survive his confirmation vote in 2006 after being rejected by the Gang in 2005? The answer is because none of the damaging information and accusations disclosed in the Supreme Court confirmation hearing was publicly known in 2006. He was known to be controversial, to be sure, but not to the extent of being a case of "extraordinary circumstances." I can assure you, had he behaved in his Senate Appellate Court confirmation hearing as he did in the Supreme Court hearing, I believe there's no question but that he would not have survived the sixty-vote threshold (still in place at that time) and thus would not have received an up or down vote. Judicial temperament is a critical tenet for the Judiciary. Whether you call it "thin skin" or a "temper tantrum," he displayed for all to see the wrong temperament to sit on any bench, let alone the highest court of the land.

He drained all the blood from my head.

Compared to Lindsey Graham, I just feel distress for Susan Collins. By 2018 there were no centrists-moderates left willing to watch her back or to work with her on consensus legislation. As I've written earlier, both the Republican and Democrat caucuses had been pulled to the far right and far left, leaving the center a lonely place where anyone standing there would come under fire from both extremes. In the end, Collins voted for Brett Kavanaugh's nomination. She delivered an hour-long speech on the Senate floor, where she laid out her reasoning. Yes, she said, the #MeToo movement is real, she found Kavanaugh accuser Christine Blasey Ford's testimony that he had assaulted her in the early 1980s "sincere, painful, and compelling," but professed to be troubled by what she called a lack of corroborating evidence.

On October 5, with support from Sen. Joe Manchin (D-WV), the Senate voted 51–49 to invoke cloture, by using the nuclear option—a simple majority—and Kavanaugh was confirmed the next day 50–48. This is why I say that if Reid and McConnell hadn't done away with the sixty-vote filibuster rule for judicial nominees and the Supreme Court respectively, Kavanaugh would not be on the Supreme Court. He never could have mustered the sixty votes needed for cloture to move to an up or down vote in 2018.

Kavanaugh should not be an associate justice on the Supreme Court. He is simply too partisan, too likely to alter the strike zone when he is just supposed to call balls and strikes, too likely to be an activist judge, creating law and not interpreting the law, to serve on our country's most important judicial bench, not rule in line with his personal political ideology or emotions.

To me the Kavanaugh case is the poster child for one way to restore the Senate. There was no hint of bipartisan support for his nomination. Contrast how the Senate handled that nomination—with no bipartisanship—compared to the Gang of 14, where seven Republicans and seven Democrats worked together to successfully negotiate a compromise to overcome the organized use of the filibuster to block nominations and set a standard for future nominations to be opposed only in "extraordinary circumstances." "That standard served the Senate very well for many years," Collins said recently, "until, regrettably, the rules changed in the Senate, and that was part of the downward trajectory, in my view."

As soon as possible, senators should join together and vote to put the filibuster rule, requiring the Senate to secure sixty votes to move a judicial nominee forward, back into the Senate's guiding rulebook. The filibuster is much more than a legislative tool. It helps force bipartisan consensus. It's a foundational part of what makes the Senate what it is. Back in 2005 we heard a lot from constituents at home and nationally about whether the Gang of 14 was a good idea, and arguments for and against deploying the nuclear option. The letter I received from Ms. Tommie M. Wilson, president of the Omaha branch of the NAACP, said it best:

> The filibuster has been an accepted parliamentary maneuver for almost 200 years; it has been a respected means of ensuring that the most ardent concerns of the minority party were taken into consideration," Ms. Wilson wrote. "It is the filibuster, or the threat of the filibuster, that makes the Senate the deliberative body; the ability to filibuster is the primary difference between the U.S. House of Representatives and the US Senate. The change that is being proposed by the majority party is known as the 'nuclear option' not only because of the tremendous rift it would cause between the two current parties, but also because of the impact such a change in the rules would have on the traditional ways of

the Senate. Furthermore, by eliminating the possibility of a filibuster for judicial nominations, the Senate would be abdicating its Constitutional role of providing 'advice and consent' to the Executive branch when it is making lifetime appointments to the Judiciary . . . Given all my concerns I urge you again, in the strongest terms possible, to support the integrity of our democracy, along with that of the United States Senate, and oppose any change to the existing rules.

SIX

Rescue, Jobs, and the Loud Crowd

I WASN'T BORN WHEN the Great Depression hit America, when unemployment climbed to 25 percent, when millions lost jobs and despaired, when our country teetered on collapse. But I had a front row seat when the Great Recession unfolded in 2008. It was pretty unsettling. It dragged America once again to the edge. Many have forgotten how bad it got in 2008 and 2009. Many still blame irresponsible banks for causing the turmoil they alone should have fixed. Others, too, believe that the federal government had no business bailing out Wall Street for its years of excesses, risk-taking, and duplicitous book-keeping. From my point of view, we had no choice.

At that time, I focused on the impact the recession had on real people, on my constituents back home in Nebraska, and on working people across the country. They were getting hammered. The economy shed jobs at an alarming rate. Three hundred thousand to five hundred thousand a month, for many months. Jobs, jobs, jobs—that was my focus. The actions taken in response by Congress and the Bush and Obama administrations in the fall of 2008 and early 2009 may not have been the best steps.

They do, however, stand in stark contrast to how Washington addressed the next great crisis, the deadly coronavirus pandemic in 2020, under the deeply flawed leadership of President Trump. With COVID-19, Congress and Trump initially joined to pass massive bipartisan relief, but Trump then politicized the response, putting both millions of lives and millions of jobs at risk. To many, the rescue and recovery of 2008 and 2009 was a lesser crisis not on par with COVID-19. Granted. But so was Washington's response and the result. The proof is that the economy quickly rebounded in 2009, consumer confidence returned, the stock market rose, and people got hired to work.

This unruly episode in American history began, for me, in the summer of 2008, when I joined a bipartisan group of ten senators to try to develop a comprehensive bipartisan energy package. We called ourselves the Gas Gang. The camaraderie and trust among us were similar to the Gang of 14 on judicial nominations. We met behind closed doors away from the TV cameras and hallway reporters, and hashed out, through detailed and honest debate, a proposal for a twenty-first-century energy agenda. By early August, before the congressional recess, we had a "New Era Energy Plan," which would seek, among other things, to improve U.S. domestic production, including offshore drilling, and to move about 85 percent of America's cars and trucks to alternative fuels in the following two decades. In one of our last meetings in early August, Sen. Kent Conrad (D-ND) said he hoped to push it forward in September as legislation, but was worried that a brewing financial storm might explode. He proved prophetic.

I remember the fear in Henry Paulson's voice. I remember the grim tone in Ben Bernanke's. It was mid-September 2008 and the treasury secretary and the chairman of the Federal Reserve called a special briefing for congressional leaders. Large financial institutions were on the brink of failure, they warned. Watching 401Ks drop value hourly traumatized investors and sent major shock waves through the economy. Congress needed to provide hundreds of billions of dollars to stem the enveloping financial crisis, the Treasury and Fed chiefs said, and immediately—or the nation's economy would collapse, maybe worse than in the Great Depression.

The problem traced its roots to 2006 when housing prices fell and banks began engaging in a number of dubious practices—

derivatives, mortgage-backed securities, low-interest loans, collateralized debt obligations, mostly based on too little real money and too much risk—to try to boost housing sales. By the summer of 2008, mortgage giants Fannie Mae and Freddie Mac were sinking under a subprime mortgage crisis, prompting the Bush administration to take over the institutions to prevent their collapse. On September 15, Lehman Brothers, a finance giant with assets over $600 billion, filed for Chapter 11 bankruptcy protection, triggering the largest bankruptcy in U.S. history.

The next day, the Federal Reserve Bank of New York gave American International Group (AIG) an $85 billion loan to keep it afloat. The global company which once had $1 trillion in assets relied heavily on selling credit default swaps and, when its credit rating was suddenly lowered, it owed people a lot of money. Less than twenty-four hours after the AIG bailout, it was clear the financial crisis hitting Wall Street was getting worse. It threatened to balloon into a global contagion.

According to news reports, Bernanke had just told Paulson they had to stop treating the symptoms and attack the underlying problem, that Congress must be engaged. Bernanke and Paulson proposed a program referred to as TARP, or a Troubled Asset Relief Program, for the government to buy $700 billion in banks' wobbly assets. Sometime later this morphed into a forced loan system for certain banks. This pushed aside the Bush administration's usual reluctance for the government to get involved in private enterprise. "There are no atheists in foxholes and no ideologues in financial crises," Bernanke famously said at this time.

On September 18, President Bush spoke from the Rose Garden, flanked by Bernanke, Paulson, and SEC Chairman Chris Cox. He made the case for the unprecedented bailout and urged swift action by Congress. "We believe that this decisive government action is needed to preserve America's financial system and sustain America's overall economy. These measures will require us to put a significant amount of taxpayer dollars on the line. This action does entail risk. But we expect that this money will eventually be paid back." Bush reminded the nation that it had weathered other storms, including the 9/11 terrorist attacks, the dot-com bust and recession, and come through stronger. "We will weather this challenge too, and we must do so together," the president said.

It seemed clear that something had to be done pronto. So, I consulted the Oracle of Omaha. I called Warren Buffett to seek his advice and views on whether the TARP response was the right solution. Buffett said he wasn't sure, but doing nothing was not an option. Wise counsel.

The U.S. House took up the Emergency Economic Stabilization Act of 2008 and on September 29, defeated it, 205–228. Ninety-five Democrats opposed the measure, as did 133 Republicans. Partisan squabbling preceded the vote, with Speaker Nancy Pelosi blaming the financial turmoil on "failed Bush economic policies," and Republicans complaining that the bill would strike a blow against economic freedom and that once the federal government got into the financial marketplace it would never leave. The Stock Market reacted harshly. It lost more than 770 points in one day, the largest single-day drop in history (at that time). Wall Street investors didn't think much of the House's childishness.

Then cooler heads took over. On October 1, the Senate approved a revised version of the $700 billion package on a strong and bipartisan vote of 75–24. I voted aye. The House recovered and two days later approved the plan 263–171, and within hours Bush signed it into law. The bill authorized Treasury Secretary Paulson to establish TARP and gave him immediate access to $250 billion, with another $100 billion released by the president's authority. The last $350 billion would be released later, only with approval by Congress.

While the Treasury Department got immediately to work buying up preferred stock in shaky banks to shore up their solvency, the economy continued a freefall. Paulson and Bernanke shifted how the TARP funds would be used, from buying troubled assets and selling them at auction to sending direct infusions of cash to near-failing banks. Still, hundreds of businesses pulled back their work and hundreds of thousands of Americans found themselves out of a job.

By the end of 2008, a total of 2.6 million Americans had lost their jobs, most in the final months. In November, 584,000 lost jobs, joined by another 524,000 in December. The Bush administration altered again how it would use the TARP funds to try to revive the securitization market for consumer credit. This would be the objective for the second TARP installment.

It is often said that presidents are defined not by the campaign promises they make or the plans they outline for when they take office. It is how they handle and react to crises that arrive unforeseen, unwanted and unavoidable, that defines them. That was true for George Bush after 9/11, after the Katrina Hurricane and the economic meltdown of 2008.

Barack Obama, who defeated John McCain (R-AZ) in the November 2008 presidential elections, seemed also to know that how he responded to the Great Recession would define his presidency, at least its first days. In December, as president-elect, Obama called for Congress to be ready to pass a significant economic stimulus measure aimed at creating or saving about three million jobs over the following two years.

"Our government has already spent a good deal of money," Obama followed up in a January address, "but we haven't yet seen that translate into more jobs or higher incomes or renewed confidence in our economy. That's why the American Recovery and Reinvestment Plan won't just throw money at our problems— we'll invest in what works. The true test of the policies we'll pursue won't be whether they're Democratic or Republican ideas, but whether they create jobs, grow our economy, and put the American Dream within reach of the American people." He also admonished Congress to not try to fund every pet project. "I understand that every member of Congress has ideas on how to spend money. Many of these projects are worthy, and benefit local communities. But this emergency legislation must not be the vehicle for those aspirations. This must be a time when leaders in both parties put the urgent needs of our nation above our own narrow interests."

On January 15, 2009, the Senate voted to release the second $350 billion in TARP funds. Under the TARP legislation the second installment could be blocked only if both houses of Congress voted in favor of blocking the release. So, the Senate rejected a resolution on a vote of 42–52 to disapprove the obligations under the Economic Stabilization and Recovery Act of 2008.

I voted to hold up the second batch of funds. "Too many questions remain about how the first $350 billion was spent, and too many surprising turns were taken by the Treasury and institutions receiving funds," I said at the time. "Although I have the utmost trust and confidence in President-Elect Obama and his team, I have not seen a concrete plan for how the additional funds would be used." I urged Obama to work with the Senate to ensure real transparency and accountability for the funds and use the money to reduce foreclosures and put people back to work.

When in office, Obama made an economic stimulus his first and highest order of business. In January, 585,000 Americans would lose their jobs; unemployment would rise to 7.6 percent; Obama had said that further delay was inexcusable; we had to find a way to ease economic hardships that were the worst in generations, back to the Great Depression. Most Republicans pledged to support only tax cuts, and allot nothing for job creation.

The House, under leadership from Speaker Nancy Pelosi (D-CA), basically grabbed everything off the shelves that might be deemed economic stimulus and lumped it into an $819 billion package that won approval on January 28, 2008, on a vote of 244–188, without a single Republican vote in support. Republicans complained that the measure leaned heavily toward new spending instead of tax cuts. House Democrats and the administration said they were open to a provision in the draft Senate package that would adjust the alternative minimum tax to hold down income taxes for many middle-class Americans. This would have raised the total cost even higher, above an $850 billion limit the president had set for the overall package, to nearly, if not more than, $900 billion.

The Senate, split with fifty-seven Democrats, forty-one Republicans, and two Independents, would decide the package's fate. The Senate's initial package was about $880 billion. During a vote on another issue, I caught sight of Susan Collins across the Senate floor. We made our way to each other. Both of us saw problems with the stimulus package, it was too big, too unfocused, and had items that were of dubious positive impact. The House bill, for instance, included $50 million for the National Endowment for the Arts and $100 million for catfish subsidies. We agreed to work together and I let it be known publicly that she and I had teamed up to try to refocus, and perhaps reduce, the size of the package. It was a new gang.

It wasn't clear how many Democrats would support the big package, let alone Republicans. Republicans already were grumbling that the House rushed a plan to the Senate that was too large, and had a lot of room for cuts. Senate minority leader Mitch McConnell (R-KY) said that Obama had asked for a stimulus without wasteful spending that creates jobs now, adding, "Republicans have better ideas for doing both." They didn't, as would become clear within days. Some Republicans also saw this an opportunity to knock the new president to his knees and made this a centerpiece for driving anger among its base. The main problem was that majority leader Harry Reid lacked the sixty votes needed to overcome a likely GOP filibuster. He would need Republicans to advance any bill.

When the White House got wind of my partnership with Collins, alarm bells went off. The president's key adviser, Pete Rouse, called my chief of staff, Tim Becker. The two knew each other from Rouse's days as chief of staff for former Sen. Tom Daschle. "Where the hell are you?" Rouse said to Becker, who told him he was driving toward western Nebraska on business. "When can you get back here?" Rouse said, and Becker responded, "Tomorrow." Good, said Rouse, and added in his gravelly voice, "I've got a question: Can

Nelson do this?" Becker responded, "I don't know. But if he can't, no one else can."

There were doubters and questioners about my motives. Some suggested that it wasn't a good idea for me, a member of the Appropriations Committee, to try to rein in the president from my party. A full spectrum of pundits, staffers, reporters, and elected members of Congress expressed exasperation saying essentially, "Oh no, not another gang." Even if I fell in with my party, that wouldn't be enough. Someone needed to reach across party lines or this effort to jump-start the economy and give people jobs again was destined to fail. So, on Friday, January 30, Susan Collins and I got to work.

We pulled together a meeting in my office with Sens. Bob Corker (R-TN), Mike Johanns (R-NE), Claire McCaskill (D-MO), Amy Klobuchar (D-MN), and Mark Warner (D-VA). We shared ideas about how to reshape the stimulus package. I talked later that day with Obama's treasury secretary Timothy Geitner and shared my thoughts on next steps.

On Sunday, February 1, Collins and I appeared on the CNN program *State of the Union with John King*. I raised concerns about items in the bill such as research for smoking cessation that didn't seem to be about a jobs stimulating effort. King asked whether the bill should be divided into two bills, stimulus items and long-term Democratic objectives neglected under the Bush administration. "There's no pork in this," I said, "but you may have identified some sacred cows."

Collins said the bill had become a Christmas tree that members were hanging a lot of their favorite programs on, and she wanted to make sure the bill created or saved jobs. We agreed that substantial spending on infrastructure projects would put a lot of people to work and help turn the economy around. King asked if we'd vote no on the House bill if it came to the floor in the Senate. Very difficult, we both said, and I added, "One of the differences, John, is we are talking in a bipartisan basis and trying to bring things together in the center. That didn't happen in the House, it rarely happens in the House."

The next day or so, Collins and I invited another group of interested senators to talk stimulus, including Corker, McCaskill, Klobuchar, Warner. And another with Joe Lieberman (I-CT), Klobuchar, Kent Conrad (D-ND), Jon Tester (D-MT), Mark Begich (D-AK), Evan Bayh (D-IN), and Michael Bennet (D-CO). Soon after that, Collins and I held a meeting with a large bipartisan group of colleagues, about twenty, that included most of the aforementioned Democrats and a few new ones, and Republican senators Lisa Murkowski of Alaska, Arlen Specter of Pennsylvania, and Mel Martinez of Florida. Many Republicans fell away after this meeting.

This occurred because by early 2009, the numbers of senators who might truly be considered centrists, who might be willing to join colleagues from across the political aisle sharply declined, even though some of the formerly centrist champions remained. Bipartisanship was beginning to take on negative baggage, and a new factor would make matters worse.

There was a new element in Congress, a kind of political virus that would virtually kill bipartisanship. There was a restive mood emerging in the conservative areas of the country, a movement of small-government, or antigovernment activists who had been, since the TARP bailout, demanding that their elected representatives stop working on a bipartisan basis with Democrats—who they derided as hopeless big-spending, big-government, left-leaning elitist liberals.

I call them the Loud Crowd. This group is in no way even remotely connected to the valuable Parkinson Voice Project that developed a program combining education, individual speech therapy (Speak Out!), and group sessions (The Loud Crowd). The group I call the Loud Crowd doesn't help people, it divides them.

While the movement wasn't yet fully formed, it had a noticeable effect on the stimulus negotiations. The political Loud Crowd, soon to be formally organized, funded by antigovernment donors and taking on the name of the Tea Party, fired thousands of shrill phone calls and emails into Republican offices on Capitol Hill.

This crowd would have a much bigger impact later in 2009 over development of the Affordable Care Act.

For the stimulus, it drove previously bipartisan Republicans away from our negotiating table. Soon, it was just me working with Susan Collins trying to woo GOP senators Olympia Snowe of Maine and Arlen Specter of Pennsylvania to join us. Joe Lieberman was something of a Specter Whisperer, so he joined our negotiating crew. We weren't much of a gang. We called ourselves The Jobs Squad.

President Obama invited me to the White House on February 4. Susan Collins came out of the Oval Office as I prepared to go in. While under stress, she was lighthearted about her talk with Obama. When my turn came, Obama asked about Collins and others with whom I'd been talking. He asked whether we would get the votes needed to move a stimulus bill. Depends on the product, I said. If I can lean mostly to bricks and mortar projects that create jobs, provide tax relief and not fatten federal programs, maybe.

I gave the president a letter that day, stating that while I understood that the economic situation was dire, "we need to craft *bipartisan* stimulus legislation." As a result, senators from both parties were working on cutting or reducing spending from the draft Senate bill that "we believe will have a marginal effect on stimulating the economy." Our group, I wrote, had identified $77.9 billion in cuts or reductions and asked the president basically if he could accept those cuts. I gave him a document outlining each of those cuts, including $300 million for upgrade of USDA facilities, $750 million for NASA exploration, $100 million for new Defense Department vehicles, $390 million for a uranium enrichment, decontamination, and decommissioning fund, and $5 billion for smoking cessation and other health initiatives. All of that was worthwhile spending, but it wouldn't create many jobs.

I had met that morning with Republican senators Collins, Martinez, Murkowski, Specter, and Voinovich, I noted, whose main concerns centered on the overall cost. They believe, I wrote, that a balance of tax cuts and spending would best stimulate the economy. This would be hard for Democrats to swallow, I acknowledged, and asked where there might be added areas the administration could ID for cuts.

"Finally, I realize that some of the largest amounts of spending in the bill are in areas which are major priorities for our party, such as education. I am wondering whether there might be any flexibility to commit to address these priorities later," I wrote. What was the president open to cutting a deal on? How would he give something to get Republicans on board?

The negotiations dragged on for days as most Republicans melted away, save Collins, Snowe, and Specter. Lieberman also actively participated throughout. He and I met often with Harry Reid and Rahm Emanuel, Obama's chief of staff, and each of the Republican holdouts individually, in Reid's offices just off the Senate floor. Reid listened to ideas and concerns and kept pressing our group for results.

We also met late that week with the larger Democratic leadership team—Sens. Reid, Durbin, Schumer, and Murray—to keep them apprised. Lieberman said, adding that on the stimulus he thought, "If we stick together we might succeed."

Through our negotiations, we cut programs, added programs, trimmed spending, added spending. Each of us was pushing for different kinds of cuts and had ideas for ratcheting up spending in some areas. In one of the meetings in Reid's office, Specter, who had survived a terrible bout with cancer, and would several years later pass away from the disease, announced he needed something to secure his support. What was that, we asked. What he wanted, he said, was substantial additional funding for the National Cancer Institute to conduct cancer research overseen by the National Institutes of Health.

"How much?" Reid asked. "Ten billion," said Specter. "*What*?" Reid responded, adding, "It's a wonderful cause but how can we do that?" He and Rahm offered $1 or $2 billion, Specter rejected it. I thought $10 billion was too high, funding for research would only produce so many new jobs, and at that size it would likely become a target for opponents, I suggested to him. We'll lose the argument that our entire package was laser-focused on stimulating the faltering economy as soon as possible.

"Specter was tough," Lieberman said, recalling that he said to the Pennsylvania senator: "We said this is a very noble cause, but, honestly, Arlen, how can we say that $10 billion for cancer research is going to get our country out of the great recession we're in now?"

"This was the power of one," Lieberman said. He recalled that when he was first elected to the Senate he quickly befriended the Senate's reining centrist, John Breaux, the Democrat from Louisiana. "Never forget," Breaux told Lieberman one day then, "everybody says we need fifty-one votes to pass things in the Senate, or more likely sixty to break a filibuster. But that's not really true. You need probably the last one or two that you don't have. So, if you and I stick together on something and particularly if we get one or two Republicans, we could make something happen." Sage advice, Lieberman thought.

Specter kept listening to our protests that too much money for the NIH might sink the whole effort, then kept pressing for a big plus-up for the NIH. I was exasperated. At one point I said, "Arlen, that's it. I don't want to lose this and neither do you. If we go too far, the deal will collapse." I had to play a little hardball in those discussions—even threatening to walk out at one point!

That really ticked off the famously short-tempered Rahm Emmanuel, who confronted Joe Britton of my staff and demanded that we not leave. Joe defended me and my work. Rahm snapped at him, "You can't bark at me!" Well, Joe's voice was always raspy and now was particularly rough from days and nights of working on our package, with little sleep and a lot of coffee. Rahm eventually backed down, and our Senate stimulus bill moved ahead. In the end, Specter got most of the money he sought for NIH.

We remained uncomfortable with the size of the package and elements in it. We had piles of wrinkled spreadsheets with red lines through spending items. But finally we got close. Objection arose over funding for infectious disease research, which while worthy didn't seem likely to create many jobs. It was recast as funding for capital building projects at community health care centers.

We offered a package to the Democratic leadership and they came back with a counteroffer, at a much higher level. Joe Britton was summoned to an obscure office he'd never been to before in the Capitol. It turned out to be Specter's hideaway, one of the small unmarked offices accorded to senators to work from so they wouldn't have to rush back and forth from their main offices during a series of votes. Britton knocked on a door, it flung open, and he was dragged inside. I'd told Collins and Specter I trusted him to help cement a deal, and was elsewhere at a meeting with leadership. Britton thought it highly unorthodox for a Democratic staffer to help advise Republicans on such a sensitive and volatile issue. I had faith in him.

Collins grew increasingly agitated as the group talked, Specter seemed close to scrapping the whole thing and walking away. Suddenly, the numbers jumped off the page to Britton. We three had offered an $808 billion version of the bill; leadership had countered with $852 billion. He thought why not round it up or down and mentioned this quietly to Specter's senior adviser who said it sounded fine to him, but he would have to sell it himself to the senators. Specter was known to be irritable at times, and he certainly was now.

Right about this time, I came into the room and heard Britton broach the idea of rounding the package, offering to split the difference and propose a package of around $830 billion. Specter's eyes lit up and referring to the Democratic leadership he said, "Do you think they'll take it?" In a mix of delirium, exhaustion, and bravado, Britton proclaimed, "We'll make them take it!" With a guarantee like that, Specter and Collins pointed to the door and told him to run with it.

We called Reid's office to say we had reached agreement. It was the first time a "yes" was on the table from the three of us. When we pitched our plan to Reid and his aides face to face, they were cool to us. "We'll think about it," we heard. Specter's staff was shocked. Here we were on the brink of an agreement on Obama's first legislative priority, one aimed at keeping the U.S. economy from sliding into a depression, and they wanted to think about it?! Forty-five minutes later, Reid called me. We talked a moment, I thanked him, hung up the phone. I turned to Joe Britton and others on my staff with a smile. "They are queuing the cameras in fifteen minutes. We have ourselves a deal."

Reid recalls working with us on what he viewed as a very important bill. "I felt we had to get something to stimulate the economy. I would have liked to have gotten more money, but in an effort to compromise and get this thing passed past us, I agreed with the lessening number on the stimulus." He recalled that they needed three Republican votes and that none of the three in the negotiations, Collins, Snowe, and Specter, wanted to be the sixtieth vote. That would make them a target for the far right. Ultimately, Reid says, the bill could not have passed if it wasn't bipartisan. "But for that, it just simply wouldn't work."

Our plan would deliver a tax cut of up to $1,000 for working couples, even if they earned too little to have to pay taxes. And it cut spending from the original Senate plan by $110 billion. Plenty of senators on both sides of the aisle didn't like the package, but they didn't have the votes for a different plan. In the end, the only Republicans to sign on and make the Jobs Squad's plan bipartisan were Collins, Specter, and Snowe.

At the press conference, Collins, lamented that the small support from her party showed how hard it would be, from then on, for Obama to overcome the widening party divisions. "It's really unfortunate as I think the American people really want us to work together and really are sick and tired of all the partisanship," she said.

That evening I appeared on news commentator Rachel Maddow's show, where she pressed me on cuts we'd made to the stimulus package. She honed in on why our group had cut funding for school construction. Wasn't that a job creator? It didn't seem to satisfy her when I frankly admitted that Republicans in the group, like many in their party, had an aversion to federal involvement in local education, and that extended to school reconstruction. They viewed federal funding for school construction as the camel's nose under the tent that would lead to much more federal intrusion into how we educate our kids.

The package still had a ton of stimulus that would largely be spent within the first year and-a-half, I said, for broadband deployment, electricity grid support, and construction money for roads, bridges, highways and sewer projects. Plus, there was $100 million for education, to support teachers. Maddow parried, saying that before our compromise emerged there was more money going to states for school construction and for food stamps, which she viewed as stimulating the economy. I responded, "I can tell that without any question, that without the intervention, without the three Republican votes, they would get zero, because this bill was going nowhere. With fifty-eight votes from the Democrats, that's not sufficient to pass anything. I think you can do the math. It was a matter of bring bipartisan support to get something done, rather than losing everything." Besides Rachel Maddow, plenty of pundits and people around the country found a lot to criticize in our plan. But here's the reality. Compromise was necessary to get any bill through.

When the Senate took up our bipartisan plan, I spoke on the floor about how we'd worked together to "cut and tailor our compromise, so it focuses like a laser beam on tax cuts for the middle class and job creation for millions of Americans." We had cut $110 billion in spending from the original bill. "Critics have gone to great lengths to find fault," I said. "That's the old Washington way that leads straight down the path to partisan bickering, deadlock, and a dead end. Many have said it spends too much, others have said it cuts too much spending. That's a sign to me that we got it just about right. As I say, we've trimmed the fat, fried the bacon, and milked the sacred cows." Most of the Republicans remained obstinately opposed.

The Senate approved the bipartisan compromise and over the next forty-eight hours the House and Senate approved the final conference report. The final agreement provided $237 billion in tax incentives for individuals; $51 billion for companies; $155 billion for health care measures, including $10 billion for research and construction at the National Institutes of Health; $100 billion for education aid to special education, teachers' salaries, and Pell Grants; $105 billion for infrastructure including highway, bridge, rail, and other transportation projects; $21 billion for energy infrastructure; $27 billion for efficiency and renewable energy research and investment to help curb U.S. dependence on foreign oil; $82 billion for low-income workers and retirees; and more.

Congress funded hundreds of billions of dollars in "shovel ready" projects that would save and create jobs, as I hoped all along. On February 17, President Obama signed into law the American Recovery and Reinvestment Act of 2009. America got to work.

ALSO, DURING THE FALL of 2008 and into 2009, in addition to the bank bailout and stimulus bill, there was a worsening automobile crisis underway due to a major drop in sales. New car sales in particular were vanishing creating the almost certain demise of the U.S. auto industry and perhaps the world's auto manufacturers. In particular, by the spring of 2009 General Motors was financially upside down. The Big Three—GM, Chrysler, and Ford—were on the brink of collapse. Employment in the auto industry had fallen by six hundred thousand jobs in two years, and those jobs weren't all just in Detroit and Ohio. Nebraskans made a lot of auto parts.

The Obama administration stepped in and offered what would be an $80 billion bailout of the auto industry, a bailout that would be similar to the bank bailout but would help keep alive a huge player in the American manufacturing sector that helped employ hundreds of thousands of Americans, either directly at auto plants or at the many auto parts suppliers.

Doing anything that bordered on a bailout triggered immediate opposition from a growing Loud Crowd. Some were so cavalier as to suggest bankruptcy not knowing the size or shark fest of such a corporate failure congesting our judicial system. They opined it would just amount to a reorganization. That naive assessment was rejected and elected officials who had supported the Bush administration's plan to bail out the industry and invest in General Motors got enormous heat from the crowd who had now assumed the mantra of the "smart crowd!"

Nevertheless, Congress decided to invest in General Motors stock, thereby infusing cash with a payback requirement. In the years following the auto crisis GM repaid the U.S. with a significant profit to taxpayers.

BACK TO THE LOUD Crowd. In February 2009, CNBC commentator Rick Santelli, speaking from the floor of the Chicago Mercantile Exchange, decried Obama's mortgage relief plan and proposed a Tea Party to protest government intervention into the housing market. His message spread like wildfire among *Fox News* devotees, conservatives, the militia movement, and those who had always distrusted government, even as it kept them financially afloat. There was an ugly twinge of racism in the Tea Party movement, with some leaders questioning whether Obama, the country's first black president, was not U.S. born and a secret Muslim. This mob struck fear in the hearts of mainstream Republicans in the Senate, made the 2009 stimulus package politically charged in a way that hadn't existed during President Bush's 2003 stimulus debate and would wreak havoc on the next big item on Washington's agenda, health reform.

The Tea Party initially had no one leader, but that is not to say it was a movement that grew only organically. It was quickly commandeered by Republican activists. The billionaire brothers Charles and David Koch helped fund astroturf groups like Americans for Prosperity, which established faux grassroots organizations in the states to organize Tea Partiers to attack politicians who dared work across party lines—mainly targeting Republicans.

The word "primary" became a verb. The fear of being "primaried" was almost palpable and you could see it when Republicans who had begun working with Democrats on the Senate's stimulus legislation soon chose to be spectators with safe seats on the sidelines. During this time the Tea Party crowd rejected all proposed financial solutions that involved government, and took to shouting at public officials at town halls and political gatherings, trying to intimidate. There was a change in the air. You could sense it and feel it. These crowds showed up at events all over the country, shaking their fists and shouting "We will replace you!"

Some of my colleagues, I noticed, appeared to fully embrace the trend. One Democratic senator—well, technically an Independent—Bernie Sanders of Vermont, made his point of switching his desk in order to be in better view of the C-SPAN cameras that pointed down to the Senate floor. I saw bipartisan friendships start to deteriorate, as any sort of cooperation became seen by the bases of the party as a sign of weakness and heresy. I sensed a great danger to the entire institution of Congress.

In the last several years, leading up to 2020, the debate over immigration reform provided a microcosm of how ineffective and paralyzing the discourse became. Everybody painted with the broadest brush they could. There were no individual strokes. Nobody cared about what worked and what didn't work for individual people. Things like humanity and reality were brushed over. Attacking people for looking different or coming from "shithole countries" is reprehensible.

What gets lost in the shuffle are the only questions worth asking: What is best for the security of this country, and what is in the best interest of humanity? In my last campaign, the Tea Party and the Loud Crowd would lump all immigrants together with the worst illegal gang members and drug dealers to try to "win" the issue. They wanted to just shut it all down. But little did they know the bad people will still find ways to come in. They will still need to be stopped. And there's no sense in shutting out the decent people who want to make America home. That kind of nuance is simply not accepted in the public debate today. It should be once again.

A CONTAGION OF ANOTHER kind spread across the nation in early 2020. As of this writing, the highly contagious coronavirus has sickened 111 million worldwide, taken the lives of 2.46 million, and in the United States sickened more than 28 million and killed nearly a half million people. Around the world and in the U.S. hundreds of thousands of businesses, schools, retail stores, restaurants, sporting events, concerts, performances, parks, and large public gatherings were all shut down in an unprecedented battle to slow the virus's spread. The stock market recorded its largest drop since the 1987 crash, the economy sank, by early May thirty million Americans had filed for unemployment benefits, and Congress came together to pass a series of economic stimulus plans in the midst of an unprecedented health crisis. That included the largest ever in U.S. history, a $2 trillion rescue package sending direct payments to millions of Americans and providing a huge boost to unemployment benefits, business loans, and billions for hospitals battling the coronavirus.

After fighting for more aid for workers out of their jobs in the economic shutdown, Senate minority leader Chuck Schumer called it the "largest rescue package in American history." Majority leader Mitch McConnell sounded almost bipartisan when he said, "We occasionally have these great crises, and when they occur, we're able to rise above our normal partisanship—and many times our normal positions—because these are not ordinary times. This is not an ordinary situation, and so it requires extraordinary measures."

But that message was a 180-degree shift from the 2008–9 economic crisis and the $787 billion stimulus package that McConnell and most Republicans derided as too much government spending, even in the face of a crisis that threatened to plunge the country into another Great Depression. It's hard to not see some hypocrisy in the shift. Back then, Democrats controlled the

White House and both the Senate and House. In 2020 Republicans held the White House and the Senate, while Democrats led the House under Speaker Nancy Pelosi. Back then, Republicans were being obstructive. McConnell at one point called the 2009 effort a "trillion-dollar mistake," and would go on to famously say in 2010, "The single most important thing we want to achieve is for President Obama to be a one-term president."

Of course, McConnell voted against the 2009 stimulus. He justified his switch to supporting massive federal spending related to the coronavirus, double or triple the "trillion-dollar mistake," with the words "extraordinary measures." Extraordinary measures, like supporting a president when he's—in contrast to 2009—a member of your political party? How does that show one is rising above "normal partisanship?" The terrible coronavirus has, indeed, been a unique and horrible shock to public health and our economy. But it shouldn't take a crisis of this magnitude for Republicans, particularly in today's Senate, to be more supportive, no matter who is in the White House, of strong federal government.

For only the federal government can help the entire nation respond to, pull together needed resources, tackle a major threat—be it an economic meltdown, a pandemic, or a major natural disaster like hurricanes pounding the coasts, wildfires scorching the West or drought and floods that upend the lives of millions. It's too big to fail.

SEVEN

For the Health of the Nation

THE AFFORDABLE CARE ACT, also known as Obamacare, was a landmark piece of legislation that almost never saw the light of day—and not just because of Republicans. Although their political gamesmanship, played out amid a serious national crisis in health care, caused the bill to become so politically charged and is why controversy continues today, a decade after passage.

The GOP had played these games before, with the creation of Social Security in the 1940s and with the establishment of Medicare in the 1960s. Leading Republicans tried in those instances to block a crucial financial safety net for workers in retirement and to stop the government from providing health care coverage for elderly people without insurance. Kind of heartless, in my view. The position of the Republican Party writ large on those two historic humanitarian gestures was the reason I am a Democrat. Time and again, my party demonstrated it cared for the less fortunate in our society, and still does. It's important to note so did many, many enlightened Republicans, including a lot in my home state. Just not the national party leadership. Not then, not today.

With the Affordable Care Act there also was infighting within the Democratic party about its signature provisions, and there was a strong pull from the left flank to push through universal health care for all Americans, which would likely end the private health insurance system millions of Americans either enjoyed or were comfortable with. As a consequence of these multiple opposing forces, I ended up having to conduct "shuttle diplomacy" between the White House and the more liberal and moderate senators to make sure everyone got just enough to make them happy. The debate, development, and passage of the Affordable Care Act, as it would turn out, left true bipartisanship in the Senate on life support, and it's still waiting to be revived today. A lot of internal politics and external forces, both on the right and the left, turned the word bipartisan into a kind of scarlet letter of shame.

But I didn't know all that in the spring of 2009. I simply saw an opportunity to bring my insurance background and my record for bringing people together to bear upon an issue that had not been successfully addressed in years, maybe even decades. So, I threw myself into the health reform effort. I had come out against Hillary Clinton's health care reforms in the 1990s as governor, and I knew this time it had to be done right. But I would get battered by the winds of change blowing through Washington in 2009, a tornado of vitriol that shredded any chance of a bipartisan product on health reform.

There were other challenges on the road to major health reform. For one, by 2009 the Senate Lions I was privileged to serve with earlier had lost their roar. These players had been giants in previous major debates, resulting in bipartisan agreements on everything from Medicare and education reforms, taxes to federal spending, war to peace. Another factor was that the number of centrists, those who could be counted on to work across the aisle, had dwindled to at most six. That was one-fourth of the roughly two dozen serving when I first arrived in the Senate just eight years earlier. Taken together, there was hardly anyone with enough gravitas to pull senators together, hardly anyone to work with and hardly anything to work on in a bipartisan way. During this troubled year, it became clear that anyone who dared walk, much less look, across the aisle in the Senate chamber soon suffered the wrath of extremists, on both the left and right.

Health care reform was hampered by another complication. It wasn't anyone's fault. It was simply reality. The Senate, and Congress as a whole, often has worked best and in a spirit of bipartisanship when trouble bears down on it like Vesuvius. In modern times, Congress came together with President Ronald Reagan in 1983 to rescue the near-insolvent Social Security system. Reagan praised the deal he struck with the GOP-led Senate and the Democrat-led House, saying, "By working together in our best bipartisan tradition, we have passed reform legislation that brings us much closer to insuring the integrity of the Social Security System."

After battling each other publicly during work hours, the Republican Reagan and Democrat House Speaker Tip O'Neill famously shared many a drink at the White House. Former House minority leader Bob Michel, who also got along well with O'Neill, once told me that those White House get togethers were "as social, courteous, professional, and business-oriented as always described." I guess that is what can happen when you have a president you can trust.

In 2001 Pres. George W. Bush got major tax cuts through with bipartisan backing. After the terrorist attacks on 9/11, Congress and Bush joined arm in arm to pass bipartisan legislation seeking to make sure another attack didn't arrive soon on American soil, and oversaw the bipartisan creation of the Department of Homeland Security. In 2005, when Senate majority leader Bill Frist had his finger hovering over the nuclear button on judicial nominations, the bipartisan Gang of 14 bridged party divides over stalled judicial nominations and kept Frist from blowing up the Senate.

With health care, America definitely was in trouble. More Americans were being denied health coverage and affordable care because of insurance company decisions and rising premiums. In fact, premiums had doubled over the previous decade three times faster than wages. Small businesses couldn't afford to cover their workers. Fifteen years before, 61 percent of small businesses offered health care, a number that had dwindled to 38 percent. More than forty million Americans were uninsured in early 2009. Many of them couldn't pay for routine health screenings to identify problems early, when treatment would generally be inexpensive. Many were forced to wait until they were in a full-blown health crisis, then threw themselves on the mercy of hospital emergency rooms. There, highly skilled doctors and nurses would undertake emergency and costly measures to save or stabilize patients knowing full well the patients could not pay. The costs of uncompensated care would be absorbed into hospitals' budgets, which were rapidly climbing and threatening their solvency.

There were myriad other flaws in the health care system: children were kicked off parents' insurance plans at age twenty-one; coverage was denied to patients with preexisting health conditions; when people changed jobs they often lost coverage; the costs of prescription drugs skyrocketed and veered toward unaffordability, and so on.

But the Obama administration didn't effectively convey the sense our health care system was in the emergency room and Congress had to deliver a bipartisan cure. There was no agreement on the problem and no consensus on the solution. Further, the public was divided. The political parties were divided within themselves, with Republicans feuding over doing nothing or modest reforms and Democrats separated into camps favoring creation of a public option, or a government-run health care insurance program and those who wanted significant reforms that stopped shy of undermining the private insurance marketplace serving more than two hundred million Americans.

Through no fault of its own, the Obama administration did not tackle health reform early enough. The financial crash of 2008 and the need for a major economic stimulus in 2009 made sure of that. When the administration was able to focus on health care reform it lacked the broad political goodwill that often is available for only a short while in a president's first term.

In hindsight, we might have been able to develop a bipartisan measure to address costs, drug prices, preexisting conditions, and expanding coverage without going to any form of government-run health care. I have my doubts, though. What the Loud Crowd did to the Republican caucus, to me, and ultimately to the country, may have occurred anyway. The Loud Crowd killed any chance of bipartisan health reform. Since then, as well, the Loud Crowd has gone on to wreak havoc across our society and altered the Senate I served in, maybe forever.

HEALTH CARE REFORM GOT started in early spring of 2009. In March, President Obama convened a health care summit at the White House that drew members of Congress from both sides of the aisle, regular citizens, doctors, nurses, and health insurance executives. Obama told the gathering the nation's health care system provided too little coverage, cost too much, left millions without health insurance, led families into bankruptcy every thirty seconds, and presented the biggest threat to America's fiscal health. The status quo was untenable and those who sought to block reform would not prevail, he argued. "But I'm confident if we come together and work together we will finally achieve what generations of Americans have fought for and fulfill the promise of health care in our time," he said. "And what a remarkable achievement that would be, something that Democrats and Republicans, business and labor, consumer groups and providers, all of us could share extraordinary pride in finally dealing with something that has been vexing us for so long."

The White House, apparently operating on the belief that the path to success in 2009 meant doing the opposite of what President Clinton tried in the early 1990s with Hillarycare, chose not to deliver a fully baked plan to Congress. It let reform develop from the bottom up. For a while, lawmakers, insurers, medical professionals, business leaders, religious leaders, progressives, conservatives, and moderates acted in good faith and put wide-ranging ideas on the table for how to fix a health care system no one viewed as sustainable. Key House and Senate committees held extensive congressional hearings addressing the panoply of faults and an equally broad array of options to improve delivery of service, quality of care, access to insurance, and affordability, all with an eye on reining in the soaring costs of health care and not bust open the federal deficit.

In July, House Democrats unveiled a behemoth thousand-page health care reform bill. It held a couple of especially interesting ideas. One was a requirement that insurers must accept applicants without charging based on preexisting medical conditions—like diabetes, asthma or other continuing illnesses. To counter adverse selection, the bill included an individual mandate, requiring that individuals buy health insurance, or pay a fine or fee if they refused, and that insurance companies provide coverage for a basic set of essential benefits. This wasn't a Democratic plan. It was a Republican one.

It first arose in 1989 in a Heritage Foundation report authored by Stuart M. Butler, who offered it as an alternative to national health insurance. The idea was for government to mandate that heads of households buy at least a basic package of health insurance for their families—which could include a catastrophic provision limiting a family's total costs for a medical issue, preventive care, and other services. Insurers would be mandated to provide that basic package of coverage. Butler wrote: "Many states now require passengers in automobiles to wear seatbelts for their own protection. All others require anybody driving a car to have liability insurance. But neither the federal government nor any state requires all households to protect themselves from the potentially catastrophic costs of a serious accident or illness. Under the Heritage plan, there would be such a requirement."

The plan was based on two principles: that the family carries a responsibility to obtain health insurance for its members and that a mandate would ensure individuals had insurance in the event of sudden and costly illnesses or accidents that society would pay, even if the person didn't have insurance, out of a moral obligation. A mandate also would force households with means to obtain insurance, ending a problem of middle class "free riders" taking advantage of society's sense of obligation to care for those in health crisis.

Newt Gingrich, the firebrand Georgia Republican who became Speaker in the 1994 GOP takeover of control of the House, had backed the Heritage option in the midnineties. So did a lot of other Republicans. Mitt Romney, the Republican presidential nominee in 2012, had backed the individual mandate years earlier as governor in Massachusetts.

But by summer of 2009, Republican politicians had sworn off the individual mandate. Why? Could it be because Democrats proposed it? And maybe too early in the debate? Looks that way to me. Partisan politics elbowed its way to the front of the debate.

The Tea Party movement also caused a lot of trouble for health care reform. During the August congressional recess that year, Tea Party members staged angry protests across the country, at the offices of members of Congress and during their public meetings. They virtually took over lawmakers' town hall meetings demanding they oppose the Democrats' health reform proposals, on grounds they cost too much, involved too much government, and would further raise the burgeoning federal deficit. This was back when Republicans cared about the deficit, kind of quaint in hindsight. The Tea Party fervor infected many.

Seemingly even Sen. Chuck Grassley, the Iowa Republican who had worked with Democrats on the Finance Committee for years, became afflicted with Tea Party–itis. At an Iowa town hall meeting, Grassley said Americans "have every right to fear" government health care reforms because the House bill provided counseling for the end of life. There should not be, Grassley said, "a government-run plan to decide when to pull the plug on Grandma."

The administration was unprepared for the fury hurled at its reform effort. During this pivotal month, the Democrats' mantra of "quality, affordable health care" was drowned out by Republicans' bogus warnings of "death panels" and a "government takeover" of health care.

In Nebraska, I held eight town hall meetings across the state, in Lincoln, Norfolk, Kearney, North Platte, South Sioux City, McCook, Scottsbluff, and Omaha, to explain principles I could support in any health reform effort, and to respond to my constituents' questions. The meetings were packed and some were tense.

Interest was so high in Omaha, speakers were set up on the plaza outside so an overflow crowd of several hundred people could hear the back-and-forth discussion. Among those attending was the "Oracle of Omaha," Warren Buffett.

These meetings were invaluable to me for an opportunity to hear directly from Nebraskans, and to clear up misinformation about what health care reform could mean. While many people attending these sessions listened and asked good questions, some who couldn't get into the meetings because of space limitations just wanted to yell, some of them at me.

After that turbulent recess, in early September Obama delivered a speech to Congress urging lawmakers to keep working toward reforming health care by year's end. "We know we must reform this system. The question is how," Obama told Congress in a special address in the House chamber. Obama praised the work of five congressional committees to develop reform ideas and laid out his own plan with three goals: to provide insurance for people who don't have it; to require individuals to carry basic health insurance—the individual mandate; and a public option available in an insurance exchange—a government-provided health insurance plan.

Obama, who as a presidential candidate the year before opposed an individual mandate, had changed positions and now was viewed as at least open-minded. The president said an individual mandate would not disrupt the private insurance market or stop people from seeing the doctor of their choice but would vastly improve coverage and services for millions. And he vowed that health coverage would not apply to people living in the United States illegally. Amid loud grumbling from the Republican side of the aisle, Rep. Joe Wilson of South Carolina shouted "You lie!" It stunned everyone. Seated behind Obama as is the custom, Speaker Pelosi looked shocked and Vice President Biden shook his head. Health reform had taken a dark partisan turn.

Within days, about sixty thousand Tea Partiers rallied at the U.S. Capitol against health care reform as too much government, too much spending, too much deficit-hiking. Some people waved signs likening Obama to Adolph Hitler. The crowd chanted "Obamacare makes me sick!" Several Republican lawmakers were in the audience, including Rep. Tom Price (R-GA), who would later become a sharp critic of the Affordable Care Act and serve as President Trump's first head of the Department of Health and Human Services—only to resign over ethics matters. Obama flew to his own pro–health care rally in Minneapolis and told fifteen thousand supporters that a public option would not keep people from getting the coverage they needed.

In early fall, the noise volume on health care reform got turned up, all across America, to a roar. On the right was a loose-knit cabal of *Fox News* and the far-right media, conservative groups like the Heritage Foundation, the Tea Party, the anti-Washington Loud Crowd, and their Republican allies on Capitol Hill. Their message: Stop this government takeover of health care. On the left was left-leaning MSNBC, the progressive media, progressive think tanks, former Vermont governor and physician Howard Dean, labor unions, liberal activists, and their Democrat leaders on the Hill. Their message: Only government can help insure the millions dying, getting sick, and going broke.

I saw the noise level rise in daily reports staff prepared documenting the rising number of calls, letters, and emails to my Senate offices in Nebraska and Washington. Professional advocacy groups on the right, left and center ginned up massive letter writing and phone-calling campaigns for and against the health care reform bills. Many called with talking points disseminated by organized campaigns.

I also got dozens of personal letters from Nebraskans offering compelling stories, narrated without talking points, to explain their personal health care plights—including losing their homes to bankruptcy, marriages to financial stress or lives of parents, siblings, or children because of a lack of health care coverage. One Nebraskan wrote that she and her husband had lost jobs, had preexisting conditions, couldn't secure health insurance, and would be happy to have the government try to help. But all she'd heard from Washington so far was "pull yourself up by your bootstraps." Well, she wrote, "My bootstraps are frayed and torn and I find myself out here on my own . . . and very scared."

Another Nebraskan wrote that she had a good job and health insurance but its rising costs were making life "very stressful . . . I feel like I'm falling through the cracks and nobody cares." On the other end, I heard from people urging me to oppose "socialized medicine," "government health care" and pretty much anything congressional Democrats laid on the table. One irate caller told one of my aides, "You tell Senator Nelson to keep his government hands off my Medicare!" Clearly, the message was lost.

No one knew what might emerge from these flames. The people who wanted nothing rather than something, and those who wanted nothing if not everything, were prevailing. But there was a lot of time ahead. The Senate Finance Committee headed by Max Baucus of Montana moved ahead with a Senate version of health reform, and while most Republicans had abandoned even the pretense of supporting the Democrats' effort, Republican Olympia Snowe of Maine continued to work with the Finance Committee Democrats.

By late October I had honed a core set of goals for health reform to gain my support. They were: a national exchange providing a range of insurance coverage for people to buy—with subsidies if needed—would have to also have similar counterparts available in the states that wanted to set them up; health reform that would not raise the deficit; and health reform delivering coverage to Nebraskans at lower cost, with improved access to care, and improved quality. I knew I could never support any bill, however, if it included a public option, if it allowed federal funding to pay for elective abortions (violating the Hyde Amendment), or if states would be required to expand their Medicaid programs to extend health care to uninsured people—they should be given an opt-in option. Each of these would be deal breakers.

Every time I headed to the Senate floor for a vote, reporters swarmed. Time and time again I said, "I'm not looking for a reason to vote against health reform. I just haven't seen yet a reason to vote for it."

As a longtime insurance man, the public option was particularly troubling. Before entering politics, I had worked for a private insurance company, served as state insurance commissioner in Nebraska and executive vice president of the National Association of Insurance Commissioners, the organization representing state insurance commissioners or directors in all fifty states. I knew something about insurance. I also knew many of my Democrat colleagues and advocates for health reform thought the public option was the silver bullet that would magically hold down costs and promote competition.

I saw it another way. A public option, if enacted, would have been exposed to the grave threat of adverse selection, whereby the premium costs of a less-healthy population of individuals— who would choose to enroll in a government-backed plan—would overpower the revenues gained from young, healthy individuals in the plan. This would have resulted in higher premiums for everyone in the public plan and create a death spiral of mounting costs.

This bad idea could eventually lead to government intervention to defray the costs of its insolvency. In addition, a public option could have undermined the private health insurance system that then covered more than two hundred million Americans. While certainly some, perhaps many, did not like the health coverage largely provided by their employers, and many plans had significant shortcomings, many other people preferred to stick with the health insurance coverage they knew, offered by companies like Blue Cross and Blue Shield, Cigna and United Health.

I wasn't alone in my opposition. Fellow Democrats such as Sens. Blanche Lincoln of Arkansas, Mary Landrieu of Louisiana, and Joe Lieberman of Connecticut had either explicitly said they'd vote no on a public option, or said they preferred private insurance cooperatives to a government-run health care provider. Lieberman was all for health care reform, he'd been working on it since the Clinton administration. He could see that some in the Democratic caucus saw this as an opportunity to usher in national health insurance, a governmental takeover of health insurance.

"I thought, that wasn't the American way. It wouldn't work in the U.S.," Lieberman told me. "The reality is I was convinced that what the advocates of the public option wanted, and I wasn't dreaming, I was basing my belief on what Democratic colleagues said they wanted in the caucus lunches, was what Bernie Sanders advocated for in the last election, that is Medicare for all, which wasn't very popular then but has become so." Lieberman was convinced that move to a Medicare-for-all system would seriously undermine, if not wreck, the employer-based private insurance that covered 150 to 180 million people. Besides that, the costs would be enormous, on the order of $30 trillion over thirty years.

In late September, the Finance Committee defeated a public option plan proposed by Jay Rockefeller (D-WV) on a vote of 8–15—five Democrats voting against. But on October 29, the Democrat-led House, under leadership from Speaker Pelosi, formally introduced a revised measure proposing major reform to the health care system in America. Late on the night of Saturday, November 7, the House approved the Affordable Care for America Act on a vote of 220–215, with just one Republican in support and thirty-one Democrats voting no. Its centerpieces were the public option and the individual mandate once championed by leading Republicans.

Joe Lieberman and I drew a line in the sand against having the public option in a Senate health care bill. "I was really grateful for Ben's support," Lieberman said. Obama, meanwhile held his cards close to the vest. He favored a public option, but did not threaten to veto a final health reform measure without one.

With the possibility of a bipartisan bill slipping away, extra attention came my way from Harry Reid and his team. At least, that's how it seemed to me when, in October, Chuck Schumer accepted my invitation to come to Nebraska to see the state, catch a football game, and go out on the land for some pheasant hunting.

We both knew what he was up to but were good friends. If there were several objectives afoot, no harm, no foul.

So, on a Friday evening in early November, Chuck and his wife, Iris, flew out to Omaha. On Saturday afternoon we headed to Memorial Stadium to watch the mighty (still so at the time) Nebraska Cornhuskers take on their longtime rivals, the Oklahoma Sooners. We sat in box seats and I remember Chuck leaning out to look at the sea of red in the stadium and marveling, "Wow this is just like the Giants!" As we made our way into and out of the stadium, he couldn't help but hear the many Nebraskans call out to me and urge me to oppose the health reform effort.

On Sunday morning we went out hunting. But first, we asked Chuck, a Brooklynite through and through, and a longtime proponent of stricter gun laws for the nation, if he'd ever shot a gun. Of course, he had, at a camp growing up, a .22 caliber rifle, lying on his stomach aiming at a paper target. Well, a shotgun's different, I told him. For one, it's got a kick. When you shoot, a recoil jams the gun into your shoulder.

We got him to go through a quick gun safety training class where he shot a shotgun a few times, and learned the dos and don'ts. As a college student, he'd had a basketball scholarship to attend Fordham University and now years later still had good hand eye coordination.

We headed into the fields walking down separate rows and keeping a safe distance from each other. Chuck was on the edge of our group. I walked next to him. Suddenly, a pheasant flushed right in front of him. His shotgun swung up and he fired. The bird fell.

"Who shot that?" he immediately shouted. With a big smile, I said, "You either shot it, or scared it to death, Chuck. But you got it because you were the only one who fired." To anyone, Chuck Schumer looked the part of a veteran hunter. Dressed in his borrowed camouflage clothing and hunter orange hat, and grasping a shotgun in one hand and a pheasant in the other, he looked like he'd done this for years. We snapped photos to record the event.

Back in Washington, I brought several of these images in eight-by-ten prints to our weekly caucus lunch. I flashed them before a gaggle of reporters gathered outside and delighted when they recoiled in shock at the image of Chuck Schumer in hunter regalia, bird and gun in either hand.

When I passed the photos around at our caucus lunch the howling was unbelievable. "You killed a pheasant?!" Barbara Boxer asked him, incredulous. "Yeah, I did, Barbara," he responded, saying it would play well in upstate New York. He enjoyed every minute of the ribbing he got.

I stood up and in a reference to a certain former vice president who accidentally shot a friend on a hunting trip, I told the crowd that Schumer and I had a very a successful time in Nebraska. The tally: "Three pheasants, no dogs . . . and no lawyers." They howled again. In a few weeks Schumer would play a key role in the health care endgame.

In mid-November, Karen Ignagni, head of America's Health Insurance Plans, the national association of private health insurers who provide coverage for hundreds of millions of Americans, invited me to speak to her organization's board meeting in Washington. Around the table sat men and women running some of the country's biggest insurance companies. I told them I was involved in the negotiations to make sure that any bill that emerged gave fair treatment to Nebraskans.

I also leveled with them: If a bill moved forward in the Senate I would fight to keep a public option out, but there were many other provisions that could have a significant impact on their industry. Rather than walk away, I counseled, the insurers should stay closely engaged, and keep lines of communication open with House and Senate members drafting the bills, and the White House. That would maintain leverage they needed try to minimize, or alter, provisions they viewed as unworkable for their businesses. Walk away, I said, you'll still have to live with whatever becomes law, if a bill passes with fifty-one votes through the reconciliation process. Stay engaged, you may make the product better if we hold the threshold for passage to the normal sixty votes.

As I left, Ignagni followed me into the hallway. Senate GOP leader Mitch McConnell had just spoken to the group before me, she said, and told them not to worry because he was going to kill the public option, kill other major provisions under discussion and kill the whole health reform effort. While some in the room liked hearing that, Ignagni said most welcomed my advice because it seemed sound and gave them something to work on. They didn't want to sit on the sidelines. They didn't want to forfeit their ability to influence the bill.

Abortion coverage was another especially thorny issue. As health care reform emerged from the House, it included an amendment authored by Rep. Bart Stupak (D-MI) barring coverage for abortion in the government-run insurance option in the House health care reform bill. His amendment also prohibited people who would get federal health care subsidies from buying private insurance policies that provided abortion coverage. Supporters of abortion decried the Stupak amendment after the House passed bill and some Democrats asserted they had gathered votes to block any bill that eventually came back to the House if the Stupak language remained.

I teamed up with Sens. Bob Casey (D-PA) and Orrin Hatch (R-UT) to introduce the Stupak language as an amendment to the Senate's health care reform bill. On December 8, the Senate defeated my amendment 54–45. I then said I would be ready to filibuster a final bill that opened the door to federally funded elective abortion coverage. That wasn't a threat. It was a promise.

President Obama invited me to the White House twice in early December to press me to support the Senate's health reform measure, listen to my continuing concerns and urge me to stay in the negotiations. I would. People would view it as a cruel hoax if, after a yearlong debate, we refused to even consider a reform measure on the Senate floor. We were, however, far from a final bill. I had rarely voted against cloture to obstruct consideration of an issue in my Senate career. I thought I might have to in this instance. It was hard.

One thing was pretty clear. If I voted yes for cloture, there wouldn't be a constituency to come to my defense—the tens of thousands, or more, of Nebraskans and the millions of Americans who wanted health reform were not organized or united. But there would be a constituency ready to attack if I voted yes—the Tea Party, conservative media, antigovernment activists and many Republicans, and they were organized.

I WOULD NEVER BE able to please everyone, I knew. During one recess while the reform was being crafted, I was bouncing along in my old truck driving back from our cabin on the Platte River when I got a call from Jay Rockefeller, my longtime friend and ally. He was calling to argue for a greater role for the Federal Trade Commission in the regulation of what would become to be known as Obamacare. With my insurance experience, I was against more FTC regulation of the industry already struggling to meet all the federal rules, and I told him so. He made several fine arguments, but my mind was made up and I politely held the line.

Finally, sensing he was out of options but ever the gentleman, Jay simply implored: "Please?" Now that was playing dirty. "Now you're being unfair and unkind," I told him. "You know I hate having to tell a friend 'no' after they've said 'please!'" We both chuckled.

Rockefeller and I continued to be friends and work on health reform. On December 12, for instance, he and I joined Lieberman on CBS's Sunday show *Face the Nation*. I told host Bob Schieffer that I was trying to be a friend to the process, but that as structured, I couldn't agree to vote for cloture to move a bill forward. By this time, all Republican senators had abandoned the health care negotiations, a factor I lamented: "Well, I think every piece of landmark legislation has had bipartisan support. In many cases, two-thirds or more of the Senate voting for that legislation. That's one of the things that is missing right now. It's not easy to reach across the aisle under the circumstances we find ourselves, highly politicized."

I also raised concerns about a buy-in Medicare proposal Rockefeller favored as being the opening to a single-payer government-run health care plan. Rockefeller disagreed, saying that the buy-in Medicare plan wouldn't lead to a single-payer plan. He believed, however, that the public option was a fundamentally correct way to provide competition with the private insurance industry—in his mind "Public Enemy No. 1."

Lieberman chimed in that there weren't sixty votes for the buy-into Medicare idea Rockefeller wanted, that the bill already would bring millions of Americans into coverage and it could gain sixty votes that very week—if a couple things were left out. Namely, Lieberman said, "no public option, no Medicare buy-in, CLASS Act which will add to our debt in the future." And, Schieffer offered, the abortion language had to be changed? Lieberman and I nodded our heads.

It was hard to see how reform could happen under these circumstances and with such a gulf to bridge, Schieffer said, especially by the Christmas deadline just two weeks away that Reid had set. Lieberman and I again nodded. Rockefeller, ever the optimist, got the last line, saying "History calls us!"

Immediately after our segment, McConnell joined Schieffer. "Well, it's noteworthy that you had to have three Democrats on to explain the Democratic position. In fact, there are more Democratic positions than you'd find in a stack of newspapers, and therein lies the problem." Republicans were united against the key provisions of the Democrats' plan, he said, and had a few modest ideas to advance some reforms, without a public option.

While McConnell held forth, Lieberman headed back home and on the way Harry Reid called him. "Did you just say . . ."? Reid said. "Yes," Lieberman responded. Come to my office, Reid said. When Lieberman arrived there he was met by Reid, Chuck Schumer, and Rahm Emanuel who immediately brought up the public option. "If we take it out, will you support the bill?" Emanuel said. Lieberman responded, "Yes I will."

Lieberman to this day thinks that the White House thought the underlying bill would do so much good that it didn't have to have the public option. "But a lot of people were not happy with Ben and me but so be it," Lieberman said.

An avid Bible believer and reader, Lieberman, who is Jewish, recalls that around these times he shared with me the story he'd read about Rachael, wife of Jacob, who had two favorite sons, her youngest, Joseph, and Benjamin. Lieberman said, "So, after that, he would greet me by saying, 'Brother Joseph!' and I would respond to him, 'Brother Benjamin!'"

Another issue loomed—Medicaid. For months, I'd publicly raised concerns about a proposal in health reform to expand Medicaid, the joint federal and state partnership that helps cover medical costs for millions of Americans, including low-income people, families and children, pregnant women, elderly people, and people with disabilities. Under the program, the federal government kicks in some funding and establishes guidelines; states pick up the tab for the rest of the funding, which varies across the states because they get to define who is eligible for Medicaid support, with some casting the net broadly and others narrowly.

Since my days as governor, I'd called the Medicaid structure an unfunded federal mandate passed onto the states that came with a lot of strings attached and plenty of requirements for states to provide health care coverage, but too little funding to effectively meet those obligations. Medicaid was eating up state budgets. The Senate's health reform effort included an expansion of eligibility for Medicaid to extend coverage to millions more Americans, many of whom lacked coverage and were without health insurance.

In December, Nebraska's Republican governor, Dave Heineman, and I traded letters, agreeing that the Senate version of reform included a substantial unfunded Medicaid mandate for Nebraska. I wrote to him that I was seeking an option for states to opt into the Medicaid expansion, giving flexibility to states "to allow states to avoid the issues you have raised. Under my proposal, if Nebraska prefers not to opt in to a reformed health care system, it would have the right."

As late as December 17, I would be quoted in a Nebraska radio interview that I was still a no-vote on the Senate bill without further changes, notably on the unresolved issue of abortion coverage in the proposed federal insurance exchange, and on the financial burden the bill placed on states for Medicaid. The latter could create "an unfunded federal mandate for the state of Nebraska," I said.

By the second week of December, the battle lines were drawn. Reid needed all sixty Democrats to advance the bill. My staff and I were immersed in marathon negotiations with Reid and his leadership team. I had a decision to make. I wrote down my thoughts, and they went like this.

In considering whether to vote for cloture on the Motion to Proceed to End Debate, the first issue is what happens if the Reid bill fails for lack of sixty votes, the second is what happens if it passes with sixty votes. If cloture fails to receive sixty votes, the White House and Democratic leadership have no alternative but to turn to the Reconciliation procedure which reduces the threshold to pass such legislation from sixty votes to a simple majority. Moreover, the current protections against federal funding of elective abortions in the underlying bill, which were still not good enough, would not survive in a new bill. It was not only possible but likely there would be no such protections. The Public Option, or Medicare buy-in provisions, could be reinstated because they now would just need a simple majority of support.

In short, I wrote, all of the improvements I have insisted on would be lost. How Nebraskans would benefit from this is hard to see. How most would suffer is transparent. The results, on the other hand, of a cloture vote receiving sixty votes is equally transparent. A much-reinforced bill could advance. If health care reform altogether died in Congress, the problems with the health care system would continue. Health care costs and health insurance premiums would continue at an alarming rate. Millions of people would remain without health insurance.

After writing down those thoughts, I decided to keep pressing for restrictive abortion language, an opt-in or opt-out for states on the expansion of Medicaid, and preservation of the private insurance system preferred by more than 250 million Americans. The dilemma, in short was this: Vote no on cloture and a bill including a public option and new abortion coverage in the federal plan would emerge, or nothing would move at all, and people would continue to suffer, including several hundred thousand of my constituents, and health care costs would just go higher and higher. Or vote for cloture on an imperfect bill.

Ultimately, I thought that if I could keep the public option off the table, secure an opt-in or opt-out provision giving all states flexibility on expanding Medicaid and ensure that no federal funds would be used for elective abortion, I might be that sixtieth vote. That was a tall order.

IN OUR CHAMBER, THE key senator on abortion was Barbara Boxer of California. I knew I had to sell her on whatever I came up with, and it wouldn't be easy. She was a fierce champion of abortion rights. I was just as adamant in my opposition to abortion. This wasn't a political issue to me. It was a personal belief and I had two children adopted at birth to make that clear. But Barbara Boxer and I were close friends; we worked well together on many other issues; we had decided to try to work out a compromise.

One day in December I was walking off the floor after a vote and felt an arm wrap around me. It was Barbara. She was beaming. She had compromise language on the abortion issue and I was going to love it. That's great news, I responded, I couldn't wait to see it. But I already knew I would not love it. So, after hearing details of her compromise I went back to work.

In nearly all-day negotiations Thursday and Friday, December 17 and 18, in Reid's office, I and my key staff worked through various sticking points—abortion, Medicaid, the public option, the insurance exchanges and more—with Reid, Schumer, White House adviser Jim Messina, and staff policy experts.

For part of the time, I was camped out in one of Reid's offices with my team, Barbara Boxer was in another room nearby with hers, and Schumer shuttled back and forth like a diplomat negotiating an international deal, trading our ideas. Finally, I came up with a counterproposal on abortion I thought might work, I dubbed two checks and a staple. Here's how I thought it could work to keep both Barbara and me happy.

Under the Senate's current draft of health care reform, some health insurance plans receiving federal subsidies could offer coverage for elective abortion. Under my amendment, an insurer would offer a plan, or plans, with varying coverage. This would be the base policy. The insurer would then issue a separate rider for the abortion coverage. The separate rider would be attached to the base policy figuratively, "with a staple." The use of riders in the insurance business to add or eliminate coverage in certain circumstances is common. In my proposal, individuals seeking health insurance coverage in a federally qualified plan that included elective abortion services would have to pay for that part of the coverage with private funds. So, when someone paid their insurance premium they would have to write two checks.

One check, which could include federal subsidies, would pay for the premium for the base policy coverage. The other check, written from personal funds only, would pay for the actuarially determined part of the premium for abortion coverage covered by a separate rider. This two checks safeguard meant that only private funds could pay for a premium in a federal plan that included abortion services. I was satisfied the Hyde Amendment would not be breached. Taxpayer money would not cover an elective abortion. But what would Barbara Boxer think?

I went to meet with her and entered a room packed full of her staffers, mostly young women, all of whom I believed likely to be strongly pro-choice and not happy about having to make a deal of any kind on abortion. They seemed to be angry with me for even raising the issue. But it wasn't them I had to sway, it was Barbara herself. I explained how our "fix" would not restrict abortion coverage any more than existing law did, which left it up to the states. That was our best way to protect the legislation from Republican attacks on its constitutionality.

As usual, she was very methodical, and asked me to explain the details of the separate checks twice. Then maybe three times. Finally, she repeated it back to me, and I nodded. "I get it," she said. Then, as I remember, we sealed the deal with a fist bump. To top it all off, she then turned around and laid out for her staff just how this was what was needed to save this legislation, and how I was working to do that despite being pro-life myself. When I reported back to Harry Reid, I said: "We have a deal with Barbara. Maybe not a deal with her staff, but she's the one who has the vote!"

Late in the day on the 18th, Reid accepted my abortion amendment and agreed to add it to his Manager's Amendment, the final provisions tweaking what would be added to the bill. He and his team agreed to leave out the public option. Other measures I sought to help small businesses, health insurance co-ops, rural physicians and parents who adopt children also were accepted. We were close.

But at the eleventh hour in a late evening session, with heavy snow falling outside, trouble arrived. The Reid team balked at my proposal to allow states to opt in or out of the Medicaid expansion. Reid's policy advisers told us that they were unable to get a "score," or cost estimate, from the nonpartisan Congressional Budget Office, the gold standard for fair economic analysis of legislative ideas. It was unclear, they said, how many states would choose the option to join. Estimating the impact of those decisions yet to be made by each of the states was not possible.

They asked, how about an alternative? What about inserting a provision in the Manager's Amendment, Reid's amendment, providing $100 million to Nebraska to pay for the Medicaid expansion? Maybe. I saw that idea as a placeholder. It would give more time to work out an acceptable opt in or out provision for *all* states.

We could tackle that option for the states as the bill progressed. I agreed to their Medicaid offer.

Around 9:00 p.m., I told everyone I now would vote for cloture. I would cast the sixtieth vote, enabling major health care reform to move forward in the Senate. Everyone looked extremely relieved. There were smiles all around, handshakes and high-fives. We had a deal.

I went home a few blocks away and slept a few hours. I awoke Saturday morning, December 19, to a world buried in still-falling snow, now about a foot deep. I made my way to the Capitol for an early Democratic caucus meeting on the day's procedures. I wanted to give a speech on the floor explaining how I had come to support the health care reform bill and why it was crucial for the country to fix health care now.

But Republicans, in a highly unusual move, objected. They forced me to deliver my floor speech outside the Senate chamber in the hallway at the media stakeout area near the Ohio Clock. Well, okay, if that's the game they want to play, I thought. At mid-morning I lined up behind the stakeout podium festooned with microphones and began.

"Change is never easy . . . but change is what's necessary in America today. I will vote for health care reform because it will deliver relief from rising health care costs to Nebraska families, workers, rural communities, and employers," I said.

On the floor of the Senate, in town hall meetings throughout our states, and in one-on-one meetings with our constituents, we have all heard heart-wrenching stories of people who are left behind, or forced into bankruptcy, or caught in the grip of a health care system that just doesn't work as well as it should. While each of my colleagues may differ on how to fix the system, I know of no member who suggests the current system is satisfactory; I know of no member who doesn't think we need to change our health care system. I believe that the free marketplace is the foundation of our economy. It is the primary focus that should drive us in our debate.

I believe that a competitive health care system will lower costs and provide better health care for the American people.

I also addressed the abortion issue head-on. "As you know I have strongly held views and I have fought hard to prevent tax dollars from being used to subsidize abortions. I believe we have accomplished that goal. I also fought hard to protect the right of states to regulate the kind of insurance that is offered, and to provide health insurance options in every state that do not provide coverage for abortion. I know this is hard for some of my colleagues to accept, and I appreciate their right to disagree, but I would not have voted for this bill without those provisions."

I continued, "I truly believe this legislation will stand the test of time and be noted as one of the major reforms of the twenty-first century, much like Social Security, Medicare, civil rights are milestones of the twentieth century. Because of Senator Reid's dedication and hard work, the lives of millions of Americans will be improved. Lives will be saved and our health care system will once again reflect the better nature of our country."

Then I turned to the tenor of the debate, which I said might fall on deaf ears: "The debate has been passionate and that has been good for the country in many ways. From the far right to the extreme left, the American people have voiced their opinion. That is good. That is part of our democracy. What has been disheartening about this debate are the reckless and ludicrous claims that have been hurled at one another from both sides in the heart of the debate. Opponents of this legislation are not less patriotic or insensitive to the health care crisis we face in America. And supporters would not be standing here if for a moment they thought this legislation would cause harm. But yet to turn to the news, read the statements from both sides of the debate, you would think otherwise. This quality of this debate has not always measured up to the quality of the American people. We can do better."

Finally, I acknowledged that the bill was far from the finish line and if material changes were made in conference with the House bill, I reserved the right to vote no on a final bill.

I didn't realize at the time just how poisoned politics had become. Within the hour some Republicans pounced on the Medicaid placeholder and labeled it a "Cornhusker kickback." It seemed like they had been lying in wait, ready to latch onto any provision I secured and attack. They decried the Medicaid funding, along with provisions Bernie Sanders, Carl Levin, Patrick Leahy, Mary Landrieu (dubbed "The Louisiana Purchase"), and Bill Nelson (labeled "Gatorade") got benefitting their states. Because I was the sixtieth vote, I got special (mis)treatment.

Surprisingly, at least to me, some of my longtime Republican partners got into the act and repeated the kickback theme. It had never been my intention to get a special deal for just Nebraska on the Medicaid expansion. All along, for months, I had lobbied for a deal for ALL states to be able to avoid an unfunded federal mandate if they felt they needed to in order to balance their state fiscal books.

In the following weeks in January, I would ask Reid to remove the Nebraska Medicaid provision, which he would do and replace it with a provision offering some flexibility for all the states I supported. But I learned once again the old aphorism that misinformation travels farther and faster than the truth.

Abortion was another issue that was misinterpreted, and not by abortion rights supporters but by the some in the anti-abortion movement. Sens. Barbara Boxer and Patty Murray of Washington, both staunch backers of abortion services, issued a joint statement that the bill was acceptable to them. Right to life and Catholic bishops' groups, however, issued statements that, in my mind, intentionally misread the bill and my unmistakable goal to ensure it did not cover elective abortion. I never would have countenanced taxpayer money used to pay for abortion, and I didn't. I asked one of Nebraska's leading law firms to research the issue and shared its findings widely (see figs. 28 and 29).

On Sunday morning, December 20, I appeared on CNN's *State of the Union* program. Host John King asked if the health care fight was the most contentious I'd seen in my career as governor and senator. "I used to have to deal with a unicameral legislature," I responded, "and occasionally we'd have a contentious subject we had to deal with, a policy issue. But the high intensity here is as harsh and as unforgiving and unrelenting as I have ever seen it in my nine years."

My old friends Lindsay Graham and John McCain were among those who made it so, along with others in the Republican caucus. They kept it up for days. I went on the Senate floor to try to set the record straight and said, once again, that I had been seeking help for all states in the Medicaid expansion, and that the federal government should stop passing unfunded mandates like these onto the states.

Finally, on the morning of Christmas Eve, capping months of divisive debate an exhausted Senate voted 60–39 to approve the Senate's Patient Protection and Affordable Care Act. I voted aye. No Republicans did. Republican Jim Bunning of Kentucky did not vote because of family commitments.

The bill would cut the deficit $132 billion over a decade, subsidize insurance costs for millions of then-uninsured people, keep children on parents' health insurance plans to age twenty-six, stop insurers from kicking people out because of preexisting medical conditions and create nonprofit private health insurance plans overseen by the federal government. There was no public option. The private health insurance system remained intact. It didn't allow federal funding for abortion.

On January 15, I sent a letter to Senator Reid formally asking to remove the Nebraska-only Medicaid provision, treating all states the same; he did so. Over the course of the next couple months, the House and Senate worked on a compromise. The White house negotiated a further change on Medicaid I fully supported providing millions of dollars in additional money for states that expanded Medicaid. On February 23, Linda Douglass, a White

House spokeswoman on health reform, issued a statement that I had been trying "to make sure that all states were protected from additional burdens (an unfunded mandate) as they try to cover low-income people through the expansion of Medicaid in their states. That's really what he wanted."

I voted for the final Senate version, but opposed the last-minute take-it-or-leave-it vote on House-added reconciliation package that would penalize a Nebraska student loan business employing thirty thousand people, and add a new payroll tax that could lead to more extensive payroll tax hikes down the road.

Long after President Obama signed the Affordable Care Act into law, the partisan rancor continued, as we've all seen. Court challenges to the Medicaid provision and the individual mandate were lodged. That culminated in a highly anticipated decision in a U.S. Supreme Court ruling on June 28, 2012. With Chief Justice John Roberts siding with the majority, the court ruled 5–4 that the individual mandate was constitutional.

The high court also found that the federal government could not cut off Medicaid federal matching funds if a state refused to expand its Medicaid program, but if a state accepted the Medicaid expansion under the Affordable Care Act, it had to abide by the new expansion coverage rules. This was exactly the argument I'd made when I pushed for states to be able to opt-in and take federal reimbursement, while not being penalized if they chose to opt-out by having to come up with state matching funds.

Harry Reid, who served as majority and minority leader for more than a decade, to this day stands by the Affordable Care Act as one of the most important bills he worked on during his career, and calls me courageous for supporting it. "I have no one I worked with in the Senate that I ever worked with more legislatively courageous than Ben Nelson," he said in 2020. "The Affordable Care Act wouldn't have happened without Ben Nelson. I want that in the book, that's for damn sure."

From my viewpoint, I had no better friend and ally than Harry Reid.

On the ACA, I believed that if you do what you think is right you have to stand and fight for it. As time has gone by, things worked out well. Millions of Americans have gotten health care coverage and health care services under the bill, including many who would not have otherwise been covered during the novel coronavirus pandemic in 2020.

As you've seen, this chapter sheds yet more light on the complexities of negotiation over contentious issues, but highlights the successes that can be achieved when everyone acts in good faith. For my part, I had faced a critical choice in mid-December, to legislate or to vacate. I choose to legislate. Had I chosen the path taken by the Republicans I could have just sailed along saying no, no, no. I could have mouthed their attack lines and the result would have been a broad bill with a public option and new tax dollars for abortion would have emerged from Reconciliation—or maybe the whole year-long reform effort would just die.

The political consequences in my largely red state would be considerably less for vacating than the benefits accrued for legislating. But I couldn't have lived with myself. That's the key. I couldn't accept the only options of walking away, a bad bill or millions of Americans continuing to suffer in a broken system. It's also worth noting that eight years after passage of the Affordable Care Act, Nebraska finally exercised the option I provided the state in those final negotiations. By a vote of the people, with 60 percent support, Nebraska chose to join the Medicaid expansion, not because it was required to by the federal government, but because it determined it was the right time to do so.

One final point I'd like to make. When Democrats passed Obamacare without a single Republican vote, they were lambasted as overly partisan. That was even though the law included as many as 180 Republican amendments and ideas, including the individual mandate requiring people to buy health insurance and allowing small businesses to join together to provide coverage to employees. In 2017, when Senate Republicans pushed their own health plan, they tried to jam it through without accepting amendments from

Democrats or even seeking their votes. Given the slim GOP majority, 51–47 and two Independents who sided mostly with Democrats, this was not very smart. What happened? Failure. Why? Maybe they were just playing to their base and never wanted a win. But the reality is that bipartisanship is fundamental to getting good legislation through the Senate. Pure and simple. It sands down the partisan edges, it brings people together, it increases buy-in, it produces durable results. Obamacare could've been bipartisan—if Washington hadn't become such a divided town.

EIGHT

Heart of the Deal

IN DONALD J. TRUMP'S autobiography *Art of the Deal*, he extols his unmatched ability as a dealmaker. There's never been anyone like him. No one is as good. No one is that uncannily smart, uncompromisingly tough, unyieldingly dominant.

But in 2016 he eked out an Electoral College win despite losing the popular vote by nearly three million votes and became president. Too many voters overlooked the obvious business failures and multiple bankruptcies and his reputation for reneging on deals in contracts or agreements with partners, banks, contractors, subcontractors, and employees. His response to these unfortunate folks: "Sue me."

Lots of people had no other option but to take Trump to court, where cases languished, thanks to his lawyers' stalling tactics, until the plaintiffs ran out of money. As long as he's gotten to affix a gold-lettered TRUMP sign onto a building, golf course, resort, or real estate project, Trump counts the predictable battle as a sign of his superior skills in making a deal. He seems to believe that the ideal Trump deal involves the other side abandoning its goals no matter how modest and giving in to what he wants—a capitulation often exercised to escape abuse.

Anyone, including myself, who truly hoped that once in the White House Trump would develop a sense of honor in his dealing with Congress, or with people on the left, right, and center in our country, or with our allies around the world, watched in abject

dismay as he acted like a bully, autocrat, and dictator. His administration was sued hundreds of times for breaking faith with the laws
of the land that govern our civil society. He lost far more than he
won of those cases in court.

Trump seemed oblivious in his pursuit of the next so-called deal
he could force upon Congress, the American people, on world
leaders, and attempt to burnish his reputation as the best ever
leader of the free world. But Trump's deals are lopsided and leave
people feeling dirty.

For reasons known only to himself, Donald Trump once called
me the "best senator" from Nebraska, and credited me with "one
of the greatest deals in the history of politics." He did so in a 2017
interview with the *New York Times* in discussing Obamacare and
health reform. He was probably referring to the Medicaid provision I accepted for Nebraska in the health care reform effort in
2009 but had intended for all states, which is where the issue ended
up. I guess that's nice of him to say, but what does praise like that
matter when it comes from a guy who doesn't know the first thing
about how real deals get done?

Trump likes to talk about the "art of the deal," but it's not about
art, it's about *heart*. There doesn't need to be a complicated for-
mula or framework, and you certainly don't need a whole book on
this supposed "art" to tell you how to make a deal. The heart of any
deal is trust, along with respect and confidence in the integrity of
all parties. That leads to true partnership.

Moderation helps, too. Some people might think that to be
moderate, or a centrist, is to be so flexible that you don't have any
principles. Really, it's just about recognizing which things need to
be looked at in black and white, and where there is room for gray.
Very few things exist only in black and white.

I don't support murder, for instance, but I did carry out the
death penalty as governor. I had to do it three times. In each case,
I reasoned out that that was what the law called for. Each case
was examined on its individual merits, not through any ideological lens. And if I could follow the law there, I could follow the same

path on most any other issue serving as a governor or a United States senator. I knew I couldn't always get everything I wanted, but it was better to get 75 percent or even 50 percent rather than nothing.

I would argue that the deals I worked out in the Affordable Care Act—keeping the private health insurance system intact for 180 million Americans, stopping the public option that would have destroyed it and ensuring that no taxpayer money would cover abortion—were worthy of presidential praise, even from Trump. Those deals were forged not by forcing colleagues to bend to my will. They came together by working with heart, all parties to a deal included. The Senate once functioned well and mainly because senators, in groups small and not so small, came together and spoke honestly, candidly, apolitically, with a sense of trust and not playing to the cameras on big problems in America, and how to fix them.

When I got to the Senate in 2001, I learned that the most successful "dealmaker" was the Democratic senator from Louisiana, John Breaux. I looked up to him as a mentor. I watched Breaux and worked with him on the first Bush tax cut and the Medicare prescription drug legislation. He was experienced from years working in the center aisle, finding areas of common agreement and seeking bipartisan solutions on legislation. He always shared credit when successful and shouldered responsibility during criticisms. He was always prepared. He had excellent staff and he was trusted. Accordingly, he could be persuasive! But he knew the limits of his colleagues as to how far they might go, their comfort level.

Unlike the hunting dog that goes on so many false points, frustrating its master, John knew who to seek out and what issues to pursue, when the time was right and when it was not. Well, John retired. I had learned that you carefully pick and choose your issues to pursue or like that overanxious hunting dog, you will soon exhaust your colleagues. When they see you coming, they are likely to turn and go the other way.

John Breaux also operated in a different era. In the 1990s and 2000s deficit hawks were everywhere in Congress. Moderates were so plentiful they could have fielded a full offensive and defensive football team, with extra team backups. Senators got rewarded in the media and back home for finding common ground with colleagues across the aisle. The Senate leaders, Tom Daschle and Trent Lott, gave members of their caucuses a loose leash, they often had to. That's not to say Daschle and Lott were moderates, they weren't.

Lott used to say he most certainly was not a moderate; he just wanted to make the trains run on time. Daschle, his friend despite party differences, also wanted to keep the Senate functioning and acting on issues for the benefit of the broadest swath of the American people.

Breaux and John Chafee (R-RI), launched the Centrist Coalition in the midnineties, which comprised of several dozen senators who genuinely liked getting together, and they established a power center outside of the Senate's leadership teams. After Chafee passed away, Republican Olympia Snowe of Maine stepped in to co-chair the coalition.

There were about ten regulars but in a 50–50 Senate, Breaux said, he didn't need more than a few from both sides for the centrists to flex their muscles. "We didn't need sixty votes, or fifty-one. Give me five and we could control the balance of power," Breaux said in 2020. Looking outward, Breaux said he believed that 60 percent of the American electorate wanted Congress to work together and he didn't want the 20 percent on either end of the political spectrum, those who wanted their way or no way at all, to dictate. The centrists made sure of that.

The coalition was like a bullpen of colleagues willing to discuss ideas, tactics, and opportunities on issues they might work together on. Often called moderates, most were just willing to work together to get something done and not be obstructionists. The common attitude seemed, "There might be a way to make this work. So, let's try." Susan Collins says the centrists were motivated by a sense of trying to develop compromises that could deliver results. Because this mirrored my experience with the Nebraska Unicameral, I felt at home.

Washington in the 1990s was in transition, though. With the election of Newt Gingrich as House Speaker after the GOP takeover in 1994, politics began driving policy. Gingrich wielded a partisan club on most House activities, and he encouraged his members to spend more time in their districts and less on working with colleagues on the other side of the aisle. He made colleagues choose sides, with us or against us. He forced government shutdowns that sharpened political differences among House members. Gingrich also threw political niceties and courtesies out the window and honed a combative style that rubbed off on many GOP colleagues and some Democrats. To me, Gingrich is the godfather of the political polarization rampant today.

During my twelve-year tenure, which ended in 2013, voters also sent an increasing number of House members to the Senate. These former House members brought their partisan baggage to the Senate floor. The result being that today, the world's greatest deliberative body doesn't deliberate much anymore. Both sides mainly just lob accusations across the aisle.

The leaders egg them on as they turn their backs on each other. And centrists? You could fit them in a phone booth, with room to spare. Senators like Lamar Alexander and Patty Murray talk about their ability to work together. Both now are retired. Lonely Susan Collins is a centrist coalition of one. There has been no one to watch her back.

IT'S MY VIEW THAT there are three basic relationships all senators have with their colleagues that determine how they operate and the degree to which they collaborate: personal, professional and political. Each is important. Each can determine success or failure on legislation.

First, unlike forty years ago, members tend now rarely to live in Washington or surrounding suburbs, preferring to travel to their home states most weekends—meaning that personal relationships are less common. Official congressional delegation trips ("CODELS") are rarely bipartisan these days. But when I served, bipartisan fact-finding trips could create personal as well as professional interaction and bonds.

Finally, the political element. Voters are sending many more politically driven people from more clearly red and blue states than when I served. Gerrymandering House districts contributed to the change in Washington. In both houses, gaining partisan political advantage seems to become a chief goal, but to what end?

Walking across aisle on the Senate floor is less daunting when personal relationships exist and they quite often break down or lessen political and partisan barriers. John Breaux showed the way for many of us to work together despite party affiliation. He was always prepared, positive, and pragmatic. He was always ready to listen, and listen hard. He liked to build legislation that incorporated ideas from both sides, that developed consensus and commitment. He taught me a lot about how to make deals that were creative, sound, durable, and gave everyone credit.

"Here's my philosophy," Breaux said in 2020. "It was always better to work across party lines and get an agreement on something and get it passed. And then, if people in California wanted to tell people there that they did it, that's fine because I'm going to be telling people in Louisiana I did it. But at least we'd be arguing about success and who accomplished something, as opposed to arguing about failure and whose fault it is that it failed. That's a much better argument as far as the government is concerned, to be arguing about success as opposed to arguing about failure."

For my part, I developed a checklist for times I wanted to reach out and try to bring senators together. It goes like this:

Before taking an idea or issue to your colleagues it is necessary to do your homework. Test it against the obvious questions:

Does it make sense?

Good policy? For whom? Constituents? For enough?

Bad policy? For whom? i.e. opponents?

Among colleagues who will/may be interested?

Chances of success? Dead on arrival?

Can I sell the idea? How many votes?

Are you ready to buck your caucus, if necessary?

These and other analyses, should be considered before proceeding. One of Breaux's selling points was quite simple: Do you want a half loaf or no loaf? This is persuasive if all of the above have been considered.

Now comes the most important factor. Trust.

The basis for any worthwhile compromise, deal or agreement is mutual trust. You must trust and be trusted. Mutual trust involves believing in one another and the capacity each has to make the deal work. Questions like these come into play: Are you competent? Can you be trusted if someone joins with you? Will you stick with those who join with you? Can you trust those who support you to be there when necessary? When there's pushback from their leader? Their caucus? And the president? Reliability and experience and competence help develop sound compromises. But *trust* is the Heart of the Deal.

Trust permitted both the first and second Bush tax plans to pass. Trust helped the nation recover after 9/11. Trust phased U.S. troops out of the conflict in Iraq. Trust among the members of the Gang of 14 avoided pushing the nuclear option button. Trust between the Jobs Squad got Americans back to work. Trust got through major healthcare reforms, without destroying the uniquely American health insurance structure.

You might think the phrase about nuclear arms reduction deals with Russia, "trust but verify" would be operable for the Senate. It's not. If you have to verify, almost by definition you don't have trust. Trust but verify for arms control agreements, sure, but not in the Senate. In the Senate it's just "trust but trust." If you don't have trust nothing works, nothing lasts.

Standing up to caucus chairs and opponents involved another quality—integrity. Without integrity, trust is virtually impossible.

IT WAS CLEAR DURING Brett Kavanaugh's Supreme Court confirmation there was neither trust nor integrity. His tirade and undisguised threats displayed a vindictive and emotional temperament that should have been reason number one to disqualify him from the nation's highest court. Lacking respect for his questioners, he accused minority members of the Senate Judiciary Committee of exacting revenge for his role in the Ken Starr investigation of Bill and Hillary Clinton when they were in the White House as president and first lady.

Remember Kavanaugh warning the Dems that "what goes around comes around?" His lack of respect for others, joined with a hot temper and a tendency to be untruthful, was lost on the majority. They just wanted to push President Trump's conservative partisan onto the Supreme Court as quickly as possible, before any other personal or professional indiscretions might emerge. They acted like lemmings rushing for the cliff because a Twitter rant told them to.

Only a cautionary flag from a Gang of Two—Sens. Jeff Flake, Arizona Republican, and Chris Coons, Delaware Democrat— interrupted the warp speed of the nomination. Flake and Coons pushed for an immediate, albeit scaled down FBI investigation. Senate majority leader Mitch McConnell (R-KY) blamed Democrats for "moving the goal posts" and vowed a quick vote on the nomination, despite President Trump's statement favoring a "comprehensive" investigation. But McConnell had moved the biggest goal post, having invoked the nuclear option and lowering the threshold for confirmation from sixty to fifty-one votes.

Democrats decried the FBI investigation as inadequate and a sham. They, rightfully to me, pointed out that potential witnesses were not being interviewed, particularly character witnesses about reports of Kavanaugh's excessive drinking while in high school. One eyewitness to Kavanaugh's behavior, Lynne Brooke, said she was aware there had to be a number of times Kavanaugh couldn't remember events because of heavy drinking. This was central to Kavanaugh's contention he had never "blacked out" and therefore knew he had never assaulted former classmate Christine Blasey Ford. A case of mistaken identity was his defense.

That was acceptable to the Republicans on the committee who voted to send his nomination to the floor, where the Senate confirmed him on a vote of 50–48, with Joe Manchin (D-WV) the only Democrat to support him for a seat on the world's most important judicial body. Lisa Murkowski (R-AK), who opposed Kavanaugh, voted present to allow for Steve Daines (R-MT) to miss the vote so he could attend his daughter's wedding. Contrast this with what happened to Kavanaugh and other judicial nominees in 2005 during the Gang of 14's closed-door deliberations. Senators agreed that some judicial nominees could be trusted to put ideology and emotion aside to uphold the law, and thus deserved up or down votes, and some—like Kavanaugh—could not.

Simply put, Kavanaugh could not then, and cannot now, be trusted. And he lacked the integrity, then and now, required for a Supreme Court justice to rule with fairness and by the law. It would be hard to believe the Senate would approve of a nominee of such low caliber as Kavanaugh to the Supreme Court bench during any other period of its existence. 2019 was the perfect storm of partisanship with a divisive president, a compliant Senate majority and a mob-mentality electorate demanding partisan blood over political progress.

I'M WELL AWARE THAT reestablishing trust in the Senate will be a herculean effort and require time and patience. Redeveloping personal and professional relationships will be necessary. Electing people of competence and prior experience, not in politics, will help as well. Unless senators set aside their partisanship and are willing to stand up to their leaders and partisan caucus, and to work across the political aisle, the obstruction and division over all the important issues the Senate should be addressing—such as jobs, taxes, health care, education, immigration, and national security—will simply continue unabated. How sad! Unfortunate. And detrimental to America!

It may be almost too late to save the institution of the Senate from within, so that means the best hope lies—as it so often does—with the American people. If they demand a higher standard from the people they send to the Senate, if they demand senators respect and protect the institution to which they belong, if they elect senators eager to work together—not always in their own self-interest—to get things done, together, if they vote for people of integrity and trustworthiness, then maybe the Senate can rise again. There were lions, once, whose roars echoed in those marble halls. Maybe the lions can roar again.

There is one additional player. The president of the United States. Successful bipartisan efforts I worked on included, in every instance, a president willing to work in a bipartisan way. In napkin diplomacy in 2001, the White House initially opposed our compromise but chose to find common ground. They treated us with civility. In the Gang of 14 deal in 2005, we corralled a sufficient number of Republicans and Democrats to block the nuclear option. We found a way forward for up or down votes for federal judgeships—because we trusted one another. Our leaders, and the president, did not support the effort at the beginning. It wasn't a coup, but merely fourteen senators deciding to hunt for a shared solution to overcome a political standoff.

In 2009 the Jobs Squad, although small, brought enough members together to develop a consensus bipartisan package to get our national economy humming again. In healthcare reform in 2009 and 2010, Republicans offered constructive ideas for months that were tucked into the Senate bill, until they didn't. They gave up on bipartisanship.

In the bipartisan successes, even though leadership and the president were not aligned with Senate efforts, there was no fear of reprisal. President Bush applied public pressure on the tax cuts, extremely tame by today's standards. Behind the scenes, though, he was cordial, respectful. Our efforts on war and peace were driven from within the Senate. Everyone allowed the Gang of 14 space. In all these instances, social media wasn't yet weaponized for the parties to deploy against each other.

It's interesting to remember the quaint tweets in the 2000s from Iowan Chuck Grassley, an early Twitter pioneer in Congress and when there was a 140-character limit. One day he tweeted: "Work on farm Fri. Burning piles of brush WindyFire got out of control. Thank God for good naber He help get undr control PantsBurnLeg-Wound." Another time, after accidentally hitting a deer: "U hv herad saying: 'deer in headlight look. It is a frightening xperience when a real deer is there." And another Grassley missive took on TV programming: "I turn to History channel frequently bc I like history. There is nevr any history unless u r an antique dealer. Change name!"

There was a sense of ire and intimidation emanating from the White House with the president's absurd, mean, partisan, and false tweets. These had a chilling effect, to say the least, on those who think differently. Ask Sen. Mitt Romney, the lone Republican to vote to convict the president on an article of impeachment in early 2020, and with the Republican senators who did so in 2021.

Concern about a White House stockade raises the consequences of stepping out of line. Senators feared they would be banished to the wilderness, surrounded by their own irate constituents who come baying and snapping. This is no way to run a country. This is no way to lead the world. The world's greatest deliberative body is better than that, or it should be.

In addition, Trump's record of ignoring and defaulting on verbal agreements elevated the whole question of trust. His lies and leadership style made it impossible to expect that a trustworthy agreement could ever be forged. He can claim that he's always been a great dealmaker. In realty, there was never a deal. Before the ink dried, Trump often changed his mind, then ignored terms or sued to break the deal. That unwillingness to stand by an agreement was reflected in his dealing with Congress. It's been clear for all to see, if it wasn't before. You can't make a deal with someone you can't trust. You can't make a deal with someone who has, throughout his life, lied to advance his cause.

The problem with Trump deals is Trump himself. With Trump, every day is a new day. A new episode on the screen of his reality-show life. A new opportunity, for a novation and perhaps an ovation. He and his deals never have staying power. No continuity. No connection to the past and no commitment for the future. Why? Because neither matter to him and no one else matters to him. This is his alternative reality—not ours. This is what you get: hour-by hour chaos.

The rest of us live in a world where history matters, where connections count, where promises made are promises kept, where the impact on the future guides how we act today and plan for tomorrow. For Donald Trump, there is only today. Right now. He lives only in the present. Every sixty seconds is a new minute, disconnected to the last and the next sixty seconds. As a consequence, any deal he's struck yesterday, last week or last year has no relevance to what he wants to do today in his new episode. That attitude may have drawn viewers to the next installment of *The Apprentice*, but it was no way to lead the greatest nation on Earth.

Trump's response to the novel coronavirus pandemic is a poster child for why trust matters. From the earliest days in office in 2017 he sought to undermine the public's trust in the institutions of government. Then in 2020, as the novel coronavirus emerged in China and began sickening and killing people with alarming speed, he ignored warnings from health professionals, even those he'd hand-picked to run key offices, that it could explode into a global pandemic.

He didn't trust them. He trusted his own "gut." He called it a "hoax." He barred travel to and from China, only after weeks of genuflecting to China's misinformation on their containment of the virus, then . . . nothing for weeks . . . and the virus silently took off in the U.S. In mid-March, when presented with evidence that the virus was spreading rapidly in America and could kill upward of one hundred thousand people without preventive steps, he suddenly declared a national emergency—at least a month too late.

While governors led the country toward safety with stay-at-home orders and mandates to wear masks, Trump dithered over using his executive authority to drastically ramp up testing, production of ventilators and medical safety gear like masks, gowns, and gloves. He took to Twitter, of course, to attack the governors while they were fighting for the lives of their constituents.

Meanwhile, hundreds of thousands of people tested positive for the virus, many became seriously ill and thousands died, even after he said cases would go from fifteen "down to zero, or almost zero, soon." The stock market plunged, the economy stalled, unemployment soared by millions week over week. Trump, fashioning himself a "wartime president," began holding daily White House briefings that quickly devolved into chaotic, contradictory, and confusing events for him to mainly praise the "incredible" job he was doing to fight the virus.

Millions of Americans holed up at home to try to slow the spread of the virus. But by mid-April Trump had had enough. Again ignoring the advice of health professionals who advised that that people should continue social distancing and staying at home and that all nonessential businesses should remain closed—because illnesses and deaths were still rising—Trump illogically began pushing to reopen the country. His motive was transparent. The staggering economy could doom his reelection prospects.

Willing to trade lives for higher stock prices. A deal with no art involved. In a short succession of days, he declared he had "total" authority in the pandemic crisis, backed off when faced with a rebellion from governors, announced reopenings would be up to them, then fomented a backlash by tweeting support for armed protestors calling for their states to reopen in states with Democratic governors. What chaos!

Amid this gravely dangerous health threat, we needed more than ever, a steady, measured, and forceful response from the federal government and the president of the United States. Instead we got a tin-star show-boater, a huckster for untried and unsafe treatments (maybe injecting bleach will kill it!), a leader who "takes no responsibility at all," more worried about his poll numbers than the rising numbers of sick and dead Americans. At this writing in 2021 more than 600,000 Americans are dead from COVID-19—far more than the 58,200 who died in the Vietnam War. It's horrifying.

SO, THIS IS WHY I say that the heart of any deal—from cutting taxes to saving lives—must be trust and integrity. Trust is most important and it's got to be "trust but trust," not "trust but verify." Any way you paint it, there is not art involved. And any way you look at it, Trump comes up short. We are paying the price, a heavy one.

We, all of us, must take matters into our own hands, and demand that trust once again becomes the heart of the deal for how Washington operates by sending people to Congress and the White House who believe in trust, are trustworthy, and who put developing trust with colleagues and the American people ahead of seeking political gain. Restoring trust in all aspects of the U.S. Senate—from its members to its policies to its actions—is where we can start. And we must put heart back into the deals made in Washington.

NINE

Save the Senate

IT SHOULD NOT TAKE a global pandemic and the worst health crisis in a century to make the Senate work. But that's about the only event in recent years that has forced senators to cross the aisle and craft, together, important legislation to help the American people. In early 2020, relief bills surpassing $3 trillion went to medical care for hundreds of thousands of people struck by the coronavirus, and millions of people who lost jobs, income, insurance, and capital for their businesses as the nation went into an extraordinary lockdown to stem the unprecedented outbreak.

I, and likely many of the ex-Senate club, was gratified to see both houses of Congress pass stimulus packages by overwhelming bipartisan votes, and have the president sign them into law. This is how Washington should work. Not every day, but much more often. I wish that spirit of unity would emerge again. I know it can. In this chapter I'm going to offer some solutions that can get the Senate back on track, which would be good for certainly the Senate, and also the country. We need again to have a functioning upper chamber legislative body that can help improve the lives of all Americans, can address their problems and demonstrate its value in preserving and strengthening our democracy. The American people need it. The world needs it.

Now I'm not going to suggest that my dozen years as a senator was an idyllic, harmonious period of brotherly and sisterly love, bipartisan partnership, and great achievements. Hardly. Turbulence, strife, partisan politicking, tension, and failure marked those years, at times. But when America was attacked by terrorists, when the administration launched an ill-conceived war, when judicial nominations stalled, when the economy melted down and when health care costs spiked like a runaway fever—what did the Senate do? The Senate did its job.

My colleagues and I, for the most part, addressed big problems head-on. We handled matters of war and peace, taxation, education advancements, job creation, energy production financial bailouts, economic recovery, and many more issues, almost always with bipartisan agreements. Sadly, the flame of bipartisanship—and the willingness and openness needed to build consensus to get things done—over the years flickered. With healthcare reform it got snuffed out.

After I left office in 2013, forces from all sides pushed senators to the extreme wings of their parties, not toward the center. The changing media made things worse. Where once *Fox News* stood out as a mouthpiece of the right, now MSNBC speaks out for the left. Meanwhile, CNN, ABC, NBC, CBS, and major newspapers struggle to maintain the appearance of presenting the news without an ideological slant. This contentious atmosphere reached its peak in 2016 with the election of Donald Trump—the "Loud Crowd" had finally and completely taken over.

But I can trace these more recent developments back to trends I noticed toward the end of my time in the Senate. I saw it in the transition of Susan Collins to a centrist attacked by both sides, and especially in that of Lindsey Graham, who transformed from reasonable to irrational. The Senate—which should be the legislative engine of the country—has broken down.

With the Senate's inability, outside of COVID-19 response, to pass meaningful, bipartisan legislation, it has ceded its authority to the executive branch, which has been all too happy to set national policy through executive orders and regulatory action outside the scope of Congress's legislative intent. Robert Byrd would be furious.

Many who have served in the Senate are alarmed as Byrd would be. In early 2020, I signed onto a letter that seventy former Republican, Democrat, and Independent senators sent to all members of the current Senate. The world's greatest deliberative body was failing to perform its duties as the framers of the Constitution intended, we wrote. It had abdicated its legislative oversight and checks and balances responsibilities. And it had ceded its authorities to the executive and judicial branches, which are by their nature less democratic. We called for creation of a bipartisan caucus:

> We believe a bipartisan caucus of incumbent members that promotes a fair opportunity for senators to participate in meaningful committee work as well as on the Senate floor could help restore the Senate to its essential place in our constitutional system. Its members would need to stand firm in the face of what could be strong opposition from partisans who prefer politicians who take intransigent positions over those who champion a legislative process that celebrates compromise. Our hope is that all of you will accept this challenge to advance that timeless and higher purpose. The Senate—and the proper functioning of our republic—are simply too important to be allowed to continue on their present course.

Indeed, the Senate cannot keep going on like this. I'd like to offer a roadmap to return the Senate to, if not greatness, functioning as the Framers of our country intended. These ideas aren't just what I'm thinking. Others are thinking about how to return the Senate to effectiveness, too. I'm just the one saying it here. It's not that we think we did things better. But because we all care deeply about this great institution. We want the Senate working for all Americans.

I'm well aware that the shrillest voices on the right and left will pounce on and pummel these suggestions. They are a destructive, not constructive force. I don't want to subject friends and allies to the Loud Crowd's mischaracterization and mistreatment so

I'm not going to identify authors much. These ideas may not be enough. Other approaches might work. Fine. Let's have the debate. Let it be guided by honesty, rigor, experience, and facts. Doing nothing is not an option. The Senate is in crisis. Its current mode of operations leads to a path of oblivion and irrelevance. That's not a future I want to see, nor do many Americans.

Here's my first recommendation. It may be the most important. It's certainly one of the most controversial. I believe that senators should vote to reinstate the filibuster rule. They should restore the filibuster for all judicial nominations, Supreme Court included. Doing so would require sixty votes to advance controversial judicial nominees to the Senate floor for an up or down vote. It would require bipartisanship to move big and important bills.

My friend Harry Reid inched open a door that Mitch McConnell drove a Mack truck through by ending the ability to filibuster judicial nominations. Ending the filibuster is the single biggest contributor to the Senate's current dysfunction. "The filibuster used to be used but not overused," Reid said in 2020. "And now every vote, every vote takes sixty votes. So, they are down now to where they don't do [meaningful] legislation." Restoring it, and demanding that it be used only sparingly, could force senators to once again act collegially and to work out agreements for votes on legislative issues with a simple majority and not force everything to meet the sixty-vote threshold. "Collegiality is the key," says Reid.

Eliminating the filibuster for judicial nominations virtually killed bipartisan agreements on seating judges on the federal bench. Why is that bad? For one, it means that a nominee has most of his or her support from partisans, either left or right. For two, it enables the majority party to install political partisans in charge of the judicial branch of government, thereby diminishing its independence.

To see how this plays out just look at Senate majority leader Mitch McConnell's underhanded blocking of Merrick Garland for the Supreme Court, which drew sharp criticisms, including from Susan Collins, when he refused to hold a hearing or vote contending the voters should help decide the next justice when they voted nine months after the death of Justice Antonin Scalia. McConnell followed that by invoking the nuclear option to get two political partisans, Neil Gorsuch and Brett Kavanaugh, on the high court with just simple majority votes. Neither would have made it, in my view, if the sixty-vote rule remained in place. Restoring the filibuster for all judicial nominees should be Job One.

In the cases of Gorsuch and Kavanaugh one can look to an often-used baseball metaphor for how they indicated they would rule on the high court. When John Roberts's nomination to the Supreme Court was before the Senate, he said in his confirmation that the responsibility of a judge, like that of an umpire, is just to call balls and strikes. Acting in this manner, he suggested, would limit judicial activism. The problem is that Gorsuch and Kavanaugh want to stretch and expand the strike zone to accommodate less-than-impartial rulings and opinions. Redefining the strike zone allows the umpire to let a conservative ideological curveball to be called a strike, not a ball.

Gorsuch and Kavanaugh are certainly not the first to seem to expand the strike zone. When Chief Justice Earl Warren led the court he expanded the strike zone to push through a series of liberal decisions that marked a period of judicial activism. As president, Franklin D. Roosevelt tried to pack the high court with liberal justices, ostensibly who would issue rulings favorable to his New Deal legislation. By proposing to add up to six justices for every justice over seventy-plus years and serving more than ten years on the court, Roosevelt sought to enlarge the strike zone so that just about any pitch, even beanballs, would be called a strike.

This redefining of the strike zone was a bad idea in Roosevelt's time, in the Warren Court era and remains so now, with Gorsuch and Kavanaugh as umpires. Restoring the filibuster for judicial nominees would increase their bipartisan backing and tendency to just call balls and strikes within a fixed, narrow strike zone.

In the case of the U.S. Supreme court, does it not make more sense for the country for justices to have been approved on a bipartisan basis and not on party line votes? Restoring the filibuster would force future presidents to send qualified, mainstream nominees to the Senate, not just partisan ones.

Along with that, senators should not give into calls from right and left advocacy groups to end the filibuster entirely in the Senate. It should remain for use to advance legislative action. The filibuster rule is the beating heart of the U.S. Senate. Without it, the Senate becomes a smaller version of the fractious, always partisan House. Without the filibuster, senators could jam through any partisan bill with a simple majority.

Please remember this: Whatever is accomplished through a simple majority can be taken away through a simple majority. Bipartisanship dies. Vindictiveness rules, as we've seen since 2016. Ending the filibuster is one of the biggest contributors to the Senate's dysfunction and the fuel that drives the partisan divide that is crippling its work.

Second, senators should start working *with* colleagues across the political aisle and stop working against them. By that, I first mean that senators should stop campaigning against their fellow colleagues. When Bill Frist of Tennessee was the Senate Republican leader in the mid-2000s, he traveled to South Dakota to campaign for the candidate running against Tom Daschle, the Senate Democratic leader, who in Washington stood just a few feet apart from Frist at the leaders' lecterns. Frist's partisan move undermined the trust he and Daschle needed to work together to set the Senate's schedule and handle critical legislation. Frist was hardly alone.

Nowadays, campaigning against fellow senators is done all too often. Campaigning to unseat a colleague destroys trust. It throws ice water on bipartisanship. I'd note that when you are standing on the floor of the Senate, the room is not very big. Colleagues across the aisle are just a couple dozen feet away. It's an intimate place where friendships can flourish but so, too, can distrust. There's no rule change required for this fix; senators should just stop running against their colleagues. And maybe let them know. They'd probably appreciate it.

Next, senators should sometimes campaign *for* colleagues in the other party. When he retired from the Senate in 2010, Indiana senator Evan Bayh wrote an op-ed in the *New York Times* about how the Senate used to be. He recalled that after his father, Birch Bayh, also a Democrat, announced he was running for reelection in 1968, the Senate's Republican leader, Everett Dirksen of Illinois, approached him on the Senate floor. Dirksen came up to Birch Bayh, put his arm around his shoulder and asked how he could help. "That is unimaginable today," Evan Bayh wrote in 2010. Still true today, maybe more so.

In a similar vein, senators also should ignore pressure they might feel to avoid working with colleagues across the aisle. In 2006, when Republicans held the majority, I served on the Senate Agriculture Committee. That year the committee was working on the most important piece of legislation for farm country, the Farm Bill. Congress approves a Farm Bill about once every five years. The committee's chairman was Republican senator Saxby Chambliss of Georgia. Chambliss and I had taken a bipartisan congressional trip together overseas. We worked well on the Ag Committee and were in my mind friends and allies.

I asked him to hold a field hearing in Nebraska, whose economy was driven by agriculture. Under Senate rules, he'd have to set up and chair the hearing. He agreed to do so. One day, he told me some GOP leaders were urging him not to do it because it could help my reelection campaign. He ignored them.

And so, during the August congressional recess, Chambliss, my Nebraska colleague GOP senator Chuck Hagel, and I flew out to Nebraska and conducted a field hearing in Grand Island. I viewed it as legislatively valuable—we heard directly from farmers, ranchers, farm groups, and local citizens. Chambliss also held field hearings in Georgia, Missouri, Pennsylvania, Iowa and Oregon, represented by both Republican and Democrat senators. Buck party leaders when they try to quash bipartisan collaboration.

Third, real bipartisanship needs to return to the Senate. Bipartisanship not only improves the product by leavening partisan elements, it forces senators to work with colleagues from other parts of the country and act in the best interests of the entire nation. Senators should get back to doing the hard work of building cross-party alliances, of listening to one another, of respecting each other's contributions and opinions, and of incorporating ideas from both parties in any important legislation.

In recent years, Lamar Alexander, a Tennessee Republican, and Patty Murray, a Washington state Democrat, teamed up to advance bipartisan legislation addressing the opioid epidemic, mental health care, and medical innovation. They forged compromises to advance progress. Susan Collins has teamed up with Joe Manchin, the West Virginia Democrat, in what they call the Commonsense Caucus and have worked together and played a key role in ending two government shutdowns.

So, while there are some senators who continue to try to work across the aisle, it's usually in small groups, not large ones that wield real power.

Another idea would be for senators to form a gang or two, go behind closed doors, limit staff, and talk candidly about a tough issue. Keep the leaders informed, though, because they can be needed allies if you come up with a bipartisan agreement.

For the Senate to truly breathe with vitality again it needs bipartisanship like we all need oxygen. "Anything I did that I feel really good about," says Joe Lieberman, "was done on a bipartisan basis." That's true for me as well, 100 percent.

Maybe someone should reinvigorate the Centrist Coalition and pull in senators interested in getting something done. It wouldn't have to start with a big group. Breaux remembers that, when the Senate was split 50–50 in the early 2000s, he teamed up with Lieberman to form what they called the "Kosher Cajun Caucus."

"We had the smallest, most powerful caucus in the Senate," Breaux fondly remembers. They even put out a Kosher Cajun cookbook. It told people how to make blackened lox.

One way to foster bipartisanship is for senators to travel together again on congressional delegation trips, or CODELS. In the Senate and serving on Armed Services, I joined or led about a dozen of these official congressional trips, all bipartisan, to places in our national interests, Iraq (four times), Afghanistan, Pakistan, Kuwait, China, Korea, Morocco, Turkey, and Russia. Each yielded invaluable insight and information we couldn't get sitting behind a dais in Washington. The trips also are fertile ground for developing friendships.

For example, I worked closely with Trent Lott, the Mississippi Republican, on Armed Services Committee matters. One was our mutual effort to engage our legislative counterparts in the Russian legislature in a post–Cold War rapprochement we hoped could develop ties, instead of suspicions, between our countries.

We hosted Russian lawmakers in Washington and they hosted us in Russia. Congressional trips, often labeled fact-finding trips, can at times unearth earthshaking facts. That's what happened in one memorable congressional trip to Russia and Turkey that Lott and I took in 2007 joined by Republican Judd Gregg of New Hampshire and Democrat Evan Bayh of Indiana.

One afternoon, Lott and I got into a taxi to take a tour of Gazprom, the Russian multinational energy corporation and the largest public natural gas company in the world. On the tour, we were shown a map of Gazprom's vast pipeline network across the continent. We saw a line depicting a major pipeline supplying gas to Europe, which we knew quite a bit about. But there on the wall was something we didn't know—a dotted line representing a planned gas pipeline across the Atlantic Ocean into Canada . . . and down into the United States. It was an omigod moment.

We raised eyebrows but didn't say a word about it the rest of the tour or on the taxi ride back to our hotel, figuring we were being watched. But after we got out and stood on a street corner we shared our amazement about the pipeline project. If that dotted line became solid it could make the U.S. beholden to Russia. That was shocking.

As soon as we got back home to the United States, Lott and I contacted the State Department to fill officials there in on what we'd seen, and we think we shared Russian plans of which it was unaware. These official congressional trips are all about gathering firsthand intel, cementing alliances, and developing friendships and partnerships. Senators should keep taking them—with senators across the aisle. At times, and not infrequently, they can be revelatory.

Fourth, this might be a contrary position, but senators should spend more time in Washington. Even an additional day a week would seed the ground for friendships to develop, for partnerships to emerge, for cross-party collaboration to push legislation forward. "If you have dinner with someone on Saturday night, you can't stab them in the back on Monday," says Breaux.

Trent Lott told me that his Democratic counterpart Tom Daschle had a two-word explanation for Washington's biggest problem: "The airplane." Lott agrees and says, "Back when we served in the Senate, we lived in Washington, our kids went to school there, we talked to each other. Now senators come in Monday or Tuesday and only want to know what time they can catch a flight back home on Thursday." That leaves three days at most to conduct legislative business—to hold hearings, to debate bills in committee and on the floor, and to vote.

The Senate could remain in session at least one day more each week, two would be best. The leaders could make this happen by a simple schedule adjustment. Why not a five-day workweek? Why not a forty-hour workweek, where business is done during the light of day and votes don't happen in the dead of night. No evening sessions. No overnight drama where cots and pizza are trucked in. Can't get it done by 6:00 p.m.? See you tomorrow at 9:00.

This could give senators a regular schedule to go home, cool off, maybe have dinner with someone from the other party and work together all day, just like Americans not elected to the Senate do. Most working Americans can handle it, why not senators? It would foster relationships made impossible if everyone's always smelling jet fumes.

"You can't minimize the importance of personal relationships," former senator Joe Lieberman recently said. "The Senate is, ultimately, behind the headlines and squabbling and everything else, a hundred people going to work at the same place every day. And your ability to gain the trust and even affection of your colleagues is really critically important into how successful you will be to advancing legislation that matters to you. In the Senate it's particularly true because you are in the constant process of proposing, discussing, arguing, debating, and then hopefully negotiating a compromise to get something done."

One way to foster friendships is to have a little fun with each other. But your idea of funny may not be someone else's. You have to read your colleagues well. That means you have to know them, too. One example from my experience might help senators today. You may remember early in the book that I pulled a practical joke in 2001 on Hillary Clinton by causing her momentary panic when I asked her what scripture she planned to read right before her swearing in ceremony. Well, I did it to Claire McCaskill, too, at her swearing-in ceremony in 2007. Except the Missouri senator looked for revenge.

Over a year later, I walked off the Senate floor one day to take a call in the senator's lobby from one of my adult children. They informed me they had just bought an expensive boat. Living in a landlocked state. A boat I thought I might end up having to help pay for. As I hung up, I saw McCaskill and Sen. Amy Klobuchar sitting on a sofa, chatting. I was distracted. McCaskill looked up and asked if I'd heard the news that the Obama administration had named one of my least favorite people to a plum job. I immediately called my chief of staff to demand to know what he knew about this. He just said, "Senator, do you know what day it is?" It was . . . the first of April, April Fool's Day. "Gotcha!" McCaskill said. I'd been had. I was delighted, but also competitive

A few months later, I got her back. With her staff's full permission, I gained access to her office. I hung a red Nebraska banner with a big white "N" on the wall next to the entrance so she couldn't miss it, rearranged her furniture, and taped color photos of me and my hunting exploits over nearly every picture and placard in her inner office. It looked good to me. On one of the photos I wrote "Gotcha!"

Then, months later in the fall of 2009, ahead of the Missouri-Nebraska football game (and they were great rivals then), McCaskill struck back. With my staff's equally full complicity, she snuck into my inner office and taped photos with the Missouri Tiger black-and-gold logo on every darn picture, placard, and surface. It took weeks for me to find them all. We never declared a truce, I always was ready to continue the game, and she knew it. Her attitude was "bring it on." So, I'd suggest senators look for ways to have a little fun, not at the expense of a colleague, but with their participation.

Fifth, the Senate should set up a regular all-senator lunch. They used to have them years ago. Today, senators meet weekly for caucus party lunches, Republicans in one room in the Capitol, Democrats in another. These luncheons serve their purpose. I remember hearing many a candid comment, attending many a revealing political strategy session, and hearing many an interesting speaker from our side of the political spectrum at our lunches. They fostered friendship, as I recount early in this book about Ted Kennedy and I sharing weight-loss drinks at the lunches. I often chattered with Barbara Boxer so much that Harry Reid treated us like bad school kids and said if we didn't quiet down he'd separate us—to everyone's amusement.

But mostly these separate lunches foster division: Democrats plot ways to beat Republicans, Republicans plot ways to beat Democrats. They do this instead of talking to each other, which is made all the more difficult because the extremes of both parties won't let them. If Republican and Democrat senators gathered for all-Senate lunches bipartisanship could gain a foothold. The lunches could feature outside speakers with expertise to educate senators on tough issues in hourlong tutorials. Everyone would have, at least from these lunches, one set of facts. No alternative facts.

Sixth, senators should regain courage. The opposite is true, don't be so cowardly. There aren't many profiles in courage in today's Senate. Senators must again show some spine like George

W. Norris, the Nebraska legend, did when he essentially took over the Senate to fight what he thought was morally right. As noted before, he filibustered President Woodrow Wilson's request for approval to arm American merchant ships because he believed engaging in a war would lead to death and destruction and benefit only money men and stockbrokers. He was labeled a traitor and denounced all over the country.

But when Norris went home and gave his "I have come to tell you the truth" speech the public roared its approval. Norris was known to be a man of integrity, honesty, and courage. Today's senators, I'm sorry to say, look fearful at the idea of standing up to the left-and-right-leaning advocacy groups always hammering them. Getting primaried looks like a death sentence to too many.

Senators also should have ignored the irrational and vindictive missives from the Tweeter in Chief. Except when he singled one of them out for punishment, in which case, the offending senator should have tweeted back, "Thanks, POTUS, for validating my point and the views of my constituents." Don't let a bully in the pulpit control your destiny down in the pews of democracy. There are worse things than being chased from public office by a narcissistic, vindictive liar. As Speaker Nancy Pelosi said, impeachment is forever. I would add this: Trumpism is not. So, members of the Senate, be courageous!

Seventh, senators should choose their Senate leader wisely, not based on their political power but on trustworthiness, and willingness to try to work across the aisle. Then, senators should respect the chain of command. When you choose a leader wisely, it's easier to follow their advice for legislative action.

In earlier times Republican Bob Dole of Kansas and Democrat Daniel Inouye of Hawaii, though both in party leadership on opposite sides of the aisle, were like brothers. Both had served and been seriously wounded in World War II. They never let party interrupt their friendship.

Trent Lott and Tom Daschle were political adversaries on the floor who never let the competition get personal. Both had respect of their caucus as well. Lott recalled that one year when he was leader his leadership team decided and announced publicly what the topline number would be for Senate's federal budget measure. His phone soon rang. It was the feisty Appropriations Committee Chair Republican Ted Stevens of Alaska. Stevens shouted, "We can't live with that number, we'll have to cut defense, what are you doing?!" Lott got heated up and the two argued until they both had enough and hung up.

Next thing Lott knew, he heard Stevens barreling into his office, past his office receptionist, past his key administrative aide, right up to Lott's desk—full of fury. Lott stood up and thought incredulously, "I'm going to have to fight this little son-of-a-gun." Stevens then barked, "I don't agree with it. It's not enough. But you've made a decision. I'll make it work."

He spun around and sped back out of the office. Lott was greatly relieved. "He understood chain of command and followership," Lott said. "That's part of the problem now. You've got the far-right nut cases and you've got the far-left nut cases. A leader is only as good as his or her followers."

Remember 2010, when Mitch McConnell said the most important thing he wanted to achieve "is for President Obama to be a one-term president." When McConnell came under fire for pursuing a political strategy of conflict with the White House, his spokesman dug in his heels. "Ending the Obama administration's liberal agenda as soon as possible is Senator McConnell's top political priority," the aide said. Notice he didn't say that was the top priority of the Republican conference he led, nor did he say he would act in the best interests of all Americans—right, left, and center. This was his personal priority, a political ploy to get rid of a president in another political party.

How could the Obama White House, or how could any White House, work with a leader who has drawn such a sharp, political line in the sand? McConnell is the marquee reason I say that both parties should choose Senate leaders who put country ahead of politics, who are respected across the aisle and who seek to work together.

These days, McConnell and Democratic leader Chuck Schumer seem to rarely talk to each other. "Tom Daschle and Trent Lott spoke more in one day, or certainly more in one week, than Chuck Schumer and Mitch McConnell probably speak in six months," Breaux said in 2020. Breaux suggested leaders, including the whole leadership team on both sides, set a regular time to get together, maybe for a bi-monthly breakfast, lunch or an after-hours cocktail. They should get to know one another personally. They should discuss the Senate's agenda for the upcoming week or two. They need to develop relationships and trust, Breaux said.

Eighth, presidents need to open lines of regular communication with senators. Back in the day, Ronald Reagan met with groups of senators in both parties weekly. George H. W. Bush and Bill Clinton worked the phone lines to Capitol Hill to try to persuade senators not push them. Breaux recalls playing tennis frequently with the elder Bush. And Clinton, even though he was impeached by the House and narrowly not convicted by the Senate, came right back to the Hill seeking people to work with on legislation.

"He never held grudges," Breaux said of Clinton. "You could impeach him on Friday and on Monday he'd be back to you trying to work a deal." That paid off with bipartisan legislation on welfare reform and balancing the budget.

George W. Bush called up to the Hill often and invited senators, like me, to the White House for social gatherings. He tried to charm and befriend lawmakers in both houses of Congress. Barack Obama was less attentive to this relationship building practice, but it wasn't his fault. The Republicans resented his election and turned on him before he could try to establish connections.

Donald Trump didn't seem to have many friends on Capitol Hill. He reached out to lawmakers, inviting them to his Florida home at Mar-a-Lago or to the White House—but Republicans only. That's hyper-partisanship. Trump still has people who fear him, or fear the mob he can incite to attack a wayward senator or House member.

Breaux says back in his day it was negotiation, but it wasn't negotiation by threats. "Nowadays," he said, "it's negotiation with threats, that they'll get someone to run against you and they'll support that person if you don't agree with them. That just gets people's dander up where they say, 'I'm not going to be with you if that's how you're going to act.' You can't negotiate by threatening someone."

Ninth, address the outsized influence of money. The role of money in politics looms too large and gives big donors access to senators regular citizens do not have, and cannot get. Raising money takes up a lot of a senator's time. People give money to candidates to pull them to the left or right. Wealthy donors, big companies, and ideological groups throw money at senators to essentially buy access and influence that is closed to regular people. I'm not sure what the answer is, perhaps the Senate should convene bipartisan hearings on reducing the role big money has on politics and advance bipartisan legislation that will return a measure of independence to members of the Senate.

Tenth, and this may be the most important of all. Trent Lott makes my point when he speaks to groups of regular people. "It's your fault," he says. "You elect these people. What do you expect? What do you expect when you elect an AOC (Alexandria Ocasio-Cortez) or a Rand Paul. You get weird people doing weird things." Lott says we'd be better off to elect people willing to work together, and also those who bring something to the table in the way of life experience or expertise.

"At the end, in our democracy it's really up the people, to the voters," said Lieberman. "To get the kind of government they want, which is bipartisan, centrist and to problem solve the problems, they have to choose more wisely."

But today, there are no more Blue Dog Democrats. There are hardly any moderate Republicans. The middle is a lot smaller, Breaux says, and the ends much stronger. But people like Breaux have hope for the future because if the middle is smaller in the Senate, it's larger in the electorate. More voters are registering as Independents. They can play a key role in bringing common sense and consensus back to the Senate.

My message to readers is this: When you go to the polls vote for candidates who say—and mean it—that they want to go to Washington to work across party divisions, to work across extremes within their own party, to bring people together and get things done. Send more like Olympia Snowe, Susan Collins, Jeff Flake, Lamar Alexander, Claire McCaskill, Heidi Heitkamp, Bob Corker, Chris Coons, Joe Manchin, and Kent Conrad. These are centrist-minded lawmakers. People must be willing to elect centrist-minded candidates and send them to the Senate. Centrism can be sexy again. Bipartisanship can be restored. And, then, progress will be made.

If voters choose candidates who are committed to bipartisan deal-making and to finding the center in arguments, the Senate can get back to functioning well for the American people. Legislation that is durable, that doesn't give advantages to one party or the other, that bridges the red/blue divide in the nation, will be the outcome of electing more centrists to the Senate.

As a member of the "No Labels" coalition, Susan Collins said in 2020 that she's calling on citizens to rise up and demand that members of Congress work together. "There needs to be pressure and support for those of us who are in the middle and like to take a pragmatic approach," she said. Collins believes the vast majority of people in the country are centrists, they're just energized and vocal as the far left and right. "We need more fanatical moderates," Collins said with a laugh.

Indeed, research by the University of Virginia shows that the middle has increased; in October 2000 the country had 87.8 million registered voters, among them 44 percent were Democrats, 33 percent Republicans, and 22 percent Independents. By October 2018, with 110.9 million registered voters, Democrats declined to 40 percent, Republicans dropped to 29 percent—but Independents had increased to 28 percent. The middle is larger, stronger.

There also needs to be a counterweight to the groups on the far left and far right that have endless amounts of money and are "savage," in their efforts to push lawmakers to adopt their agenda. What does that mean? In the month of April 2020, Collins said far left groups ran 1,753 negative ads across the media in Maine blasting her. In April she was named the most bipartisan senator, for the seventh year in a row, by the bipartisan Lugar Center.

"That's just really hard to withstand," she said. "I don't have the resources to respond to that. At the same time, I'm being named the most bipartisan member of the Senate. The irony of that! But that doesn't stop Chuck Schumer from making me one of his top Senate targets. The fact that I work across the aisle more than any other senator and yet I'm one of his top four Senate targets."

Sadly, she said, that taking advantage of the political opportunity has become more important than trying to get things done for the American people, "and I think that's truly tragic."

I couldn't agree with her more. Indeed, each of us has a duty to take steps to restore the Senate. Each of us has too much to lose if we let this further slide. Everyone living from Idaho to Iowa, from Florida to Washington, from Arizona to Maine, and everywhere in between will lose if partisanship continues to reign.

We, all of you reading this, must vote for people who will cross the political aisle to get things done—to prepare for the next pandemic, to create jobs of the future, to better educate children, to make us more secure, whatever keeps people up at night. Until fundamental changes are made in the way the Senate and senators function, in who gets elected to the Senate, in restoring the role of bipartisanship, the United States Senate will not again be the world's greatest deliberative body. A beacon of democracy. And one of the world's greatest forces for good. That's a shame. We can't let that be the Senate's future. Join me, join others. Let's save the Senate.

Epilogue

AT THE END, HE STOOD ALONE, except for family and a decreasing inner circle of staff and supporters. This is how it usually ends for the autocrat. Alone in a compound or a bunker protected by a fence or a moat—no matter the age in history.

It all started as a promise for a businessman, not another politician, who would "Make America Great Again." A man who rode reality TV shows and beauty pageants into becoming a nationally known celebrity. This pop culture status and an opponent with political baggage led him to the White House. As he said to Black Americans, exhorting them to vote for him, "What the Hell do you have to lose?"

I suppose others were also answering that challenge in their own way. MAGA became a rallying call for a movement away from the current reality to an alternative reality where norms and laws could be ignored and broken with impunity, where people could completely reject whatever they considered elitist or just "being politically and socially correct." It became an "anything goes" anti-culture which had great appeal to those who felt disaffected.

But by Thursday night after the November 3 elections, it looked like it was ending for the would-be authoritarian. Or was it? A majority of U.S. voters—a record 81,283,485 Americans gave Democratic presidential candidate Joe Biden a popular vote lead of more than seven million—and an initial 270 electoral votes, and rising, and were saying to Donald J. Trump, "Enough." (Biden ended up with 306 electoral votes to Trump's 232.) The majority had seen and felt enough of a man and his followers who disdained every law or norm that stood in the way of MAGA. The would-be autocrat stood almost alone claiming election fraud and calling for the courts to overturn those local election results that said no to another four-year term. Even his niece, Mary Trump said this was the first time in her uncle's life that there was no one to turn to for a bailout. A loan forgiveness. No one to take his debt. No one to assume responsibility for his failure. For the first time in his life Donald J. Trump was facing failure. Alone.

He stood there in the White House Press Room at the podium reading a prepared diatribe about a rigged and fraudulent election. He lacked the usual bravado of his rally tirades. Only occasionally looking up, he read the text slowly with little emotion, finishing with an abrupt exit.

To some, he looked like it was slowly sinking in that the end was near. On Friday three days after the elections, some of his advisors were suggesting that. His daughter and son-in-law and others were trying to prepare him for how his presidency was ending. But Rudy Giuliani and other enablers of Trump's delusional grasp on reality were litigating and fanning the flames of chaos and confusion. Soon there were promises of another campaign in 2024, possibly a rematch like prize-fighters. Instead of extinguishing, they were adding fuel to his alternative reality that he would emerge at the end of this—the winner. Losing was not an option, he was and still would be the president. He would not fail. He couldn't. After all, he was Donald J. Trump!

In this alternative reality, others now joined in to sow discord and cast doubts on the possibility of an orderly baton-pass to now President-Elect Biden. Secretary of State Mike Pompeo said that it would be a smooth transition—to a second term. Missouri senator Roy Blunt questioned whether Trump had actually lost the election. Senate Republican leader Mitch McConnell said Trump was "100 percent within his rights to look into allegations of irregularities and weigh his legal options." To be sure, the Republican Party wasn't completely walking in lockstep with Trump as it had over the previous four years. A small group of senators, representatives, and governors stated the obvious, that Trump had lost and it was time to prepare for an orderly transition, so our adversaries wouldn't be able to threaten the security of the American people.

Denial and fantasizing fuel the existence and expansion of an alternative reality. As it grows, it adds other believers. They begin to believe their own misconceptions. Incoherence which has no basis in reality begins to make sense. We won.

By Tuesday following the election, the alternative reality was fully birthed, much like the birther movement Trump helped fan into life years before, questioning former president Barack Obama's legitimacy. Again, many who should have known better, didn't. They watched *Fox News* and listened to Rush Limbaugh broadcast falsehoods, and believed. In gear, they raced forward, most saying, even if not fully believing, he won. Those who might ask how tyranny works could see it in full gallop. What happened to those who knew better? Why had they stopped speaking out publicly in favor of a transition? Fear. What if Trump succeeds? What if the alternative reality becomes the ultimate reality? Best not to chance it. Keep quiet. Fall in line. This is how it was for Hitler, Mussolini, Gaddafi, Saddam. Their backers hung in to the end.

But wait, this is America and we don't do anything like that. We have elections. The people speak and the victors benefit from a peaceful transfer of power. Until 2020, we've had every expectation we would get that. Now, in this most unusual year amid a pandemic that took the lives of nearly a half million people in twelve months and was continuing, we had every expectation we would not.

Usually, the outgoing president acts to help the incoming president be successful. Trump took the opposite tack. He wanted Biden to not hit the ground running, but on his knees and nose. Usually, the outgoing president leaves a supportive letter in the president's desk in the Oval Office, like the one George H. W. Bush left for Bill Clinton, where he wrote, "Your success is now the country's success. I am rooting hard for you." Usually, outgoing presidents depart in a dignified way and don't armchair quarterback their successor's efforts to lead the country. Although Trump left a letter for his successor (contents not disclosed), he refused to call Biden. Did not attend the inauguration on January 20. No welcome or goodbyes. Just Air Force One to Florida.

To no one's surprise, Trump refused to concede, citing all sorts of conspiracies and voter fraud, plus his right to litigate in various state and federal courts including the United States Supreme Court. Various Republicans supported his conspiracy theories about uncounted and fraudulent ballots to the point that state canvassing boards consisting of both Republicans and Democrats found it necessary to appear on the news shows defending the thousands of American volunteers and staff contending that this was the most accurate American election in history.

It didn't matter to Trump and his legal team. They continued to file and lose frivolous lawsuits all over the country. At the risk of over-flogging Giuliani, the former "America's mayor" during 9/11, it is noteworthy to observe a major change in how the former mayor and the president's personal attorney has conducted himself and his dealings during Trump's presidency. The same person? Doesn't seem so to me. More like a hired gun shooting blanks. At a press event outside Four Seasons Total Landscaping in Florida, Giuliani, with his black hair dye melting and streaming down his sweating cheeks, pausing only to wipe the sweat from his head and brow with his hanky, ranted all sorts of baseless legal theories absent evidence or proof. With eyes bulging, and his arms waving in the air, he even cited some authoritative point from the movie *My Cousin Vinnie*. Even so, the media reported charitably only that this or that court had just thrown out one of their cases because of lack of proof. To an attorney, these lawsuits seemed not only baseless but vexatious litigation. Even Attorney General Barr informed the AP that there was no evidence of widespread fraud that would change the outcome of the presidential election. He even suggested he might leave his post early before the end of the term. He did.

The media had a heyday speculating on all sorts of gossip. Would Trump attend the inauguration? Would he really start his own news network? Wasn't Fox complicit enough? Does he plan to seek another term? If so, when will he file? And early enough to freeze out the field? Even suggesting he's considering running may be enough to put a major freeze on others such as Republican senators Ben Sasse, Tom Cotton, and Marco Rubio. At the least, they have to have a "wait and see" approach. Reelected in 2020, Nebraska's Sasse said in a November 29, 2020, story in the *Omaha World-Herald* that Trump would get the Republican nomination should he decide to seek a second term. These and countless other tidbits not only led the news while President-Elect Biden was low-key and hard at work with his agenda and populating his administration.

There were reports that Giuliani was discussing with Trump the possibility of a prearranged self-pardon. Apparently, Richard Nixon considered but rejected a self-pardon. However, he had the good fortune to be followed by his personally appointed vice president, Gerald Ford, who granted Nixon the pardon that he sought. It was such an unpopular decision that it cost Ford the presidential election to Jimmy Carter. But Trump was not followed by anyone disposed to grant him a pardon. Still, he did not self-pardon.

Given the pardons of Michael Flynn and Roger Stone, it was reasonable to expect that Trump would grant pardons to any number of his family, friends, and supporters. But he didn't.

What isn't clear is whether being holed up in the White House and largely tweeterless was somehow Trump's plan to stay in the news. What is clear is that somehow he continued to compete with Biden for the news even when Biden was busy at work. What also seems clear is that Trump has no plan to disband his seventy-four-million army of Trump voters and abandon his base. We should not have wasted time asking whether Trump would leave the White House voluntarily or forcibly; that is pure theater. He was always likely to leave the White House like a disgruntled debtor in foreclosure. The question should have been: What will he be doing (up to) during the next four years? And beyond?

I am about to ignore my father's advice about going out on that limb and give you my predictions for what lies ahead at least during those four years.

First, expect that Trump will not fade away like "W" or be a traditional ex-president. Retired. Writing a book. Reading books. Building houses with Habitat for Humanity. Fishing. This just isn't in his DNA. He will continue to seek news coverage just as any addict seeks the next fix. He will not sit on the sidelines and watch the Biden administration reverse Trump positions like he did with Obama's. He just can't.

In spite of his impeachment by the House of Representatives, Trump had already begun a campaign for the second term he was denied due to "voter fraud." Whether it will be sustainable over the next four years is not certain. Whether he will work every day to undermine the president and his administration is almost certain. The media will assist. They will report every day on Trump. Whereabouts and comments. Just as they have these past four years. They too have developed a need for that fix. Will the public tire of it? Not his base. Can he sustain the interest and support of his followers? Probably not all. But maybe just enough to keep the cacophony going. Fundraising. Occasional special event rallies. Biden and his supporters will tire of it before it begins and will have difficulty ignoring it. Trump will be that proverbial thorn in the side and a pain in the ass. A royal one. This was all speculation until January 6, 2021.

Senate minority leader Chuck Schumer said that the January 6, 2021, attack on the Capitol would be another day to live in infamy alongside the attack on Pearl Harbor on December 7, 1941. You can add 9/11. This latest attack, unlike the first two, was by domestic terrorists, enemies of our government.

We faced enormous questions as we worked our way through this unbelievable attack on the symbol of our American democracy.

Who was this angry terroristic mob which breached the security lines to illegally enter our seat of government by breaking windows and knocking down doors? Once in, they trashed and vandalized offices, occupied the Speaker's office, posing for pictures like a member of an official Capitol tour.

They threatened by name the Speaker, sought out her location and also made efforts to locate Vice President Pence, who had been presiding over the electoral college votes. Some of the invaders were carrying zip ties, possibly to find and secure Speaker Pelosi and Vice President Pence. And any other member of Congress to disrupt the electoral vote counting and constitutional acknowledgement of President Biden and Vice President Harris.

What was their intent? To reverse the outcome of the election by disrupting the electoral proceedings. Holding or harming the vice president and/or the Speaker would have worked to do just that, raising constitutional issues regarding the validity of the election. To the Trump crowd this would result in validating a Trump victory by invalidating the electoral process.

Who sent them to demonstrate at the Capitol? There is clear video taken of Trump, his sons Eric and Don Jr., and Rudy Giuliani at a rally near the Capitol shortly before the insurrection. They urged the crowd to go to the Capitol. Trump told them he would be there with them. Mitch McConnell later accused Trump of "provoking" the crowd. But at the conclusion of the rally Trump led his entourage to the safety of an official autocade away from the Capitol. Reports are that he watched the riot on TV, perplexed that his staff didn't share his enthusiasm.

Like so many of his Republican colleagues in the Senate and cabinet, Vice President Pence was finally distancing himself from Trump. To his credit Pence refused Trump's urging to upend the electoral proceedings and instead carried out his constitutional duties. As a result, he found himself being shunned by the president who tweeted that "Mike Pence didn't have the courage to do what should have been done."

Then, later, as the rioters surged into the Capitol Pence was whisked to a secret location. The mob ran wild in the halls and offices. In the end, six people died. More than fifty law enforcement officials were injured. One rioter stole the Speaker's official podium and put it on eBay.

In apparently trying to do the right and politically safe thing, Pence had found his way into a political corner by not engaging the cabinet in a Twenty-Fifth Amendment vote to remove the president? Had he pushed the cabinet to remove Trump, his political future with the Trump base would have been over. Likewise, by not having been firm in his refusal, he lost them anyway. In politics there is no safe corner.

Pence already faced competition for the Trump supporters, rioters and all. Sens. Ted Cruz and Josh Hawley have carefully courted them before and during the electoral proceedings by voting to object. Pence courageously carried out his constitutional duties. Will there be credit for him in 2024? This conundrum gives rise to the old adage from your parents "be careful who you choose for your friends." Or in Pence's case, who "chooses you."

We are and will continue to be troubled by the events leading up to and the attack on our nation's capitol. The investigations will need to shine a bright light on what was obviously a colossal failure of both Intelligence and Security. A Capitol police force of eighteen hundred officers, roughly the equivalent of the police forces of Baltimore or San Francisco, was surely sufficient with assistance from the District Police and National Guard to repel the rioters.

Like the bombing of the Murrah Building in Oklahoma City in 1995, it is hoped that all investigations will be made public. But what we know up front is that this insurrection was seditious and cannot be justified any more than our Civil War some 160 years ago. For justice to prevail all attackers of our democracy must and will be prosecuted. It is not arguable that there were good people on the rioters side. They were illegally violating the constitution and the laws of our land.

On January 13, Speaker Pelosi led the House to impeach Trump for "inciting violence against the government of the United States" in his drive to overturn the election results and called for him to be removed and barred from ever holding public office again. In a House vote of 232–197, with ten Republicans voting for impeachment, Donald Trump became the only president ever impeached twice. Both times the Senate declined to convict, but in 2021 ten Republicans joined the fifty Democrats supporting conviction, the most bipartisan vote ever—just seven votes short of the tally needed to keep Trump from seeking the presidency again.

There was a bright spot for the Democrats during the deadly sacking of the Capitol. Democrat Jon Ossoff won the second Senate runoff contest in Georgia, meaning that, along with fellow Democrat Rev. Raphael Warnock's victory, the power would shift in the U.S. Senate to a 50–50 split. This handed control of the Senate to Democrats, with Vice President Harris on hand to cast tie breaking votes. Dozens of Biden's key nominees faced a much easier path to confirmation and getting to do the work of helping him carry out his agenda; Democrats might be able to set the agenda of what legislation receives floor debate and votes. But in other ways, how the Senate functions is yet to be determined. But real change must come from within.

The best Senate I served in was in 2001 when it was evenly divided 50–50 and even when Jim Jeffords became an Independent and the count went to 51–49. We had a president like Biden in George W. Bush who realized he had to work with Democrats to get things done. My hope is that the center—and even a reconstituted centrist coalition—will reemerge in the Senate and Biden will have to make a case for legislation that draws the Democrats, Independents, and enlightened Republicans.

The wider the margin of party control, the less likely either side will be interested in making deals for the good of the country as a whole. Unless the Senate changes from within, unless political partisan behavior changes, we'll just have more of the same gridlock, deadlock and dysfunction. It'll be a case of what I've learned from my lieutenant governor, Kim Robak, about the value of considering new ideas: if you always do what you've always done, you'll always get what you've always gotten.

Something's got to change, someone's got to make that happen, and I don't think we should hang our hopes on just one person shaking the Senate back to its senses. The Senate needs an atmospheric change. One regenerated, invigorated limb won't do the trick; the whole body needs a transformation. Along with the

Senate changing from within, both political parties need to change from without and stop being knee-jerk pugilistic and start working to advance the fortunes of the entire country.

On the GOP side, I defy anyone to tell me what the Republican Party currently stands for other than Trumpism. My plea to Republican senators is this: Shake off this now former president—his incendiary policies and rhetoric, the cult-like hold he's had on too many Republican voters—and be born again. Be reborn as Republicans. Return to your roots and once again fight for what has been the Republican brand for decades. Fortunately, several Republicans have sounded that call as well, including Jeff Flake, who represented Arizona in the House and Senate from 2001 to 2019. On NPR in January right after the riots at the Capitol, Flake told host Michel Martin: "If this event—if there is ever a silver lining—it's tough to see with such a horrible event—but I think that it will cause the Republican Party to move away from Trumpism more quickly. It has to happen at some point." There's no "there" there with Trumpism.

He added that he was cautiously optimistic that would happen. "I remain a Republican and will because I believe that . . . the principles that have animated the party for generations—limited government, economic freedom, individual responsibility, strong American leadership—if we return to these principles, we can be a relevant, rational majority party in many states and win national elections," Flake said. "But if we continue down this nativist road, this kind of personality cult kind of experience, we're not going to get there."

For Democrats, I'd urge Democratic senators to find ways to work with colleagues across the aisle. That will mean avoiding intentionally antagonizing them by pushing policies of the far left. The 50–50 split is a mandate to be sure, a mandate to find common ground because neither side controls enough votes to have its way.

Centrism is the only path to progress.

The good news is that Joe Biden, as president, knows this all very well, and, I hope will make it a priority. Likewise, VP Kamala

Harris with less experience, knows it as well. Biden served in the Senate for decades, knows it and its members, quirks and all, probably better than any sitting senator. I hope, and trust, he'll use that wisdom to the country's advantage.

The biggest obstacle Biden faces, at least in getting his agenda through the Senate, is, of course, Kentucky Republican Mitch McConnell, the dark knight who lives, breathes, and eats to gain political advantage breakfast, lunch, dinner. But McConnell, who famously said his top priority was to make Barrack Obama a one-term president, doesn't have to placate the Trumpian crowd any longer, his seat is once again secure for another six years.

And in Biden, McConnell faces a leader who knows him, his tactics, his abilities, and his shortcomings very well. They were contemporaries and Biden may have McConnell's number. We'll have to see. This time around, McConnell's GOP-first tactics may be too obvious. The Senate watchers will throw the yellow flags and call penalties. He'll be less likely to pull the same shenanigans, and if he does, less likely to sustain it. McConnell should, finally, shape up and work with this president when he can, oppose when he must, and always keep the fortunes of all Americans— not just red state or far right or Tea Party or Trumpers—as his guiding light.

So, who will become born again Republicans? Maybe we should forget Lindsey Graham. He lost his McCain wingman replacement—Trump–and will be searching for a new one. Until he finds that wingman, he will continue to be rudderless even as the GOP leader and ranking member of the powerful Senate Judiciary Committee, although in January he showed nascent signs of breaking with Trump. With Graham, unfortunately, the winds of the times too often whisk him away from his core Republican roots.

What about Susan Collins, who like Lindsey, won reelection for another six years? She knows how the center works, is experienced, and in her "heart of hearts," knows what our country needs.

She's the one Republican who has crossed the aisle in the past but needs a Democratic partner.

Chris Coons is already suited up and given his close relationship with Biden could work with Collins to form a new bipartisan centrist coalition. It would have good leadership skills and instant credibility with other colleagues who likewise know what it will take to recover economically from COVID-19 and bring our country back together.

Sen. Joe Manchin of West Virginia could also become a member and a leader as well. He has demonstrated he is independent minded and marches to his own drummer. Just maybe?

I am sure that presidential goodwill could become contagious in a closely divided Senate, finding common ground on a number of fronts. But what if Trump from the outside continues to divide the country, as well as his Republican Party throughout 2021 and beyond?

The caucus leaders with their partisan agendas will be quite skeptical not knowing what way a centrist coalition may go. But in a closely divided Senate, this will be the only way to begin the process of finding legislative solutions. Obviously, the Biden White House can also play a major role just as the Bush White House did in 2001. Given the Senate background of Biden and Harris, it could very well be an all Senate team. Could be quite interesting! That could be the game changer!

Being president will not be an easy ride. Biden understands that the pact made with the left for its support created a major shadow candidacy with Kamala Harris on the ticket. While Harris may have helped with the left and certain other voters, there were also reluctant votes coming from anti Harris voters. This needs to be understood and balanced going forward. And soon.

Her smiling persona aside, during the primary debates Harris was the most vocally critical of Biden. Even so, she failed to gain traction, an indication that it didn't work. But while all may be forgiven, it's not forgotten. Her political future will be based on how she comports herself as vice president rather than assuming she is the "president in waiting." Biden knows this from his VP role with Obama and can be an excellent mentor. She needs it.

In DC some on the left are already promoting the next four years of the Biden administration as the "Biden Bridge." Bridge? To where? Or to whom? Unless this group and all others join together to support Joe Biden as they did to elect him and send Trump packing, the so-called Biden bridge will likely be the bridge to "nowhere."

I believe there's much to hope for in Joe Biden's presidency. Bringing the Senate back from the brink, restoring it as the world's greatest deliberative body, making it do the work of the people ranks high. For years, political pundits said that while many senators thought they would make excellent presidents and ran for higher office, very few ever made it. Is that because they remained at their heart legislators pushing bills through the messy sausage-making on Capitol Hill? With Biden we now have a leader who knows the Senate intimately and may have the tools to inspire it to set aside political gamesmanship for the good of the country. Maybe he can help heal the Senate, as he works to heal the nation. It matters. It really does.

American democracy is the institution itself. We say its messy because unlike authoritarian government it encourages and tolerates its people and our peaceful views. But it does not tolerate violent expression of any views. Thus, it did not on January 6. It fought back and won. It won by continuing to function. It showed the world it would not cower. It would not be broken. It would not fail.

Some authoritarian world leaders immediately dissed our American democracy as they watched the failed coup attempt. Perhaps Americans and our leaders have been too smug. Maybe we have become too self-righteous in preaching our democracy to the rest of the world. Regardless, I ask them to continue to take a closer look at how American democracy prevailed against an attempted coup.

At the conclusion of the Constitutional Convention in 1787, it was reported that Ben Franklin was asked, "Well, Doctor, what have we got, a monarchy or a republic?" He replied: "A republic, if you can keep it."

On January 6, "we kept it." We are still a republic.

In the same building a few hours earlier occupied by the mob through violent lethal force, and the presiding officers' seats still warm from the thugs who sat there for selfies, Congress reassembled and finished its job. It peacefully confirmed the next president-elect and vice president-elect of the United States of America. As it has for the last 245 years.

The Capitol insurrection and riot sent shockwaves throughout the world. The Trump brand became toxic, creating significant financial implications for the former president as he was resuming his "private person" status. The size of this unwanted financial impact is the subject of speculation but is somewhere in the range of several hundred million.

Conservative media outlets felt the swift sword of advertisers pulling their financial support for advertising. Certain conservative talk show hosts were impacted as TV audiences were dwindling.

Mike "My Pillow" Man felt the impact to his brand from his close identification with Trump. His pillows were pulled from the shelves by certain retailers reminding us once again, to be careful with whom we associate.

Rumors had been floating that Trump and the producer of *Apprentice* fame might team up again, but not after January 6. Those rumors were dashed as corporate America began to withdraw financial support for all sorts of conservative media. Trump may be a man without a network.

World leaders were left wondering whether the end of our democracy was happening before their very eyes. Could there be any peaceful transition? Or would there be a transition at all? They waited only two weeks for their answer.

On January 20, Donald Trump left the White House and DC tarnished and President-Elect Biden became the president of the United States of America.

The would-be dictator will go down in history with a painful legacy—he failed to succeed in his attempt to gain a second four-year term. His efforts to incite an overthrow of our government failed. He failed.

INDEX

bipartisanship (*cont.*)
important bills and, 180; limits on, xvii;
return of, 183–84, 193, 194; Senate and, 17–18;
Social Security and, 135; success with, 172
birther movement, 197
Blue Cross and Blue Shield, 143
Blue Dog Democrats, 192
Blunt, Roy, 196
Boehner, John, 12
Boxer, Barbara, xii, 32, 146, 188; abortion coverage and, 152, 153, 154, 157
Boyle, Mike, 5
Boy Scouts, 2, 3
Branstad, Terry, 6
Breaux, John, 9, 12, 33, 40, 44, 124, 169, 186, 192; on Clinton, 191; dealmaking by, 165–66; Lieberman and, 184; on middle, 192–93; on philosophy, 168; relationships and, 191; tax cut and, 46
Britton, Joe, 124, 125, 126
Brooke, Lynne, 170
Brooks, Ralph, 24
Brown, Janice Rogers, 99, 102, 104
Brown, Scott, 88
budget deficits, 40, 42, 45, 58
budget surplus, 37, 40, 41–42, 43, 45
Buffett, Warren, F24, 116, 140
Bunning, Jim, 13, 14–15, 158
Burr, Richard, 88
Bush, George H. W., 47, 50, 69, 197; Iraq and, 70; senators and, 191
Bush, George W., F15, xii, 51, 93, 99, 100, 113, 116, 117, 203; budget surplus and, 37; compromise with, xvii; economic stimulus plan and, 53, 129; election of, 7; Gore and, 42; Hagel and, 43; Hussein and, 72, 73, 74; initiatives by, 10; Iraq War and, 76; Jeffords and, 48; judicial nominees of, xviii, 89; McCain and, 96; nicknames and, 44, 54; September 11th and, 64–65; social gatherings with, 191; speech by, 39–40, 53, 71, 115; State of the Union Address of, 35, 42, 60–61; support for, 10; tax cuts and, 38–39, 42, 44, 45, 46, 55, 57, 91, 135, 172
Bush v. Gore (2000), 37
Butler, Stuart M., 138
Byrd, Robert, xix–xx, 25, 27, 32, 49–50, 72, 95,

96, 97, 103, 178, 178–79; fears of, xxii; female senators and, 28; nuclear option and, 91; oratory/debate and, 19; partnership with, 28–29; traditions/decorum and, 28

Calhoun, John C., 24
Calio, Nick, 41, 42, 45, 47, 50
Campbell, Ben Nighthorse, 9
Candid Camera, appearance on, 6, 7
capital gains tax, 39, 57
Carnahan, Jean, 46, 49
Carper, Tom, 9
Carter, Jimmy, 199
Casey, Bob, 147
Centers for Medicare and Medicaid Services (CMS), 13, 14
Central Intelligence Agency (CIA), 51, 107
Central National Insurance Group, 4
Centrist Caucus, xxi, 18
Centrist Coalition, 12, 40, 166, 184, 206
centrists, xiii, xxi, xxii, 8, 9, 11, 57, 96, 121, 164, 166, 167, 178, 192–93, 204–5, 206
Chafee, John, 166
Chafee, Lincoln, 9, 10, 46, 93
Chambliss, Saxby, 183
checks and balances, 73, 91, 101, 103, 106, 179
chemical weapons, 68–69, 74
Cheney, Dick, F23, 8, 41, 56, 57, 65, 69–70; Iraq War and, 76, 77; Nebraskalander Award for, 47; tax cut napkin and, 47–48, 51; WMDs and, 70
Cheney, Lynn, 47
Chicago Mercantile Exchange, 129
child tax credit, 50, 53, 57
Chrysler, 128
CIA. *See* Central Intelligence Agency (CIA)
Cigna, 143
circuit breakers, 41, 44–45, 47, 48, 49, 52–53
civil rights, 25, 156
Clay, Henry, 24
Cleland, Max, 9, 49, 71
Clinton, Bill, F9, 18, 68, 85, 105, 170, 197; impeachment of, 98–99, 191; tech bubble and, 37
Clinton, Hillary, 82, 170; health care reform and, 134, 137; Obama and, 35; practical joke and, 18–19, 187; respect for, 34; as workhorse, 18